Inscription and Erasure

Inscription and Erasure

Literature and Written Culture from the Eleventh to the Eighteenth Century

Roger Chartier

Translated by Arthur Goldhammer

PENN

University of Pennsylvania Press
Philadelphia

This work is published with the cooperation of the French Ministry of Cultue, Centre National du Livre

Originally published as Inscrire et effacer: Culture écrite et littérature (XIᵉ–XVIIIᵉ siècle)
by Gallimard/Le Seuil
Copyright © Editions du Seuil/Gallimard, 2005

10   9   8   7   6   5   4   3   2   1

Published by
University of Pennsylvania Press
Philadelphia, Pennsylvania 19104–4112

Library of Congress Cataloging-in-Publication Data

Chartier, Roger, 1945–
   [Inscrire et effacer. English]
   Inscription and erasure : literature and written culture from the eleventh to the
eighteenth century / Roger Chartier ; translated by Arthur Goldhammer.
      p. cm.—(Material texts)
   ISBN-13: 978-0-8122-3995-9 (cloth : alk. paper)
   ISBN-10: 0-8122-3995-4 (cloth : alk. paper)
   Includes bibliographical references and index.
   1. Written communication—Social aspects—History. 2. Transmission of tests.
3. Printing—Social aspects. 4. Literature and society. 5. Books and reading—Social aspects.
I. Title. II. Series.
P211 .C483 2007
302.2´24409—dc22   *2006051419*

Contents

Introduction: Aesthetic Mystery and the Materialities of the Written

The fear of obliteration obsessed the societies of early modern Europe. To quell their anxiety, they preserved in writing traces of the past, remembrances of the dead, the glory of the living, and texts of all kinds that were not supposed to disappear. Stone, wood, fabric, parchment, and paper all served as substrates on which the memory of events and men could be inscribed. In the open space of the city or the seclusion of the library, in majesty in books or in humility on more ordinary objects, the mission of the written was to dispel the obsession with loss. This was no easy task in a world where writing could be erased, manuscripts misplaced, and books existed under perpetual threat of destruction. Paradoxically, complete success in this enterprise could lead to danger of another sort: that of uncontrollable textual proliferation, of a discourse without order or limits. The excess of writing piled up useless texts and stifled thought beneath the weight of accumulating discourse, creating a peril no less ominous than the threat of disappearance. Obliteration, though feared, was therefore necessary, just as oblivion is a condition of memory. Not all writing was destined for safekeeping in archives that were supposed to rescue texts from the vagaries of history. Some of it was inscribed on materials that could be erased and used again.

The purpose of this book is to examine the manifold relationship between inscription and erasure, between the durable record and the ephemeral text, by studying the way in which writing was made literature by certain works belonging to various genres and composed in various times and places. In approaching old works, we must therefore combine the history of written culture with the sociology of texts. Defined by D. F. McKenzie as "the discipline that studies texts as recorded forms, and the processes of their transmission, including their production and reception,"[1] the sociology of texts seeks to understand how human societies have constructed and transmitted the meanings conveyed by the various languages used to designate creatures and things. By refusing to separate the analysis of symbolic meanings from that of the material forms by which they are transmitted, such an approach

sharply challenges the longstanding division between the sciences of interpretation and those of description, hermeneutics and morphology.

The same can be said of the notion of "graphic culture" proposed by
Armando Petrucci. The term refers to the whole range of written objects
and practices in any given society, and the goal of this approach is to understand the differences among contemporary forms of writing and to catalog
the multiple uses to which writing is put.[2] The studies of particular texts that
make up this book are aimed at understanding how certain works laid hold
of the "graphic culture" of their time, or at any rate of certain of its elements,
in such a way as to make the written itself the subject of writing.

If we hope to move the boundary between, on the one hand, the most
common practices and products of written culture and, on the other hand,
literature, seen as a specific domain of creativity and experience, we need to
bring together what western tradition has long kept apart: on one side, interpretation of and commentary on works of literature, and on the other, analysis of the technical and social conditions of their publication, circulation, and
appropriation. There are a number of reasons for this separation: the durable contrast between the purity of the idea and its inevitable corruption by
matter;[3] the definition of copyright, which established the author's ownership of a text that was said to remain the same no matter what form its publication took;[4] and the triumph of an aesthetic that judged works apart from
their material substrate.[5]

Paradoxically, the two critical approaches that devoted the most sustained attention to the material modes of inscription of discourse did not
counter this process of textual abstraction but rather reinforced it. Analytic
bibliographers rigorously investigated the different states (editions, issues,
copies) in which a given work appeared in the hope of recovering an ideal
text, purged of the alterations inflicted by the process of publication and representing the text as written, dictated, or imagined by its author.[6] From this
came a discipline almost exclusively devoted to the comparison of printed
objects, an obsession with lost manuscripts, and a radical distinction between
the essence of a work and the accidents that distorted or corrupted it.

The deconstructionist approach insisted strongly on the materiality of
writing and the various forms of inscription of language. But in its effort to
abolish or reconfigure the most immediately apparent oppositions (between
orality and writing, between the singularity of language acts and the repro-
ducibility of the written), it constructed conceptual categories (such as "archi-
scripture" and "iterability") that can impede perception of the effects of
empirical differences that these categories obliterate by subsuming them.[7]

Against such an abstraction of discourse, it is appropriate to point out that the production not just of books but of *texts* themselves is a process that involves, beyond the act of writing, various moments, techniques, and interventions: by copyists, bookseller-publishers, master printers, compositors, and proofreaders. The transactions between works or literature and the social world go beyond the aesthetic and symbolic appropriation of ordinary objects, languages, and ritual or daily practices, as the "New Historicism" would have it.[8] At a more fundamental level, they involve the manifold, shifting, and unstable relations between the text and its materialities, between the work and its inscriptions. The publication process, regardless of its modality, is always a collective process involving numerous actors in which there is no sharp distinction between the materiality of the text and the textuality of the book. It is therefore pointless to try to distinguish the essential substance of the work, which is supposed to remain invariable, from the accidental variations of the text, which are viewed as unimportant for its meaning. Nevertheless, the many variations imposed on texts by the preferences, habits, and errors of those who copy, compose, and correct them do not undermine the idea that work retains a permanent identity, which readers or listeners recognize immediately.

David Kastan recently applied the adjective "platonic" to the view that a work transcends all of its possible material incarnations, and the adjective "pragmatic" to the view that no text exists apart from the material object that makes it available to be read or heard.[9] These contradictory views of the text divide literary criticism as well as editorial practice, opposing those who believe it necessary to recover the text as its author drafted, imagined, or desired it, repairing the wounds inflicted in the course of copying the manuscript and setting the work in type,[10] to those for whom the multiple textual forms in which a work has been published constitute its various historical states, which must be respected, published, and understood in their irreducible diversity.[11]

A similar tension between the immateriality of works and the materiality of texts characterizes the relations between readers and the books they appropriate—even when they are neither critics nor editors. In a lecture Borges gave in 1978, entitled "El libro," he said, "One day I thought I would write a history of the book." Immediately, however, he dismissed any interest in the material forms of written objects: "I am not interested in the physical aspect of books (and especially not in the books of bibliophiles, which are usually oversized) but in the various ways in which books have been regarded."[12] For Borges, books are objects of no interest, whose particularities are of little moment. What counts is the way in which the book, taken to be the universal form of the written work regardless of its specific modality, was regarded—or, more often than not, disregarded, in comparison with the "wingèd and sacred" spoken word. Borges, in other words, took a "platonic" view.

But when the same Borges dictated his autobiography to Norman Thomas di Giovani, he spoke of his encounter with one of the books that shaped his life, *Don Quixote*, and the first thing that came to his mind was the book as object:

I still remember the red bindings with gilt titles of the Garnier edition. Eventually, after my father's library was broken up and I read *Don Quixote* in another edition, I had the feeling that it was not the real *Don Quixote*. Later, a friend obtained for me a Garnier edition with the same engravings, the same footnotes, and the same errata. For me, all these things were part of the book: in my mind, this was the real *Don Quixote*.[13]

For Borges, the story Cervantes wrote would always be that of the edition that the Garnier brothers exported to the Spanish-speaking world and that he had read as a boy. The platonic principle is of little weight compared with the pragmatic return of memory.

Borges' two contradictory views suggest that the contrast between "platonism" and "pragmatism" is probably a false debate or the result of a badly framed question. A work becomes available to be read or heard only in some particular state. Depending on the time and genre, the variations between states can be considerable and may involve, separately or together, the material form of the object, the written representation of the words, and/or the content itself.[14] Yet inevitably multiple agencies (philosophical, aesthetic, and juridical) attempt to reduce this diversity by postulating the existence of a work that remains the same regardless of its form. In the West, neo-Platonism, Kantian aesthetics, and the definition of literary property all contributed to the construction of this ideal text, which readers infallibly recognize in each of its different states. What is important, however, is not to eliminate or resolve this irreducible tension in one way or another but rather to identify the way in which it was constructed at various historical moments—and, to begin with, in and through the works themselves.

That is the purpose of this book, which aims to show how certain literary works appropriated objects or practices that belonged to the written culture of their time.[15] The authors of these works transformed the material realities of writing and publication into an aesthetic resource, which they

used to achieve poetic, dramatic, or narrative effects. The processes that bestowed existence on writing in its various forms, public or private, ephemeral
or durable, thus became the very ground of literary invention. In the chapters that follow, there is nothing systematic or calculated about the choice of
texts to comment on, and I do not claim to have exhausted the subject. The
choice was dictated by my reading and tastes, and mindful of what Erich
Auerbach wrote about the works he chose to include in *Mimesis*: "My method
was to allow myself to be guided by a small number of themes that occurred
to me without intentional effort on my part, and to set these against a number of texts that had become familiar to me in the course of my work as a
philologist. This method struck me as practical and fruitful."[16]

In the age of print, the typographic shop was the chief place where new
objects for ensuring the circulation of works were produced, for better or for
worse.[17] Hence it is not surprising that when Don Quixote visits Barcelona,
he wants to see a printer's shop, and in Chapter 3 we will visit it along with
him. Nevertheless, Gutenberg's invention did not do away with the role of the
manuscript copy as a medium for the publication and transmission of texts.[18]
Handwritten newsletters remained competitors with printed gazettes for a
long time, and clandestine manuscripts that showed little respect for authorities and orthodoxies circulated more easily than printed books.[19] Hence we
look in Chapter 4 at Ben Jonson's comedy *The Staple of News*, which stages
the bitter rivalry and widespread dishonesty among the printers of newsbooks
and the authors of handwritten newsletters. In chapter 5, moreover, we look
at Cyrano de Bergerac's *États et empires de la lune et du soleil*, which not only
inscribes the story of its own manuscript publication in the text itself but
also displays imaginative uses of the written that are at once comical, critical,
and nostalgic.

Not all written texts are destined to last. From the Middle Ages to the
eighteenth century, a variety of objects were used to record writing tempo-
rarily until, having outlived its usefulness, it could be erased. This was true
of the wax tablets that were used throughout the Middle Ages for the composition of texts that were later copied onto parchment. It was also true in
the early modern period of another kind of "table," a small notebook whose
pages were coated with a substance that made it possible to erase what had
been written and to take quick notes, not with pen and ink but with a metal
stylus with which one could record a thought, a speech, a verse, or a letter.[20]
These humble objects of written culture also became part of literature—
before they were noticed by psychoanalysis.[21] At the turn of the twelfth century, Baudri de Bourgueil wrote poems about his wax tablets (chapter 1). Early

in the seventeenth century, Cervantes saw to it that Don Quixote and Sancho Panza encountered Cardenio's *librillo de memoria*, the primary medium for recording poems and letters for later copying. For both the poetic abbot and the one-armed writer, writing, memory, and forgetfulness were closely intertwined, as if every inscription could or should be erased and as if writing invariably sought to counter its own fragility (Chapter 2).

The *mise en abîme* of text within text, of the written within writing, involved more than just objects and techniques. Numerous metaphors for the written were employed. The production of the text, from its composition to its publication and representation, was conceptualized by comparison with the various stages in the design, fabrication, and sale of textiles. Goldoni, in his last Venetian comedy, *Une delle ultime sere di Carnovale*, offers a melancholy, masculine and industrial image of the common metaphors and manufacturing practices that had linked text and textiles since ancient times (Chapter 6).[22] For Diderot, what explained the unprecedented power of Richardson's novels was the comparison with painting. Composed of a series of tableaux, they obliged the reader to adopt a new relation to works that were a source of the purest emotions and a guide for all aspects of life.[23] Writing, now mutated into images, required a different kind of reading and a break with old habits. It called for a revolution in practices and in the heart (Chapter 7). Objects of writing and processes of publication thus often turned up in a realistic or metaphorical form in the works themselves. This literary representation should no doubt be understood as one of the ways in which societies attempted to control the irresistible proliferation of the written, to reduce the worrisome dispersion of texts, and, as Foucault wrote, to "escape the heavy, awesome materiality" of discourse.[24]

When it comes time to take our leave of the works we have selected for commentary, a look at Diderot's *Letter on the Book Trade* (in the Epilogue) will afford us an opportunity to look back on the fundamental tension inherent in our approach. In volunteering his services to Parisian booksellers in order to affirm the sovereignty of authors over their works, and in discussing the trivial realities of publishing the better to bring out the immaterial nature of the work of art, Diderot formulated, with the resources and constraints characteristic of his time, the question that Borges put somewhat differently: "*Art happens*, according to Whistler, but the thought that we will never get to the bottom of the aesthetic mystery does not prevent us from looking into the facts that made it possible."[25] Among those "facts," the relations that were established between literary creation and the materialities of the written were not the least significant.

This book owes everything to the friendship of Fernando Bouza, José Emilio Burucúa, and Peter Stallybrass, who in recent years have been wonderful companions in teaching and research in Madrid and Buenos Aires and at the University of Pennsylvania.

My gratitude, too, to Jean Hébrard and all the members of my seminar at the École des Hautes Etudes en Sciences Sociales, whose questions and criticisms repeatedly obliged me to rethink what I was doing.

Finally, I would like to thank all the many colleagues who afforded me the opportunity to present versions of the chapters of this book as lectures and conference papers.

Chapter 1

Wax and Parchment: The Poems of Baudri de Bourgueil

In chapter 25 of Part One of *Don Quixote*, the knight-errant and his squire cross the lonely wastes of the Sierra Morena. Don Quixote is gripped by a desire to write a letter to the woman of his dreams. But how can he do this without paper on which to record his epistolary verse?

Since we have no paper, it would be well for us to write it as the ancients did, on the leaves of trees or a few wax tablets; although it would be about as hard to find anything like that now as it would be to procure paper.[1]

We shall see in the next chapter how the *hidalgo* overcame this difficulty. What is important for now is Cervantes' feeling in 1605 that wax tablets belonged to the remote past, indeed to ancient times. In 1540 Pedro Mexia made the same association in *Silva de varia lección*, in which he described wax tablets, *tablicas enceradas*, as one of the media that *los antiguos* used for writing.[2] Thus to contrast the Moderns, who used paper and quill, and the Greeks and Romans, who wrote on wax with a stylus, was to forget that in the medieval period wax tables were the primary instrument of writing. To remind us of this, we can turn to a poet who took writing implements and practices as the subject matter of his compositions.

His name was Baudri, and we know little about him. He was born in Meung-sur-Loire in 1045 or 1046 and named abbot of the wealthy and powerful Benedictine abbey of Saint-Pierre-de-Bourgueil sometime between 1078 and 1082. He left the abbey in 1107 to become archbishop of Dol and subsequently became involved in a series of conflicts with his fellow bishops, his chapter, and the papal legate. In the final years of his life he retired to a Norman priory subordinate to the church of Dol. The abbot traveled a good deal and visited a number of Benedictine abbeys in Normandy and England. But he was also a poet, as well as the author of various prose works, including lives of saints, accounts of miracles, a chronicle of the first crusade, and a treatise on the good death. His greatest pleasure, however, came from verse, as attested by the 256 poems contained in a manuscript preserved in the Vatican Library (Reg. Lat. 1351 [V]). These have been translated into French by Jean-Yves Tilliette.[3] Some brief, others extended, Baudri's poetic compositions are learned works, written in metrical Latin verse in a variety of genres: epistle, satire, hymn, epic, epitaph, and so on.

I will not use these categories in approaching Baudri's poetry, which I came to know through the work of Ernst Curtius. In his chapter on metaphors of the book, he quotes one of the verses that the abbot addressed to his tablets, his stylus, and his scribes.[4] By coming back to the entire collection, it is possible to take the full measure of the obsessive presence of the materiality of the written in Baudri's poems and, more than that, of the process of writing from composition to transcription and publication to reception.

Composing and Transcribing

In Baudri's poems, writing is inscribed on three materials: the wax of tablets, the parchment of letters and books, and the stone of epitaphs. With few exceptions, however, his own writing is always represented as linked to the stylus and tablets. In two poems that attracted the attention of Curtius and later of Richard and Mary Rouse,[5] Baudri gives a precise description of the medium on which he writes his poems. In *Ludendo de tabulis suis* [12], he extols the beauty of the eight small green tablets bound with straps and protected by a sack, which will accompany him even in death:

> May our common recreation continue eternally: I mean: may I never be deprived of my tablets. I shall live near you, and you, near me. May a single grave await us at the end. Amen.[6]

On his eight tablets, organized as a *codex*, Baudri could fit up to 112 lines:

> In height, the pages of which you are made contain exactly eight lines; in width, barely a hexameter. Yet since you are composed of eight small leaves, that makes two times two plus ten small pages [indeed, the two outer surfaces were not covered with wax, so that the eight leaves gave fourteen pages]. Thus they contain two times six lines, plus one hundred: the large number of pages makes this possible.[7]

Baudri's cherished instrument may remind us of the green wax tablets of Beauvais and Oslo, as catalogued and described by Elisabeth Lalou,[8] or of the six Florentine tablets studied by Armando Petrucci in 1965.[9] Bound together by a parchment backing, these six tablets (of which there were probably more originally) constitute a polyptych on which a Tuscan merchant of the late thirteenth or early fourteenth century kept his accounts and records of textile purchases and loans, possibly in connection with the fairs of Champagne.

In the poem *Ad tabulas* [196], which follows certain Latin authors in taking the form of a conversation between the writer and his tablets,[10] Baudri promises to restore the "feeble forces" of his "beautiful ladies":

I know not who or what broke the straps that bound you, but I think it was age that inflicted this harm. Tenderly I shall heal your affliction and replace the strap at my own expense. As for the wax, it is old and black with grit, and this old wax disfigures your beauty. So you are less indulgent of the writer and resist his stylus as though you found it odious. Hence I am preparing green wax to replace the black, so as to make you more tolerant and friendly toward the scribe.[11]

The little tablets of which Baudri was so fond were a gift: "He who gave you to me [the abbot of Sées] wisely offered a tearful child a bird [12]."[12] Indeed, in Baudri's poems tablets are frequent gifts, dispatched, bestowed, or promised as tokens of friendship. Baudri received such presents not only from the abbot of Sées but also from Bernard (*Pro tabulis gratiarum actio* [144]), and Eudes promised to send him some as soon as he could find a messenger (*Ad eum qui tabulas ei promiserat* [105]). Conversely, Baudri often promised or gave wax tablets as gifts himself: for instance, to the nun Agnès ("The tablets that I promised you, and that you ask for, I shall send when I can; for the time being I have none" [138]),[13] and to Guiternus, who, like an importunate creditor (*improbus exactor*), "extorts" from Baudri tablets that he must take from his own collection (*Ad eum qui tabulas ab eo extorsit* [148]), and Raoul du Mans ("I would have sent you beautiful tablets if I had wanted to. I did not want to send them, but rather to give them to you with my own hands" [205]).[14]

Why were wax tablets so eagerly desired and appreciated as gifts? For the simple reason that it was on, or, rather, *in* wax (for, as Richard and Mary Rouse observe, "one writes in, not on, a wax surface") that authors drafted their texts for later transcription onto parchment by a scribe. There is no more informative commentary on this common practice of twelfth-century monastic writers[15] than Baudri's complaints about his scribe Gérard:

I would have written poem after poem if there had been room to write in my tablets. But I filled them completely, while you lie about endlessly and put off transcribing the words I have traced in wax. So in order to make room in the wax, transcribe my work: rouse yourself and overcome your customary laziness. (*Ad Girardum scriptorem suum* [9])[16]

A fundamental distinction was thus laid down between composition and transcription. Baudri always refers to the composition of poems using the verbs *componere, cantare,* or *dictare* (the last of these verbs did not imply that the text was dictated out loud).[17] In the poem that opens the anthology, *Contra obtrectatores consolatur librum suum* [1], Baudri, alluding to himself, remarks that "he wrote poems of this sort at night or on horseback," that is, in situations in which writing was difficult if not impossible.[18] Thus composition could be done entirely in the head and committed to memory, but in Baudri's case it usually involved writing in wax, which allowed for crossing out words and changing one's mind. The poet-abbot of the Val de Loire thus offers a perfect illustration of Richard and Mary Rouse's assertion that "the wax tablet, as a support for the written word, had a longer uninterrupted association with literate Western civilization than either parchment or paper, and a more intimate relationship with literary creation."[19]

Writing on wax tablets was necessarily ephemeral. If poems were to be sent to a friend or collected in a book (referred to as *liber, libellus,* or *codex*), they had to be recopied onto parchment. Baudri describes this activity as an art requiring special skills and a form of labor worthy of remuneration. The *puer* Gautier, an "expert in calligraphy," was an artist who elegantly respected Baudri's instructions regarding the ornamentation of the manuscript of his poems:

I asked that the capital letters be made of bright metal, so that the book would be valuable for its material aspect even in the absence of ideas (it was the Arabs, perhaps, who brought us the gold that makes the initial letters of texts so resplendent). I had the other initials painted red or green, so that the whole work would make a better impression. That way, those incapable of responding to the richness of expression will at least find the appearance of the manuscript appealing. [1][20]

As Jean-Yves Tilliette notes, this description fits the manuscript preserved in the Vatican Library.

In the poem *Ad scriptorem suum* [84], which is addressed to Hugues, another copyist of the manuscript, Baudri states precisely what he will receive if he does his work rapidly and well. As was often the case, the remuneration consisted of a wage (*pretium*) plus a number of gifts: a cheese, a trip to Rome ("I also want to take you to Rome at my expense, so that our conversations can distract me from my worries. Then you will breathe the fragrance of an unambiguous friendship, while I delight in the honey of your words"), and renown ("I shall perpetuate your name in centuries to come, if my poems succeed in securing perpetuity for anyone").[21] The logic of the gift, which assumes friendship, here intersects with that of the contract, which demands payment. As Natalie Zemon Davis has noted, this was the rule in pre-modern societies, which saw no contradiction in combining remuneration with generosity, wages with gifts.[22]

The distinction between composition and transcription, between the hand of the author and the hand of the copyist, was so clear that any transgression bestowed particular value on a piece of writing. Thus, in a letter addressed to a nun named Constance, to whom he proposes a "pact of love" (*foedus amoris*) that is to bind their hearts together ("Let our hearts be united, but our bodies separated"), Baudri insisted on the fact that he himself had written (*scribere*) the epistolary poem he had also composed (*dictare*): "When you are alone, read my lines to the end, follow carefully the path they trace. Everything you find there was written by the hand of a friend. It is the hand of a friend that wrote, and it is also the hand of a friend that composed: the scribe is also the author of the poem" [200].[23]

Yet Baudri only rarely portrays himself as writing with a quill on parchment. The metal stylus with which he traces letters in the wax of his tablets is the only writing implement he describes. In a heroic-comic lament addressed to his broken stylus (*De graphio fracto grauis dolor* [92]), he meticulously describes the fabrication of this instrument, which requires "industry and skill" on the part of the artisan, and he bitterly deplores the loss of the stylus (designated as either *stilus* or *graphium*) that he had used for nine years: "There you are, dear stylus, wrenched from my hand. What other awl can trace so sharp a furrow in wax? What other stylus will be as well suited to my tablets?"[24] When he dreams of the ideal life in the poem *De suffientia uotorum suorum* {126], stylus and tablets suffice to complete his happiness.[25]

Memory and Song

Poetic creation, which according to Mary Carruthers involves an effort of recollection aimed at finding material (*res*) and giving it form (*collectio*) in a new composition,[26] was thus closely associated with writing on wax tablets. Memory was often described as a collection of tablets (*tabulae memoriae*), and, as late as Shakespeare's time, we find Hamlet obliged to erase the "tables of [his] memory" of all useless archives so as to preserve only the words of the ghost: "Remember me."[27] Conversely, tablets are the primary, if not always necessary, support of poetic invention and composition, which bring together ideas and fragments of texts filed away in memory.[28]

Memory also plays an essential role in the transmission of poems. The poet is a *cantor*, whose voice and breath inhabit his songs. The regular, expected mode of "publication" is thus a recital or declamation of a memorized text. There were virtuosos of this art, such as Godefroid of Reims, a poet who died in 1095, whose artful speaking Baudri extolled (*Ad Godefredum Remensem* [99]): "You also possess to an eminent degree a quality whereby you excel all others who read in public: when you declaim a text, no matter which one, your voice accentuates it so that the words you pronounce, as many as there are, charm all ears. Indeed, you wed words to melody and melody to words so ably that there is not the slightest dissonance between them."[29] Godefroid's art does justice not only to his own works, stored away in memory, but also to works he has heard recited by his colleagues: "Finally, what you compose, but also what you hear for the first time, you are always capable of repeating musically."[30]

This ability recalls the memory techniques that all intellectual activity requires. Thus Baudri admires young Pierre for the accuracy of his memory: "What you read and understand, you repeat with a memory so faithful that not a word is missing from your recital" (*Ad puerum mirandi ingenii* [113]).[31] Pierre's exceptional talent no doubt relates to the fact that, at a time when memory *ad res*, that is, of content and not necessarily words, normally sufficed, he was capable of reproducing what he read verbatim. This is an admirable talent, but it can also lead to rote and unimaginative repetition of the memorized material.

To what type of memory were the metrical poems of Baudri and other poet-abbots addressed? The hexameter form would seem to imply that respect for the text as composed by its author was essential, so that its "melody," or regular alternation of long and short syllables, could be correctly reproduced. In a poem inviting Avit to visit him soon, Baudri alludes to the pleasure of declaiming their works together: "So come here, my child. Come savor with me the charming garden, and let your heart and mine indulge in the comforts of this delightful setting. You will chant your poems, and I will chant mine, and we shall harmonize our voices with the caressing sounds of the lyre (*Ad Auitum ut ad eum ueniret* [129]).[32]

Yet it is also reasonable to think that the metrical forms of oral poetry, epic as well as lyric,[33] allowed for memorization and recital in which one word or line could be substituted for another, as long as the distribution of dactyls and spondees was respected. Baudri sought to fix his poems in a stable form, with a logical and aesthetic order of his own choosing, in the *liber* that he so carefully arranged. Unfortunately, we know nothing about the way in which these poems were received, memorized, or declaimed by their readers and auditors.

Books and Reading

Wax tablets were not the only writing medium mentioned in Baudri's poems. Parchment also appears, in three different forms: the book, the charter, and the letter. The words *liber* and *codex* referred both to collections of poems, such as the one copied and decorated by the scribes hired by Baudri, and to the books that he and others read, perused, and consulted. In the poem addressed to Godefroid of Reims [99], Baudri describes his own method of composition: "Composing poems actually sharpens the mind's dulled edge, for when I compose I consult books endlessly."[34]

Mental composition and memorization, aided by writing on tablets, was not incompatible with the use of books from the library of Baudri's monastery. He recommends this to Gérard of Loudun: "I know a place rich in leisure, books, parchments, and all the necessary implements of study: Bourgueil." Gérard is invited to join the Benedictine community, whose bookish treasure he will then be able to share: "The knowledge scattered throughout the world, all that you are searching for, awaits you. It fills the library of our cloister" (*Ad eundem ut monachus fiat* [77]).[35]

Books were not only preserved in libraries but also offered as gifts, loaned, and borrowed. Such circulation was not without risk. Baudri lent one of his books to an importunate borrower but was not sure that the book would be returned: "May the oath he swore be true, when he promised to return the Ovid he obtained from me with his ruses!" (*Ad eum qui ab eo Ovidium extorsit* [111]).[36] The fact that the borrowed book is a manuscript of Ovid's poems is not unimportant in a collection rife with citations and imitations of Latin poets: Vergil, Horace, Juvenal, Perseus, Lucan, Ovid himself). Baudri's great familiarity with Latin letters has led scholars to assume that he frequented one of the cathedral schools that included ancient authors in their teaching in the second half of the eleventh century. They provide Baudri with the repertoire of situations, images, and references that sustain his verse, which therefore cannot be read as an immediate description of lived reality.[37]

Learning to write on tablets inevitably went hand in hand with the frequentation of books. Baudri urges young Géraud to read as well as write:

To me the child more likable than any other is the one who applies his talent to writing tablets. So if you wish to be agreeable to me—and do wish it, Géraud—spend all your time with books and tablets. Peruse the books, and peruse them again. Search for what you do not know, and search for it again. Produce a work worthy of being declaimed before your friends. (*Ad Geraldum*, 197)[38]

This advice to Géraud envisions a close connection between the two modes of appropriating texts: by listening to a voice that declaims, recites, or reads the work, or by individual reading of the written text.

Poems, Baudri's as well as Géraud's, were written to be spoken, chanted, and listened to. Yet this intention did not preclude solitary reading. Baudri uses the verb *perlegere* to denote the attentive reading that he expected from certain of the people for whom his poems were intended. One such person is Emma, a nun and teacher, from whom he expects a critical reading: "Today I am sending you my little book in its entirety, so that you can read it closely and examine it carefully. . . . May Emma, with her lips of Sibyl, respond to my request; let her read thoroughly, give praise, make corrections, and complete where necessary" (*Emme ut opus suum perlegat* [153]).[39] Another is Constance, to whom he proposed, as we saw earlier, a "pact of love" in a letter written in his own hand. In her imagined response, Constance is indeed the reader he desires: "I have read your letter to the end, fervently following the path it describes, and I have touched your poem with my bare hand. Overcome with joy, I unrolled the parchment twice, then a third time and a fourth, and could not get enough of examining each of its details. The book delighted me, and the words could not have been more charming, so I spent the day reading and re-reading them [201]."[40]

This poem of Baudri's shows that the same object—in this case a letter addressed to Constance—could be referred to in different ways: as *carta, volumen, liber*, and, later on, *pagina*. One should therefore be wary of reading poetic language too literally as historical documentation, especially in a period when the word *volumen* no longer referred exclusively to the scrolls of the Ancients but had become a synonym for *liber* and had begun to be used as an equivalent for *codex* in colophons and library catalogues.[41] The relations between writing implements and the words of poems are never straightforward.

The reading that Baudri ascribes to Constance is not simply a careful individual reading but a reading that mobilizes the body and senses:

I placed the leaf on my chest, under my left breast, which they say is closest to the heart. If I could give your pages to my heart and not my chest, I would. Ultimately, exhausted, I surrendered my limbs to sleep, but to an anxious love night never falls.

What hopes did I not nourish? What did I not allow myself to hope? The book spawned hope in me, and night brought leisure. . . . When the time came to sleep, sleep eluded me, because your letter, lying on my breast, burned my insides.[42]

Constance's ardent reading culminates in an upheaval of the senses, an emotion of the heart and body more to be expected in a reader of Richardson than in an eleventh-century nun, even though we must bear in mind that her model came from the Ancients[43] and that Baudri's Constance was a creature of poetry. Yet her emotions warn us against the temptation to take too narrow a view of the diversity of ways in which people of a given time read, be they real or imaginary.

Baudri says nothing about the modality of solitary reading of poems and books. Was it silent or spoken out loud? Furthermore, as Guglielmo Cavallo,[44] Armando Petrucci,[45] and Franco Alessio[46] have pointed out, the opposition may not have the importance that has been attached to it in the wake of the work of Paul Saenger.[47] Three modalities of reading coexisted in the medieval period, and according to Armando Petrucci, these were practiced in some cases by different readers and in other cases by a single reader: these were "silent reading, *in silentio*; reading in a low voice, called "murmur" or "rumination," which served as an aid to meditation and an instrument of memorization; and finally, reading out loud, which, as in Antiquity, called for a special technique and was rather like liturgical recitation and chanting."[48]

These various ways of reading could be put to different purposes. Reading was first of all a means of acquiring resources for invention and composition. In the poem in which he sketched his ideal life, Baudri described the instruments that such acquisition required: "I would have plenty of books and parchment on which I would copy excerpts from what I read." [126][49] The work of preservation, here entrusted to writing, could also be entirely mental: mnemonic techniques included the use of alphabetic systems, numeric series, and architectural configurations as aids to memory, useful for classifying the various materials for storage in the mind's archives.

The second purpose of reading was *meditatio*, which was a way of establishing a relation between the text at hand and other texts stored in the "tables of memory." Although reading for the purpose of memorization could be silent, half-vocalized, or fully vocalized, nonlinear reading required concentration and silence. Such reading was obviously more appropriate for learned texts than for poetry, whose metrical composition called for a voice, which could be either a reader's voice or an inner voice. Baudri, who participated in a written culture that was undergoing mutation but prior to the transformations of the twelfth and thirteenth centuries, obviously knew nothing of the reading techniques the scholastics would later adopt. For him, reading poems always meant a slow and careful process of decipherment intended to make the melody of the verse audible to the reader or to the poet himself. This was true even when poems were read silently.

Writing the Dead

Our abbot also availed himself of one other material support for his writing: the stone of funerary monuments. The manuscript containing Baudri's poems includes 91 epitaphs, most of which were not intended to be actually engraved in stone (for example, the six epitaphs he dedicated to Cicero). These belonged to the genre known in French as *tombeau*, or tombstone writing, which imitated or inspired funerary epigraphy.[50] Baudri also practiced another kind of writing about the dead: mortuary encyclicals, or *rotuli*. On six occasions he added his own verses to a parchment scroll that made the rounds from one community to another after the death of an abbot. Twice he deplored the pointless prolixity of previous writers, who used the occasion for other than its intended purpose (namely, prayers for the dead and compassion for his brothers) and squandered a rare and expensive material, parchment.

On a mortuary scroll for an abbot named Noël [14], he addressed his fellow writers on a classic theme of such *rotuli*:

On many scrolls, writers try to trace their words all the way back to Adam. . . . If a long poem could help the believer, we would bend all our effort to the writing of poetry. But since frivolous odes are of no use to him, let us set aside odes and their frivolity. Save your strength for prayer, note your place of residence in a brief inscription below, and be careful lest the frenzy of your pen result in a useless waste of parchment.[51]

Similarly, he deplores the writerly excesses on a scroll in honor of Rainaud of Mans: "This encyclical scroll includes many irrelevant things, which, being indulgent of foolishness, we overlook without comment. But it would have been right to economize on scant parchment." [17][52]

It was such economy that called for the use of wax tablets for writing destined to be erased, and that is why the use of such tablets virtually disappeared when paper became available as a less costly replacement for parchment. At least that is how Covarrubias, in his *Tesoro de la lengua castellana* (1611), related the decline of writing on wax to the discovery of paper: "Before paper and ink were invented, people wrote on wax tablets, using a pointed instrument to inscribe the letters in wax."[53] Indeed, as Elisabeth Lalou has shown, as paper manufacturing developed, royal and municipal accounts ceased to be kept in wax tablets, and Parisian tablet makers turned to making wooden objects other than "writing tables."[54]

Exchanging Words

"Mutual exchanges take place between valued friends. It is sharing that cements friendships," Baudri maintained in a poem addressed to Payen [223].[55] Objects of writing and, even more, poems in the form of letters are tokens or offers of friendship that call for reciprocity. For Baudri, to send a poem to a correspondent was to oblige him to *rescribere*, to return the gift in kind. That is what he expects of Godefroid of Reims: "Thus shared love compelled me to write you a few lines, so as to compel you to write me many in return" [99].[56]

Yet these distant exchanges were always regarded as an inferior substitute for a meeting, a visit, or a *colloquium*. Examples abound in Baudri's writing. For example, he makes this declaration to Muriel, a nun and poetess:

O! Let it come, I beg you, the moment when I shall benefit from a second conversation! You would open your heart to me and respond effusively to all my questions, and I would do the same in return. Meanwhile, let us confide in one another by exchanging poems. May a silent loyalty be their guide and companion. (*Murieli* [137])[57]

He asks his friend, the monk Étienne, to return as soon as possible:

This parchment, this letter, contains my greetings and commands you to return, Etienne. Delay no longer. Come back, please, so that we can see each another and become reacquainted through conversation. What happiness Fortune would bring to my life if she were to bring you back to me sooner than planned! A single day without you is like a year to me, while a thousand days in your company are but the briefest of days. (*Ad Stephanum monachum suum* [90])[58]

To Avit he writes: "My dear Avitus, come see me here, come stay with me and savor with me the pleasures of warm conversation, have a good time with me." [129][59] As we have seen, the good time referred to here was time spent reciting poems together.

In Baudri de Bourgueil's world of writing, the most basic exchange is still that of speech.[60] The classical metaphor in which words were dishes and the poem a banquet is fully realized here.[61] Poems chanted by one person after another, books read by many voices, and erudite conversations passed the time in the most delightful of banquets:

These things will fill my learned friend's table: it is to this that he invites us, and by which I hope to be restored. When we re-read books, we discover varied flavors, more savory than manna. . . . Let anyone invited to this table hasten to take his seat, for here philosophy offers her breast. Since my friend invited me, I shall go speedily, putting off all other affairs and obligations. I shall dispatch my business and quicken my old man's step so as not to incur by my negligence delay after delay. I do not wish to be a cause of sadness in those to whom I would bring joy by my prompt arrival and agreeable conversation. (*Ad ipsum qui eum invitauerat* [208])[62]

Around banquet tables as on wax tablets, *verba volant*, words fly away. Parchment could hold on to them, but still more to the sweet memory of words shared among friends.

Chapter 2

Writing and Memory: Cardenio's Librillo

Just after Sancho and his master enter the Sierra Morena in chapter 23 of Part One of *Don Quixote*, they encounter "a saddle pad with a valise attached to it, both of them half or wholly rotten and falling to pieces."[1] Don Quixote asks Sancho to examine the contents of the abandoned valise. Sancho does as he is told and finds

> four fine cambric shirts and a number of other curious articles made of linen and all very clean, while wrapped in a handkerchief was a small pile of gold crowns. "Thank Heaven," cried Sancho, "for providing us at last with a profitable adventure!" Looking further, he came upon a memorandum book, richly bound.[2]

Cervantes wrote "un librillo de memoria ricamente guarnecido" to designate an object that different translators of *Don Quixote* have understood in different ways. For the French translators, the librillo was succesively "un petit livre de souvenirs richement relié" (a small book of souvenirs, richly bound),[3] or "un carnet de voyage, richement relié" (a travel notebook, richly bound),[4] or "un petit carnet de notes, richement orné" (a small notebook, richly decorated).[5] The earliest translations made a different choice and proposed another equivalent: for example, one that appeared in 1639 translated "librillo de memoria" as "des tablettes for richement accommodées" (very richly prepared tablets),[6] and another, published in 1798, as "des tablettes richement garnies" (richly decorated tablets).[7] A similar uncertainty is found in the English translations, for while the most recent choose terms such as "memorandum book," "notebook," or "diary,"[8] older ones favor renderings such as "a tablet very costly bound," "a little pocket-book richly bound," or "a pocket-book elegantly bound."[9] In other words, the translators hesitated as to the nature of the *librillo* and the meaning of the expression "ricamente guarnecido," which some take to describe the binding and others the ornamentation. What exactly was the object that Don Quixote and Sancho found in that lost valise on a dusty road in La Mancha?

Eager to know more about the owner of the valise and the reason for its abandonment, which could not have been robbery because the bag still contained the *escudos de oro*, Don Quixote opened the *librillo*, and "the first thing he found in the way of writing was the rough draft of a sonnet, in a very good hand; and in order that Sancho might hear it, he read it aloud."[10] Reading the love lamentation set as a poem suggests to Don Quixote the idea of writing a similar letter in verse to Dulcinea del Toboso and having Sancho deliver it to her. Continuing his examination of the unfortunate poet's *librillo*, the don comes upon another text: "'This,' said Don Quixote, turning a page, 'is prose and appears to be a letter.'"[11] He reads it aloud, and it confirms that the author was surely a spurned lover: "Leafing nearly all the way through the little book, he came upon other verses and letters, some of which he was able to read while others he could not. They were filled, all of them, with complaints, laments, misgivings, expressions of joy and sadness, talk of favors granted and a suit rejected."[12]

The mysterious identity of the owner of the gold crowns, quality linen, and *librillo* is revealed in the next chapter, when Don Quixote and Sancho meet Cardenio, a young Andalusian noble who, desperate and mad with love, has fled into the wilds of the Sierra Morena. As Cardenio is about to begin his tale of woe, he asks Quixote and Sancho not to interrupt him, for "I desire to relate my misfortunes as briefly as I can, since the telling of them serves only to bring me fresh sorrows."[13]

At this point, one of the key themes of the Sierra Morena chapters begins to emerge: the contrast between memory as a durable trace of the past, which can be recovered by way of a potentially painful search such as Cardenio's, and memory as vulnerable, ephemeral, and erasable, like that which is written as a "rough draft" on the *librillos de memoria*.

In the account he gives of his ill-fated love, Cardenio mentions that Luscinda's father had forbidden him to visit her. Sending poems and exchanging notes therefore did more than compensate for the absence of the beloved; they inflamed the lover's desire: "Ah, good Heaven, how many letters I wrote her! How many charmingly modest answers did I receive! How many love verses did I compose in which my heart declared and translated its feelings, painted its kindled desires, feasted on its memories, and re-created its passion."[14]

The texts that Cardenio sends Luscinda belong to the same genres as those found in his *libro de memoria*. In both cases we find poems and love letters, which speak of a love at first happy and ardent, then desperate and plaintive. Why not assume that in each situation, Cardenio wrote a "rough draft" of his poems and letters before copying them out with a pen and sending them to Luscinda?

Writing Without Ink or Paper

Plunging further into the mountain in chapter 25, Don Quixote, taking his inspiration from Cardenio, who reminds him of the knights-errant of old, decides to play "the part of a desperate and raving madman" so as to imitate the "tears and sighs" of Amadis after he is rejected by Oriana, or the rage of Orlando, driven mad by Angelica's betrayal. Dulcinea's answer to his letter will decide his fate.[15] The knight, having shed his arms and clothing so as "to remain as naked as the day he was born," gives his letter to Sancho, who is to mount Rocinante to deliver it.

"But how," Don Quixote asks, "are we going to write this letter?" To which Sancho is quick to add, "And the order for the ass-colts too,"[16] recalling Don Quixote's promise after the theft of his mount. Mentioned without further elaboration in the first edition of 1605, the theft of Sancho's ass was expanded into a brief narrative in the second edition, also published in 1605. To console Sancho for his loss (which explains why he must take Rocinante to deliver the letter to Dulcinea), Quixote assures him that he will be duly compensated: "Don Quixote, upon seeing his tears and learning their cause, consoled Sancho as best he could and begged him to be patient, promising him a letter of exchange for three asses from his house of the five he had left there."[17]

Upon receiving this *cédula* or *libranza* (letter of exchange), Don Quixote's niece will be obliged to give Sancho the three ass-colts. But before this can happen, the letter must be written, and this is no mean feat in the Sierra Morena, for as Don Quixote declares, "since we have no paper, it would be well for us to write it as the ancients did, on the leaves of trees or a few wax tables; although it would be about as hard to find anything like that now as it would be to procure paper."[18]

It is possible that in writing this passage, Cervantes used the chapter of *Silva de varia lección* that Pedro Mexía devoted to writing practices prior to the invention of paper. There, invoking ancient texts, he reviews such writing materials as palm leaves, bark, sheets of lead, fabric, papyrus, and wax tables, or *tablicas enceradas*, on which they wrote, like Baudri after them, with a stylus—a fact that affords Mexía the occasion for an etymological excursus on the origin of the word "style" in its modern sense: "From this comes the fact that we say of a person who writes well that he has a beautiful style, after the name of the instrument."[19]

How, then, is Don Quixote to write the letter to Dulcinea and the letter of exchange promised to Sancho? At this point he remembers Cardenio's *librillo de memoria*:

> It would be a good idea, an excellent idea, for me to write it in Cardenio's memorandum book, and then you will take care to have it transcribed on paper, in a fair hand, in the first village where you find a schoolmaster, or, failing that, some sacristan, but do not give it to any notary to be copied, for they write a legal hand that Satan himself would not be able to make out.[20]

The text here plays with several contrasts. The first is between the *papel* or paper onto which Sancho will have the letter of exchange transcribed and the *librillo* on which Quixote intends to write it. The point of this opposition may have to do with the material nature of the object (a separate sheet of paper versus a small notebook or pocket book), or it may suggest that the pages of Cardenio's *librillo* are not made of ordinary paper. A second contrast opposes the "fair hand" (*buena letra*) of schoolmasters and clerics to the "legal hand," or what seventeenth-century French translations called *le lettre de chicanerie*, this being the formula used to render *letra procesada*, or the indecipherable writing of chancellery scribes and court clerks.

This condemnation of a professional hand that is opaque to the uninitiated and therefore liable to suspicions of witchcraft has a parallel in Shakespeare's *Henry VI, Part 2*, when the rebels led by Jack Cade kill the clerk of Chatham because he knows "court hand," the English equivalent of the *escritura procesal* of the Spanish clerks, thus proving that he has made a pact with the devil:

Weaver: He's a book in his pocket with red letters in't
Cade: Nay, then he is a conjurer!
Butcher: Nay, he can make obligations and write court hand.[21]

Court Hand and Stenography

In the Sierra Morena, the two letters are written in Cardenio's *librillo*. Sancho then worries about the validity of the document awarding him the three ass-colts:

"But what is to be done about the signature?" asked Sancho.
  "The letters of Amadis were never signed," Don Quixote assured him.

"That is all very well," said the squire, "but that order you are to give me has to be signed, and if it is copied over, they will say the signature is false and I'll not get the ass-colts."

"The order, duly signed, will be in that same little book, and when my niece sees it, she will not give you any trouble about carrying out my instructions. As for the love letter, you will have them put as the signature: 'Yours until death, the Knight of the Mournful Countenance.' It will make little difference if it is in some other person's handwriting, for, as I recall, Dulcinea does not know how to read or write, nor has she ever in all her life seen a letter of mine or anything else that I wrote."[22]

The need for an autograph signature to authenticate a document invested with the value of a command or obligation[23] was thus associated with another common practice in early modern societies, the delegation of writing, here granted to the scribe who is to copy Quixote's letter.[24]

After Don Quixote completes a draft of the letter to Dulcinea in the *librillo de memoria*, we return to the theme of memory without books or reading, entwined with the act of writing:

He called Sancho, telling him to listen while he read it to him and to memorize it, in case the original should be lost along the way, as he had reason to fear from the ill luck that seemed to pursue him.

"Just write it two or three times in that book, your Grace," Sancho said, "and then give it to me; for it is nonsense to think I am going to learn it by heart when my memory is so bad that I often forget my own name."[25]

Cervantes plays here with the gap between two kinds of memory: individual memory, which can be defective, and collective, cultural memory, which comprises a repertoire that anyone can mobilize, including, perhaps especially, the illiterate. Sancho, who is capable of forgetting his own name and who claims to be incapable of memorizing the don's letter (an inability that will be demonstrated in what follows), is nevertheless a man of memory, whose speech is a tissue of proverbs and commonplaces (*refranes* and *sentencias*), and who, as we know from chapter 20 of Part One, is able to recite the tales that embody the oral tradition of his village. According to Pedro Mexía's Aristotelian typology, which distinguishes between the memory of subtle minds (*los agudos de ingenio*) and that of rustics (*los rudos*), Sancho exemplifies to perfection the latter, who "take things in and learn with difficulty but are better at preserving."[26]

Sancho's request that Don Quixote write the letter to Dulcinea in the *librillo* two or three times is a comic embellishment, as if copying the text more than once in the same place could better assure its survival. Yet Sancho's insistence may also suggest that a letter written in Cardenio's notebook could be erased, so that copying it onto several pages would in fact offer greater assurance. If this is correct, the question of the material nature of the *librillo* remains.

Quixote reads the two letters—one a parody of chivalric romance, the other a comical imitation of a letter of exchange—to Sancho, and in this way Cervantes reveals their contents to the reader. After the letter concerning the three ass-colts is read, Sancho once again worries about its authentication:

> "That is very good," said Sancho, "and now sign it, your Grace."
> "It is not necessary to sign it," said Don Quixote." All I need do is to add my flourish, which is the same as a signature and will suffice for three, and even three hundred, asses."[27]

In other words, the same value is ascribed to the don's mark as was previously ascribed to his signature.

In seventeenth-century translations, *librillo de memoria* is consistently rendered as *tablette* in French and *table* in English. The English translation published in London in 1687 by J. Philips illustrates the liberty that translators were allowed at the time. The translator, bringing his own concerns into the text, adds to the condemnation of "court hand," which is the phrase used to translate *letra procesada*, the handwriting of chancelleries and tribunals, a condemnation of his own, of "shorthand" or stenographic writing, which does not appear in Cervantes' text. In this English version, Don Quixote advises Sancho not only to avoid the "Lawyer," "for the Devil himself will never be able to read Court-Hand," but "more especially" to "beware of one that writes Sermons; for I hate Short-Hand mortally."[28]

The translation thus alludes to one use of the many methods of rapid writing that appeared in England in the seventeenth century: the stenographic transcription of sermons as they were delivered for later copying in "long hand" and subsequent publication, often in an edition not approved by the preacher. Thus the relation between writing and orality was not simply one of vocal transmission of a written text, as when Don Quixote read his letters out loud. It could also be transcription of the spoken word, whether of the preacher in church, the political orator, or actors on stage. Although little direct evidence of this practice has survived, it can sometimes be inferred from printed editions. The title pages of many books of sermons published in England in the seventeenth century indicate that the text was "taken by characterie," that is, recorded stenographically (the words "characterie," "stenography," "tachigraphy," and "brachigraphy" referred to different types of rapid writing). The anomalies and variants in the printed texts of some plays can be understood as errors due to poor transcription using one of several methods practiced in England after 1580.[29] The English translator of 1687 thus used Cervantes' text to express his own dislike of a technique that allowed works to be pirated without the consent of their authors and circulated in highly corrupt editions—perhaps also because the previous English translator of *Don Quixote*, Thomas Shelton, had the same name as the author of a method *for* "*Short-Writing*" that was reprinted several times under various titles between 1630 and 1650. Stenography does not seem to have had such great importance in Lope de Vega's Spain or Molière's France, since texts describing the printing of plays based on transcriptions never mention the use of rapid writing by word thieves.[30]

Having decided to emulate Amadis's melancholy rather than Orlando's madness, Don Quixote is gripped in chapter 26 by an imperious desire to describe the glories of his mistress and the pain he suffers as a result of her absence: "He spent his time walking up and down the little meadow, carving inscriptions on the bark of trees, and writing many verses in the fine sand, all reflective of his melancholy and some of them in praise of Dulcinea."[31] The reference to Pedro Mexía and to writing on bark is here coupled with the theme of the lover who litters nature with poems expressing his passion. Orlando does the same in *As You Like It* when he hangs poems to Rosalind from the branches of trees.[32] Writing on sand has more tragic precedents. In *Titus Andronicus*, Lavinia, after being violated and mutilated, writes the names of her tormentors in the sand.[33] Don Quixote's poems on bark, three of which are quoted in the text, allow Cervantes to play a familiar game—referring to supposedly authentic documents, in this instance, surviving traces of compositions by the knight: "only these three could be deciphered in their entirety."[34]

Sancho the *Memorioso*

Sancho's return to the company of the curate and the barber is marked by a similar intertwining of the book of memory (the epistolary medium) with the memory of the book, or, in this case, of the written, by a person who does not know how to read. When the curate offers to transcribe the letter to Dulcinea, Sancho looks for it and is alarmed to discover that Cardenio's *librillo* with the letter of exchange in his favor is missing: "But when Sancho put his hand in his bosom to search for the book he could not find it, and he would not have been able to find it if he had searched until now, for the reason that Don Quixote still had it, the squire having forgotten to ask him for it."[35]

Although Sancho is beside himself for having mislaid the *cédula* his master had signed, the curate calms him down by telling him that the document would have had no legal value anyway: "The curate did what he could to console him by telling him that when he returned his master would give him another order, and they would have it done on paper this time as was the usage and custom, for those that were made out in memorandum books were never accepted nor complied with."[36] A letter of exchange (here designated by the term *libranza*) is valid only if written on paper. It has no power of obligation if recorded in a *librillo de memoria*. The curate thus explains the difference between a private object, which belongs to an individual, and a public document attesting to a contractual commitment. As we have seen, however, the distinction also points to another possible opposition, between the sheet of paper and a different material medium, the "tablet," which was probably made of something other than paper.

With no written text at hand, Sancho claims that he can recite the letter to Dulcinea so that the curate can transcribe it. But his memory betrays him, and he has forgotten nearly all of the missive or remembered it only in the most confused way:

"In God's name, Señor Licentiate, may the devil take me if I can remember it. I know that it began, 'High and sufferable lady—'"

"He would not have said *sufferable*," the barber corrected him; "it must have been *sovereign* lady or something of that sort."

"That's it," said Sancho. "Well, then, unless my memory fails me, it went like this: 'The pierced and wounded one, the sleepless one kisses your Grace's hands, O ungrateful fair one and most unrecognized,' and so on and so forth, all about health and sickness which he was sending her and a rigamarole that ended with 'Yours until death, the Knight of the Mournful Countenance.'"[37]

Cervantes' characterization of Sancho's memory is quite subtle. Apart from formulas (such as proverbs and the closing signature of the letter), his memory is not like that of men of letters trained in the art of memory and capable of preserving in their minds either the verbatim text of what they have read and heard or, in the case of *memoria ad res*, the subjects discussed.[38] Sancho's memory, which is entirely aural, mixes up words (*sobajada* for *soberana*, *llego* for *llagado*) that he has misheard or mismemorized, conflates passages from different parts of the text, and mistakes meanings. This gives rise to a series of comic effects for the reader, who knows the letter, as well as for the curate and barber, who have good reason to believe that the original was not as Sancho remembers it. Sancho's memory also relies on repetition and recapitulation, as the Spanish text indicates by doubling words: "Luego, si mal no me acuerdo, proseguía, si mal no me acuerdo" ("Then, unless my memory fails, it went on like this, unless my memory fails"). This manner of expression, which here indicates the effort of recollection, also structures the recital of tales.

In chapter 20, Cervantes contrasts Sancho's way of telling tales with the expectations of the reader, which are also Don Quixote's. In recounting the story of the shepherd Lope Ruiz and the shepherdess Torralba, Sancho often goes back in time, embellishes, digresses, and goes off on tangents. He constantly interrupts his story to comment on the situation in which he and his master find themselves. Don Quixote, meanwhile, expects a linear narrative, without recapitulations, repetitions, or digressions: "If that is the way you are going to tell your story, Sancho, saying everything over twice, you will not be finished in a couple of days. Tell it in a straightforward manner, like a man of good sense, or otherwise do not tell it at all." Sancho replies that he cannot tell it any other way: "'In my country,' said Sancho, 'they tell all fables just the way I am telling this one, and I cannot tell it any other way, nor is it right for your Grace to ask me to adopt new customs.'" Resigned and possibly amused, Don Quixote ultimately accepts this manner of speaking, which is so alien to his manner of reading: "'As you like, then,' said Don Quixote, 'and since fate has willed that I must listen, proceed with it.'"[39]

Dictionary Definitions

Found by the wayside, already almost entirely filled with writing yet capable of accommodating two more letters, one in verse, the other a letter of exchange, Cardenio's *librillo de memoria* does not give up its identity easily. To understand it better we probably need to leave the Sierra Morena. In the first third of the eighteenth century, more than a century after the publication of the story of the *librillo*, the *Diccionario de la Real Academia Española* proposed a definition of the object:

Small book customarily carried in the pocket, with white pages covered with wax and in which was included a metal quill in the point of which a small piece of pencil was inserted for the purpose of recording whatever one did not wish to entrust to the fragility of memory, and which could then be erased so that the pages could be reused; also made of ivory.[40]

The characteristics of the object are clearly delineated. It was a small notebook whose pages were covered with a coating on which one could write with a stylus carried in the binding; after being written on, the pages could be erased and reused. More reliable than memory, because it fixed in writing what might otherwise be forgotten, the *librillo de memoria* was nevertheless not a library or permanent archive. The assumption was that whatever was written in it would be copied onto another medium so that the pages could be restored to their original pristine condition. As an example, the *Diccionario* cited this sentence from chapter 23 of *Don Quixote*: "Y buscando más, halló un libro de memoria, ricamente guarnecido" ("Looking further, he came upon a memorandum book, richly bound"). Cardenio's *librillo* thus became the primary example of the object described in the definition.

Before accepting this interpretation by eighteenth-century Spanish academicians, one needs to ask whether it was applicable at the beginning of the previous century. Covarrubias's *Tesoro de la langua castellana* of 1611 has no entry under *librillo de memoria*. The term does appear in two other definitions however. In the article *librero*, we read: "libro de memoria, pugilare," as if there were a possible equivalence between the waxed tablet of the Ancients, designated by the Latin word *pugilare*, and the *libro de memoria*. In the article *memorioso*, the comparison is even more extensive, emphasizing the reuse of the same writing surface: "libro de memoria, pugillares latine, vel palimpsestus." Erasable and reusable, the *librillo de memoria* is the palimpsest of the Moderns. It was described, but without using the term, in another entry in Covarrubias' dictionary, on *barniz*, or varnish, which is said to be a type of gum or glue used to coat paintings, iron, and "tablets for writing," like the Latin "tabelle gypsata, seu dealbata" or the Greek *palimpsestos*.[41] Thus it is likely that the pages of Cardenio's *librillo* were not made of paper, or at any rate not of ordinary paper requiring a quill and ink for writing and not erasable. The "drafts" of the letters to Luscinda, at first ardent, then desperate, may have been written and rewritten on pages covered with a kind of varnish (*barniz* or *betún*) that allowed for changes of heart, erasures, and alterations.[42]

The Tables of the Prince of Denmark

Even as Cardenio was leaving behind his *librillo de memoria* in the Sierra Morena, on stage in London another young man wished to erase his tables. The ghost having issued the order "Remember me," the young prince obeyed by wiping the "tables of his memory" clean of all but the ghostly injunction:

Remember thee,
Yea, from the table of my memory
I'll wipe away all trivial fond records,
All saws of books, all forms, all pressures past,
That youth and observation copied there,
And thy commandment all alone shall live,
Within the book and volume of my brain,
Unmix'd with baser matter.[43]

To imagine memory as a library of tablets containing quotations, models, and sentences collected in the course of reading was by no means original. What was more original was the fact the ancient and medieval metaphor should have been embodied in the material object that Hamlet drew from his cloak:

My tables, meet it is I set it down,
That one may smile, and smile, and be a villain
At least I am sure it may be so in Denmark.
So, uncle, there you are. Now to my word,
It is "Adieu, adieu, remember me."[44]

On stage, the actor who plays the role is thus given a notebook that can be kept in a pocket and written on while standing up, outside, without the encumbrance of an inkwell or the need for a table, and allowing for the possibility of "wiping away" what has been written and writing again on the same page.

Such things did exist in Elizabethan England.[45] Between 1577 and 1628, to judge by the dates of surviving examples, Frank Adams and Robert Triplet, two London bookbinders and "makers of writing tablets," put out a large number of notebooks designated as "Writing Tables with a Kalender for XXIIII years." In 16vo format used either in the usual way or as an oblong object, printed notebooks containing some of the standard features of almanacs (such as a calendar, a list of fair dates, distances between cities, tables of weights and measures, multiplication tables for Roman numerals, and a plate depicting coins in circulation) also included blank pages, some of which were covered with a coating of plaster, glue, and varnish that could be written on and then erased and rewritten. In the 1604 edition published by Robert Triplet, we find in the calendar for the date December 13 instructions on how to use these "writing tables":

To make cleane your Tables, when they are written on. Take a little peece of a Spunge, or a Linnen cloth, being cleane without any soyle: wet it in water, and wring it hard, & wipe that you have written very lightly, and it will out, and within one quarter of an howre you may wryte in the same place againe: put not your leaves together, whilest they be very wet with wyping.[46]

Twenty-one copies representing eighteen editions have survived. As with all widely circulated works, however, the survival rate is inversely proportional to the quantity of production, which suggests that, counting editions that have totally disappeared and a minimum print run of 1,200 copies, something on the order of a hundred thousand copies of Adams's and Triplet's *Writing Tables* were in circulation in England between 1570 and 1630. The Lord Chamberlain's theater troupe, to which Shakespeare belonged, could easily have acquired a copy for use by Hamlet as a prop.

The material nature of the object and its presence in the stage directions or dialogue of numerous Elizabethan plays give us an idea of precisely how it was used: out of doors or away from a desk, for making quick notations with a metal stylus. So these "writing tables" or "table books" could be used to record a thought, copy down an order, preserve a comment or phrase, or take down a text on the fly, to judge by what actors did with them on stage.

The texts that we find in surviving examples on both the erasable and non-erasable pages suggest other uses as well: copying down medical formulas, keeping accounts, listing dates of fairs. What all these traces of writing have in common is the fact that they were destined to be transitory, to be erased when they were no longer useful or when their content had been copied onto a more durable medium. Hence it is reasonable to assume that they were used to transcribe, stenographically or otherwise, sermons and plays, to collect quotations encountered in the course of reading, prior to being sorted under the headings of the commonplace notebooks, and, finally, to compose drafts of texts of which fair copies were later made on paper. Despite Hamlet's assertions to the contrary, it is indeed a commonplace that he writes down in his "tables" before the command issued by his betrayed and murdered father: "That one may smile, and smile, and be a villain."[47] Cardenio, for his part, used his *librillo de memoria* for drafts of his letters and poems before Don Quixote reused it to draft a love letter and a letter of exchange for subsequent transcription by an expert writer.

Is it legitimate, however, to liken Hamlet's "tables" to Cardenio's *librillo*? Surely yes, since the existence of "writing tables" was not limited to the fifty years during which Adams and Triplet published theirs in London, initially on their own and later on behalf of the English Stock of the Stationers' Company, whose profits were shared among its members. As early as the beginning of the sixteenth century, English customs registers mention the importation of "table books" or "writing tables," which we may assume were manufactured on the continent, and even after Frank Adams began selling his "tables," imports of various types continued to be sold by booksellers and stationers.[48] Thus it is reasonable to assume that pamphlets with erasable pages were in use on the continent before or at the same time as Hamlet's "tables." In 1611, two dictionaries made clear reference to the existence of such objects on both sides of the Channel. *Queen Anna's New World of Words*, by John Florio, defined the Italian word "cartella, cartelle" as "leaves of writing tables,"[49] and Cotgrave's French-English dictionary lists the equivalence "*Tablettes*, Writing Tables."[50] French dictionaries of the late seventeenth century (the Richelet of 1680, the Furetière of 1690, and the *Dictionnaire* of the Académie Française in 1693) reinforce the idea that the two objects were similar because they indicate that *tablettes* were made of "prepared" paper on which one wrote with a pencil or *touche* (i.e., a metal stylus), and that these were sometimes combined with an almanac (at least in Richelet's definition). Is it not likely that Spain, too, would have been familiar with erasable writing and the media that supported it?

The *librillos de memoria* Between Spain and the Spanish Colonies

Several pieces of evidence show that this was indeed the case. First, inventories of aristocratic and princely estates often mention sumptuously decorated *libros de memoria* (richly "guarnecidos" like Cardenio's) together with a stylus (*clavo, palo, palillo de oro*), which served, as indicated in an inventory of property brought to France in 1615 by Anne of Austria, "para escrivir en libros de memoria."[51] Clearly, then, one did not write in such books with pen and ink but, as in "writing tables," with a metal-tipped object. To be sure, not all *librillos de memoria* were as precious as these. Evidence for this can be seen in the small business that a certain Jorge Noé did in the late sixteenth century. Noé sailed as a drummer on the *Almiranta*, which crossed the Atlantic, and in 1583 he died in San Juan de Ulúa in Mexico. An inventory of his belongings included three dozen small *libretes de memoria* and two old *libros de memoria*, together with other dry goods. In addition, he had sent a Flemish merchant settled in Veracruz twenty-four additional *libretes de memoria*. The relatively low price fetched by the *libretes* when sold at auction suggests that the goods that Noé imported into New Spain were fairly common and in wide use, closer to Adams's and Triplet's "writing tables" than to the precious objects owned by the grandees of Spain.[52]

Just as the English theater did with "table books" and "writing tables," the *comedias* brought *libros de memoria* to the stage and assigned them the same uses as in England: immediate transcription of the spoken word, recording of fleeting thoughts, and drafting short texts, all carried out in the same kinds of places, such as public squares and streets or carriages. Lope de Vega's uses of the term come in three different registers.[53] First, he refers to the material nature of the object carried by various of his characters. Thus, Celia in *Ay, verdades, que en amor* declares: "Libro tengo de memoria," "I have tablets." Second, there is the image of memory as a varnished tablet, which works against the traditional idea of memory as a repository or archive and insists rather on its fragility and vulnerability. In *Amar, servir y esperar*, for example, the servant Andrés says that "memory is not bronze but like a varnished tablet that is easily erased and rewritten."[54] Finally, there is a metaphorical register, in which the inconstancy of a woman's heart is compared with writing on erasable tablets. Thus, in the first part of *El Príncipe perfecto*, Beltrán declares:

One day, a learned man said that the love of a woman is like one of those varnished tablets on whose virgin surface women record their memories. With a little saliva they erase the first name written there and replace it with another. A woman's soul is like a blank tablet. If your name is written there today, tomorrow it may be erased. It takes no more than a day, sir, for their love is like varnish, and where Don Juan was written, Don Pedro may come and take his place.[55]

In contrast to England, where some twenty of the Adams and Triplet calendars have survived, no *librillo de memoria* has yet turned up in a Spanish library or archive. The Princeton University library has one consisting of sixteen pages covered with an erasable coating. It was used at various times in the sixteenth and seventeenth centuries to copy births and baptisms in ink, but this was probably not the purpose for which this object was originally intended.[56]

All signs thus indicate that booklets whose pages could be reused did indeed exist in Golden Age Spain and that they were useful for writing in places and circumstances where the use of pen, ink, and ordinary paper would have been difficult if not impossible.[57] Cardenio had one, and so did Hamlet.

Fragile Words

The linking of *librillo* and memory reappears at the end of chapter 30, when Don Quixote asks Sancho how Dulcinea reacted to the letter he had written and who had transcribed it. Sancho must confess what his master already knows: "'Sir,' replied Sancho, 'if I am to tell the truth, the letter was not copied for me by anyone, for I did not have it with me.'"[58] But he adds that his memory was able to compensate for the absent "book," thus sparing him the need to retrace his steps: "'That is what I'd have done,' said Sancho, 'if I hadn't learned it by heart while your Grace was reading it to me, so that I was able to recite it to a sacristan who copied it all down for me, point by point. And he said that in the course of his life he had read many a letter of excommunication but never a pretty one like that.'"[59] When Don Quixote asks if he still remembers it, Sancho replies that he has erased it from his memory: "'No, sir, I do not [remember the letter]; for as soon as I had said it over to him, seeing that I had no further need of remembering it, I proceeded to forget it.'"[60]

In *Don Quixote*, words are never safe from the risks of disappearance. Manuscripts break off, as is the case with the one that recounts the adventures of the knight-errant;[61] poems written on trees are lost; pages from memory books can be erased; and memory itself is often faulty. Like *Hamlet*, the story narrated by Cid Hamet Benengeli is haunted by forgetfulness, as if all objects and all techniques for preserving memory were of no avail.

Yet there is one defense against such fragility, the one evoked by the duchess when Cardenio's *librillo*, lost in the Sierra Morena, is mentioned for the last time, in chapter 33 of Part Two. Speaking to Sancho, she says:

"Now that we are alone," she said, "with no one to hear us, I should like the Señor Governor to resolve certain doubts that I have, growing out of the story of the great Don Quixote that has already been printed. For one thing, inasmuch as the worthy Sancho never saw Dulcinea, I mean the lady Dulcinea del Toboso, and never brought her Don Quixote's letter, which was left in the memorandum book on the Sierra Morena, how did he dare make up the answer . . . ?"[62]

"Already printed," the story of the knight and his master will withstand the ravages of time, and as Samson Carrasco declares, "As for me, I have no doubt that nary a nation nor a language will allow it to go untranslated."[63] The bachelor was not mistaken.

Chapter 3
The Press and Fonts:
Don Quixote in the Print Shop

In 1615, the Madrid print shop of Juan de la Cuesta printed for the bookseller Francisco de Robles the second part of *The Ingenious Knight Don Quixote de la Mancha* (*Segunda Parte del Ingenioso Cavallero Don Quixote de la Mancha*). Ten years after his first exploits, Don Quixote set out again on the routes of Spain. In chapters 61 to 65, Sancho and his master find themselves in Barcelona, where Don Quixote has decided to go instead of participating in the jousts at Saragossa. Roque Guinart, the highway robber they encounter on their way, has delivered them to the jests and mockery of Don Antonio Moreno and his friends. To avoid the laughter of the children who are following his ridiculous cortège, Don Quixote decides to go on foot and without an escort:

In the meantime, Don Quixote wished to go out for a quiet stroll, for he feared that if he went on horseback the small boys would follow him, and so, accompanied only by Sancho and a couple of servants that Don Antonio had furnished him, he set out with this object in view.[1]

As he was going down a certain street he glanced up and saw a sign in large letters over a doorway, reading: "Books printed here." This pleased him very much, as he had never seen a printing shop up to that time and had a desire to find out what it was like.[2]

This was not the first time that a fictional narrative was situated in a print shop, as the tales told around a print shop hearth in William Baldwin's *Beware the Cat* show.[3] In Cervantes, however, the shop is more than just a backdrop. It introduces into the book itself the place and process that make its publication possible. If the work done in such shops is what allows the fiction to exist, the terms of this equation are reversed in chapter 62 of part two of *Don Quixote*, because the prosaic world of the print shop becomes one of those places where, as Borges puts it, "Cervantes delights in fusing the objective and the subjective, the world of the reader and the world of the book."[4]

Book, Body, and Soul

On entering the print shop, Don Quixote "saw them drawing proofs here, correcting them there, setting type in one place and making revisions in another—in short, he beheld everything that goes to make up a large establishment of this sort."[5] Cervantes immediately introduces his reader to the division of labor and multiple operations necessary to turn a text into a book: the composition of pages by compositors (*componer*), the correction of the first printed pages, or proofs (*corregir, enmendar*), and, finally, the printing of forms, or pages secured in a chase, for printing on the same side of a large sheet of printing paper by the workers in charge of the press (*tirar*).

The accuracy of this description of the work process of a printing shop is corroborated by the first manual of the art of printing written in a vulgar tongue (excepting the German translation, published in 1634, of Jerome Hornschuch's *Orthotypographia* [Leipzig, 1608]).[6] This treatise in Castilian, set directly in movable type without a pre-existing manuscript, was composed around 1680 by the typesetter Alonso Victor de Paredes, who was a master printer in Seville and then Madrid; only a very few copies were printed.[7] In the tenth chapter of the book, entitled "De la Correción," four types of correctors, copyeditors or proofreaders are identified: university graduates who know grammar, theology, and law but, not being printers, are unfamiliar with the techniques of the trade; master printers with a smattering of Latin; the more expert compositors, who may not know Latin themselves but can seek assistance from the author or some other educated person; and, finally, the ignorant, who barely know how to read and who are employed by the widows of printers or by booksellers who are not themselves printers.

All perform the same tasks (except the ignorant, who are not capable of them). First, the corrector must identify the compositors' errors by following the printed text while the original is read aloud (*escuchar por el original*). In addition, he also acts as censor, charged with rejecting any book in which he finds anything prohibited by the Inquisition or contrary to the faith, the king, or the republic (*algo prohibido por el Santo Tribunal, ò que sea, ò parezca mal sonāte contra la Fè, contra nuestro Rey, ò contra la Republica*), even if the work has been approved and authorized. Last but not least, the corrector is responsible for putting the finishing touches on the text by adding the necessary punctuation (*la apuntuacion legitima*) and fixing any authorial oversights (*descuidos*) or compositors' errors (*yerros*). These responsibilities require the corrector to understand not only the letter of the original text but also the author's intention (*entender el concepto del Autor*) so as to convey it comprehensibly to the reader.[8]

Some years later, Joseph Moxon assigned some of these same tasks to the compositor, others to the corrector. For him,

A good Compositor is ambitious as well to make the meaning of his Author intelligent to the Reader, as to make his Work shew graceful to the Eye and pleasant in reading. Therefore, if his copy be written in a language he understands, he reads his Copy with Consideration; that so he may get himself into the meaning of the author, and consequently considers how to order his Work the better both in the title page, and in the matter of the Book: As how to make Indenting, Pointing, Breaking, Italicking, etc. the better sympathize with the Authors Genius, and also with the capacity of the reader.[9]

All decisions made by the compositor are nevertheless subject to modification by the proofreader, who plays a decisive role in the publishing process: "He examines the Proof and considers the Pointing, Italicking, Capittalling, or any error that may through mistake, or want of Judgement, be committed by the Compositor."[10]

In 1675, a lawyer, Melchor de Cabrera Nuñez de Guzman, divided the responsibilities of compositor and corrector in an identical manner when he defended fiscal exemptions and immunities for printers on the grounds that the art of printing was a liberal and not a mechanical art, for in all its associated trades "the intellectual and speculative part is vastly greater than the manual activity."[11] In his view, the compositor should "understand the meaning and argument." He should be an expert in the Castilian language and must know how to cast off the copy, "because books are composed not in the order in which the text is written but by forms." He must be able to punctuate the text correctly, "so as to be clearly intelligible," to distinguish sentences, and to place accents, parentheses, question marks, and exclamation points where needed, "Because often the writer's expression becomes confused if these elements, which are necessary and important for the intelligibility and comprehension of what is written or printed, are missing; because if they are absent, the meaning is transformed, altered, and different."[12]

Like Moxon, however, Cabrera believed that the corrector should be allowed to second-guess the decisions of the compositor because the former was better educated. He was obliged

to know, at a minimum, grammar (there have been, and there are, some who are graduates in one discipline or another), spelling, etymology, punctuation, and where to place accents. He must have knowledge of the sciences, letters, Greek and Hebrew characters, and the rules of music; he must master eloquence, art, and elegance in order to recognize and correct barbarisms, solecisms, and other faults in Latin, Castilian, and other languages.[13]

For Paredes and Cabrera, Moxon, and Cervantes before them, textual production involved a variety of stages, techniques, and operations. Intervening between the author's genius and the reader's capacity for appreciation, to borrow Moxon's terms, the publication process did not divorce the materiality of the text from the textuality of the book.[14] Paredes stands a classic metaphor on its head to express the dual nature of the book, object as well as œuvre. Whereas countless texts describe the human body or the face as a book,[15] Paredes treats the book as a human creature, because, like man, it has both a body and a soul: "I see a book as being made in the same way as a man, who has the rational soul with which Our Lord created it, with all the graces that His Divine Majesty has deigned to bestow on it; and with the same omnipotence He has given him an elegant body, handsome and harmonious."[16] It is possible to compare a book to a man because God created human beings in the same way as books are printed. Cabrera gives this analogy its most elaborate form when he says that man is the only printed book of the six that God wrote. The other five are the *Starry heavens*, which he compares to a vast parchment on which the stars figure as the letters of the alphabet; the *World*, which is the summa and map of all Creation; *Life*, which is like a record book containing the names of all the elect; *Christ*, who is at once the *exemplum* and *exemplar*, that is, an example offered to all mankind and an authorial manuscript to be copied; and finally, the *Virgin*, the first of all, whose creation in the Spirit of God, the *Mente Divina*, preexisted the creation of the world, of time, and of the earth. Among these various works of God, all of which are mentioned in Scripture or by the Church Fathers and all of which are related by Cabrera to some object in the written culture of his time, man is an exception, because he is the product of a print shop: "God placed his image and seal on the press and clamped it down, so that the copy would come out identical to the form it was supposed to have . . . and it was also his wish to enjoy the numerous and varied copies of his mysterious original."[17]

Paredes used the image and stressed the idea that for him the soul of the book was not simply the text as composed, dictated, and imagined by its creator but the text as embodied in a form adequate to its intention: "A perfectly finished book consists in a good doctrine, presented as it should be by the printer and corrector: that is what I regard as the soul of the book. And it is a good impression on a clean and well-maintained press that makes for what I would compare to a gracious and elegant body."[18]

If the body of the book is the result of the pressmen's labor, its soul is not fashioned solely by the author but shaped by all who have a hand in its punctuation, spelling, and layout, including the master printer, the compositors, the copyeditors, and the proofreaders. Paredes thus rejects out of hand any separation of the essential substance of the work, taken to be the same regardless of the form in which it is presented, and the accidental variations of the text resulting from the printing process and alleged by some to be of no importance to the significance of the work.[19]

Sancho's Ass

An episode from the editorial history of *Don Quixote*, which was printed in late 1604 in the shop of Juan de la Cuesta and published with the date 1605, illustrates the realities as well as the risks of collaboration inherent in any publishing process. In chapter 25 of the story, in the first edition of the book, Sancho mentions in passing the theft of his ass: "Good luck to him who has saved us the trouble now of stripping the ass." Four chapters later, Sancho follows on foot as his master rides on horseback: "The knight then mounted Rocinante and the barber his own beast, while Sancho came along on foot, which led him to think once more of the gray ass whose loss he now felt worse than ever." Without explanation, however, the ass reappears in chapter 42: "Sancho Panza alone was fretting over their delay in retiring, but he was the one that ended by making himself the most comfortable of all, for he simply threw himself down on the trappings of his ass."[20]

Acknowledging the discrepancy, which was immediately noticed by his critics, Cervantes wrote two brief stories for the second edition of *Don Quixote*, which was also published in 1605 (a sign of the book's success). The first told of the theft of the ass by Ginés de Pasamonte, the galley slave who was inadvertently set free by Don Quixote; the second described Sancho's recovery of his mount after he recognizes the thief disguised as a Gipsy, chases him off, and reclaims his beloved gray ass.[21] In the second edition, the story of the theft was inserted in chapter 23, shortly after the two heroes enter the Sierra Morena, while the other story was included in chapter 30, when they leave the mountains along with Cardenio, Dorotea, the barber, and the curate, who have come to rescue Don Quixote from his sylvan folly. Everything seemed to have been set right, then, but unfortunately the first sentence of chapter 25 was not corrected. It read: "Taking his leave of the goatherd, Don Quixote once again mounted Rocinante and ordered Sancho, who was now in a very bad humor, to follow him, which the latter did *with his donkey*."[22] In other words, Sancho is still riding the ass, even though it has been stolen from him. In the edition that Roger Velpius published in Brussels in 1607, a more alert copy-editor eliminated the discrepancy, although we find it still intact in the third Madrid edition, which left the presses of Juan de la Cuesta in 1608.

The tribulations of the vanished but still present ass remind us first of all that texts, far from being fixed in their final form once and for all, are variable, unstable, and malleable. Variants are the result of a host of decisions and/or errors that may occur at any point in the publishing process. As the example of *Don Quixote* shows, the negligence of the author, the mistakes of the compositors, and the inattentiveness of the proofreaders all played a part in determining the work's successive states. How should editors and critics regard these inconsistencies and discrepancies? Francisco Rico thinks that one must try to recover the text that Cervantes wrote, imagined, and desired, which was subsequently distorted in the print shop.[23] One should follow the classical philologists, who studied the whole manuscript tradition of a work in order to establish the most probable text,[24] and compare all the printed states of a work to recover what the author wrote, or wanted to write, which in some instances does not appear in any edition.

Or consider another perspective: that of Shakespeare criticism, for which the forms in which a work was published, no matter how strange, must be regarded as different historical incarnations.[25] All states of the text, even the most inconsistent and bizarre, must be understood and eventually published, for, as the result of acts of writing and work practices, they constitute the work as it was conveyed to its readers. Every work exists only in its simultaneous and successive material forms. The search for a pure primary text that would somehow exist prior to or beyond its various material embodiments is therefore pointless. To edit a work is therefore not to recover an "ideal copy text" but to make explicit the reasons for preferring one or another of its various states, along with the choices governing the presentation (divisions, layout, punctuation, spelling).[26]

The decision is not always easy. Take a Shakespearean example: *Love's Labor's Lost.* In 1598, in the first edition of the comedy in quarto format, the couples are rearranged in the course of the play. The amorous dialogue initially links Berowne and Katherine (not Rosaline) and Dumaine and Rosaline (not Katherine). Only in the third act, following the divisions introduced into the text by eighteenth-century editors, does each of the young lords of Navarre fall in love with the woman who will occupy his thoughts to the end of the play. In 1623, the Folio edition, which for the first time brought together Shakespeare's "Comedies, Histories, & Tragedies," as the title page has it, "published according to the True Originall Copies," depicts a different situation: Berowne and Rosaline and Dumaine and Katherine are attracted to each other from their first encounter.

What are we to make of this difference? Did Shakespeare mix up the names of the characters in the original version? Did one of the compositors of the quarto edition make a mistake? Or was the original edition more faithful to the author's dramatic intention, since an abrupt shift of amorous passion is a theme that we find in other plays (most notably in the loves of Romeo), and the fickleness of the young "lords" of Navarre might explain why the young ladies of France are so hard on them in the play's final act? As Stephen Greenblatt explains, the tension between aesthetic preference and textual tradition makes the choice difficult: "Although the version printed here is based on the near consensus among recent textual scholars, Q may provide the most accurate rendition available of the romantic relations in *Love's Labour's Lost*."[27] In other words, the editor is torn between respect for the more consistent version of the text, as sanctioned by a tradition dating back to 1623, and the nostalgic allure of a more exciting version.

The episode involving Sancho's ass has another lesson to offer. The textual inconsistencies that we find in *Don Quixote*, of which this is only one example, point up the similarities that exist between Cervantes' writing and certain practices of orality. As Francisco Rico notes, "Cervantes revolutionized fiction by conceiving it not in the artificial style of literature but in the ordinary prose of everyday life." In this sense, "*Don Quixote* is not so much *written* as *spoken*, written without submitting to the constraints of writing—neither the constraints of its time, with the baroque skills required by the styles then in fashion, nor, of course, the constraints of our own day."[28]

For the first time, a novel was written in the rhythm and syntax of the spoken language, against the rules of grammar and aesthetic conventions. More than that, the narration, with its multiple digressions, parentheses, and free association of words, themes, and ideas, was composed not according to the principles of literary rhetoric but according to the codes that govern conversation and oral exchanges. Omissions, confusions, and discrepancies are of little importance to a style that constructs a narrative as though it were a manner of speaking.[29]

Glory and Profit

The time has come to return to Don Quixote in the Barcelona print shop. There he encounters an "author" who has translated an Italian book entitled

Le Bagatele into Castilian. In the dialogue that develops between them, Cervantes touches on three standard motifs of his day. First, there is an amusing reference to the success of Ariosto's poems: "'I,' said Don Quixote, 'am somewhat acquainted with Tuscan and pride myself on being able to recite certain stanzas of Ariosto.'"[30] Then there is the comic effect that comes from Quixote's admiration for the most trivial translations: "I will lay you a good wager that you translate *piace* as *place*, *più* as *más*, *su* as *arriba*, and *giù* as *abajo*."[31] Finally, there is the debate on the utility of translation. "It appears to me," says Don Quixote, "that translating from one language into another, unless it be from one of those two queenly tongues, Greek and Latin, is like gazing at a Flemish tapestry with the wrong side out: even though the figures are visible, they are full of threads that obscure the view and are not bright and smooth as when seen from the other side."[32]

In addition to these references to shared knowledge, the dialogue is filled with allusions to the practices of printers and booksellers. In his discussion with the translator, Don Quixote mentions the two forms of book publishing that existed in Golden Age Spain and modern Europe:

"But, your Grace, I should like to know, is this book being printed at your own expense or have you already disposed of the rights to some bookseller?"

"I pay for the printing," said the author, "and I expect to clear at least a thousand ducats on this first edition of two thousand copies, which at two *reales* apiece ought to sell in no time at all."[33]

By printing *por su cuenta*, that is, paying to have the book printed "for his own account," the translator has retained the privilege that was granted to him and commissioned the Barcelona printer to produce two thousand copies to be sold either by booksellers or directly by the printer (which was not unusual, as Fernando Bouza has shown[34]).

In requesting the printing of two thousand copies for the first edition of his book, the translator of *Le Bagatele* was not altogether unpresumptuous. A press run of this magnitude was the highest contemplated by Paredes, who indicates that in one working day a press could print 1,500, 1,750, or 2,000 copies of two forms (that is, the pages corresponding to both sides of a printer's sheet).[35] Cervantes may be using this detail to suggest that the translator is overconfident, or he may want to indicate that the public is enamored of translations, more so than of original stories. Recall that Juan de la Cuesta very likely printed only 1,750 copies of the second edition of *Don Quixote* in 1605, and that this was in any case a much larger than average print run,[36] and surely greater than that of the first edition.[37]

A remark by the translator contrasts two "economies of writing": "I do not have books printed to win fame in this world, for I am already well known through my works; it is money that I seek, for without it a fine reputation is not worth a cent."[38] The contrast between *fama* and *provecho*, reputation and profit, was a commonplace in Golden Age Spain. Here, however, it is linked to a sharp perception of the literary world. Translators were in fact the first "authors" to receive, in exchange for their manuscript, not only copies of the work to be given to their patrons but also monetary remuneration.[39] This marked a first step toward the professionalization of writing, linked to an activity that was related to copying. In Castilian, the same word, *trasladar*, designated both activities, copying and translating, as Covarrubias's definition indicates.[40] Concerned to earn money from his book, the translator had no intention of surrendering the privilege to a bookseller who would then reap all the profit from his eventual success.

In contrast to the classical model of writing, in which the writer was assumed to be a disinterested party by virtue either of his social status or the protection of a patron, the translator of *Le Bagatele* claims that it is possible to live on what he writes, and to live well. He hopes for what Cervantes, in his "Prologue to the Reader" in Part Two of *Don Quixote*, deemed impossible: "One of the greatest temptations [of the devil] . . . consists in putting it into a man's head that he can write a book and have it printed and thereby achieve as much fame as he does money and acquire as much money as he does fame."[41] This, for Cervantes, was an idle hope. Books could not bring both fame and fortune. For those without either status or wealth, like Cervantes himself, only the generosity of a patron—in his case the count of Lemos, viceroy of Naples, and the archbishop of Toledo, Bernardo de Sandoval y Rojas—could ensure the writer a decent life.

Don Quixote expressed skepticism regarding the expectations of the overconfident translator:

"That," said Don Quixote, "is a fine bit of calculation on your Grace's part, but it is plain to be seen that you are not familiar with the ins and outs of the printers and the way in which they all work together. I can promise you that when you find yourself weighted down with two thousand copies, you will be astonished how your body will ache all over, especially if the book happens to be a little out of the ordinary and does not make spicy reading."[42]

Here the text plays with a commonplace of the Golden Age: the greed and dishonesty of printers, who were always quick to alter their account books and use accomplices to hide the true number of copies ordered, so that they could sell a certain number of copies more rapidly than the author and at a better price.[43]

Cervantes had used the theme earlier in one of the *Novelas ejemplares*, in the story of the "Licentiate of Glass." "Your trade would please me well if there were no fault in it," Tomás says to the bookseller in whose shop he is leaning against a wall (with a "thousand precautions," because, having bitten into a quince on which a spurned lover has placed a curse, he believes that he is made of glass). To the bookseller, who asks him what that fault might be, the licentiate responds: "The charlatans who pretend to be booksellers when they buy the privilege of a book, and the trick they play on the author, if by chance he has had the book printed for his own account, for instead of 1,500 copies, they print 3,000, and while the author thinks they are selling his books, it's actually their own that they are selling."[44]

The evil ways of booksellers were a favorite theme of writers critical of the printing trade: ignorant compositors left texts littered with errors, corrupting their integrity; booksellers fobbed books off on readers incapable of understanding them, thereby distorting their meaning; and the low standards of the book trade generally degraded literary intercourse.[45] "Well, good luck and God help you" are Don Quixote's last words to the translator, who is too presumptuous to recognize the perils that lie ahead.[46]

Don Quixote, Reader of Cide Hamete and Avellaneda

When Quixote visits the print shop in Barcelona, two books are being printed and proofread. The first is entitled *Light of the Soul* (*Luz del alma*). According to Francisco Rico, and contrary to classical commentary, this cannot be an allusion to the book of the same title that was printed by Felipe de Meneses in Salamanca in 1556 and reprinted as late as the 1590s. An allusion to such an old book, fraught with Christian humanism of Erasmian inspiration, would scarcely have been compatible with Cervantes' vigorous commitment to the Counter-Reformation in the last years of his life: in 1609 he joined the Confraternity of Slaves of the Most Holy Sacrament, and in 1613 he took the habit of the Third Order of Saint Francis. *Light of the Soul* is therefore more likely a generic reference to the type of religious work that dominated Spanish publishing at the beginning of the seventeenth century, or else an allusion to a work that was one of the bestsellers of the time, the *Obras de Lodovico Blosio* (or Louis de Blois, abbot of the monastery of Liesse). As Francisco Rico observes, this book, which went through more than a dozen

editions from 1596 to 1625, was printed several times by the same printer who
did both parts of *Don Quixote*: Juan de la Cuesta printed it for Diego Guillén
in 1604 at the same time and with the same font in which he set part one of
Quixote. In 1608 and 1611 he reprinted this same work for Francisco Robles,
who was the publisher of *Don Quixote*, and in 1613 of the *Novelas ejemplares*.
Cervantes was therefore familiar with the work in the same way as Don
Quixote, from having seen it in a print shop.[47] Hence the following remark
is no doubt to be taken seriously: "'These,' he said, 'are the books that ought
to be printed, even though there are many of the sort, for many are the sin-
ners these days, and an infinite number of lights are required for all those
that are in darkness.'"[48] The second work that Don Quixote encounters is
even more interesting: "Going up to another case, he saw that here, too,
they were correcting a book, and when he asked the title he was told that it
was the *Second Part of the Ingenious Gentleman, Don Quixote de la Mancha*,
composed by a certain native of Tordesillas. 'I have heard of this work,' he
said."[49]

He is not the only one to have heard of it, for the reader of Part Two
knows, if he has read the Prologue, of the existence of this apocryphal sequel
to Cervantes' novel, which appeared in 1614 with a title page announcing the
*Segundo tomo del Ingenioso hidalgo Don Quixote de la Mancha, que contiene
su tercera salida; y es la quinta parte de sus aventuras* (*The Second Part of the
Ingenious Knight Don Quixote of La Mancha, which contains his third sally;
and constitutes the fifth part of his adventures*).[50] The "third sally" alludes to
the final pages of Part One of *Quixote*, which indicate that

The author of this history, although he has made a most thorough and diligent
search, has been unable to come upon any account—at least none based on authentic sources—of the deeds performed by Don Quixote on his third sally. There is only
the tradition, handed down in La Mancha, to the effect that in the course of this third
expedition he went to Saragossa, where he was present at some famous tourneys that
were held in the city.[51]

The "fifth part" refers to the four-part division of the book published
in 1605, which at that time was not the first part of a diptych. The book presented itself as the work of "el Licenciado Alonso Fernández de Avellaneda,
natural de la villa de Tordesillas," and claimed to have been printed in Tara-
gon by Felipe Roberto. Analysis of the fonts used in the book suggests that
the typographic address on the title page concealed the actual location of
the printing, which was allegedly the print shop of Sebastián de Cormellas in
Barcelona. The print shop that Don Quixote visited was therefore not that of

Pedro Malo, as has been claimed,[52] but rather Cormellas',[53] described by Cervantes on the basis of his own knowledge of the shop where *Don Quixote* was printed, that of Juan de la Cuesta in Madrid.[54]

In the text of Part Two, the first mention of Avellaneda's work (the real identity of which has never been established for certain[55]) occurs in chapter 59, when two of the guests in the inn where Don Quixote and Sancho are staying refer to both the novel of 1605 and the sequel of 1614. Don Juan says, "Upon your life, Señor Don Jerónimo, while they are bringing our supper, let us read another chapter of the *Second Part of Don Quixote de la Mancha*," and the other man replies, "Why would your Grace have as read such nonsense as that, Señor Don Juan, seeing that he who has read the First Part of the history of Don Quixote de la Mancha cannot possibly find any pleasure in the second one?"[56] The dialogue between the two noblemen reminds the reader of the passage in which the bachelor Carrasco, Don Quixote, and Sancho are discussing the reaction to the exploits of the knight-errant as recounted by the Arab historian Cide Hamete Benengeli (the supposed author of the narrative after chapter 9 of Part One) and printed on the Madrid presses of Juan de la Cuesta.[57] Carrasco alludes not only to the great success of the book, of which more than 12,000 copies have already been printed,[58] but also to criticisms that have been leveled against it:

Some, to be sure, have complained of the author's forgetfulness, seeing that he neglected to make it plain who the thief was who stole Sancho's gray, for it is not stated there, but merely implied, that the ass was stolen; and a little further on, we find the squire mounted on the same beast, although it has not made its reappearance in the story.[59]

The mistake made in the first edition and hastily patched up in subsequent ones was thus transformed into a theme of the narrative itself. Sancho comes back to it in the next chapter, where he tells the story of the theft and recovery of his ass, and when Carrasco, alluding to the inconsistency that still exists in the second edition, points out that the error resides "'in the fact that before the ass turns up again the author has Sancho riding on it,'" Sancho replies, "'I don't know what answer to give you, except that the one who wrote the story must have made a mistake, or else it must be due to carelessness on the part of the printer.'"[60] Well before Don Quixote visits the shop in which books are composed, printed, and corrected (sometimes quite carelessly), it thus makes its appearance in the story when Cervantes blames the Arab chronicle or the printers for his own negligence.

The fact that the characters in *Don Quixote* read and comment on the book that tells their story is one of the things that makes the novel "magical" for Borges, for whom this narrative device is one of the most effective ways to fuse the world of the book with that of the reader. The same is true in *Hamlet*, where the performance of the *The Murder of Gonzago* by the theater troupe from the city replays the murder of old Hamlet before the court of Elsinore. Borges asks "why does it disquiet us to know that Don Quixote is a reader of the *Quixote*, and Hamlet is a spectator of *Hamlet*? I believe I have found the answer: those inversions suggest that if the characters in a story can be readers or spectators, then we, their readers or spectators, can be fictitious."[61]

The protagonists of *Don Quixote* read of the *hidalgo*'s early adventures but were also familiar with the sequel, published in 1614. Let us return to the inn to which Don Jerónimo and Don Juan have brought a copy of Avellaneda's book. On hearing Don Juan say that what he dislikes about the book is that it depicts Don Quixote as no longer in love (*desenamorado*) with Dulcinea, Quixote denies the insulting accusation and reveals his identity to the two *hidalgos*. Cervantes then plays a vertiginous game with the book that was published a year before his own Part Two appeared and in which the self-styled licentiate of Tordesillas described among other things Don Quixote's pitiful performance in the tilt for the ring in Saragossa.

Quixote refutes Avellaneda's false allegations: he is and will always be constant in his love for Dulcinea. And that is not all. He says that the events described in the sequel as having already occurred will in fact never take place. He had never been to Saragossa and would not go there now: "I will not set foot in Saragossa but will let the world see how this new historian lies, by showing people that I am not the Don Quixote of whom he is speaking."[62] Cervantes "falsifies" Avellaneda's account by describing what the sequel-writer had presented as an already completed past as a future that would never come to pass. And indeed, Quixote does not go to Saragossa but to Barcelona, where we found him in the print shop.

Before setting out, Quixote leafs through a copy of Avellaneda's book, which one of the gentleman has given him. In an ironic reversal, he accuses the author of carelessness and inconsistency:

> The third [thing for which the author deserves to be censured] is the mistake he makes, and the falsehood of which he is guilty in the essential part of the story, by stating that the wife of Sancho Panza, my squire, is named Mari Gutiérrez when the name should be Teresa Panza. And it is greatly to be feared that one who errs in so important a matter as this will be wrong in all the other particulars throughout the history.[63]

This ridiculous criticism of the sequel writer is a way for Cervantes to mock not only his own detractors, such as Lope de Vega, who had made the theft of the ass "the most important point in the story," but also himself, since in Part One Sancho's wife appears under various names—Juana Gutiérrez, Mari Gutiérrez, and Juana Pança—while in the second she becomes Teresa Pança and ultimately Teresa Sancha.[64]

The Plagiarist Plagiarized

From chapter 59 on, allusions to Avellaneda's sequel abound. In chapter 61, Don Quixote, before entering Barcelona, is welcomed by one of Roque Guinart's friends with these words:

Welcome to our city . . . O valiant Don Quixote de la Mancha—not the false, not the fictitious, not the apocryphal one that we read of in mendacious histories that have appeared of late, but the true and legitimate one, the real one that Cide Hamete Benengeli, flower of historians, has portrayed for us.

Which causes our hero to turn to Sancho and say, "These gentlemen plainly recognized us. I will wager you that they have read our history and that of the Aragonese as well, which was printed not so long ago."[65] In chapter 62, he leaves the print shop in irritation, saying in regard to this same book that "in all truth and upon my conscience, I think it ought to be burned to ashes as a piece of impertinence."[66]

In chapter 70, in the vision of Altisidora, devils are playing a ball-game on the threshold of hell, but instead of playing with balls they play with books. One of them whacks a book so hard with the blazing shovels they use as rackets that the book falls apart, with pages flying in all directions:

"Just see what book that is," said a devil to his companion, and the other devil replied, "This is the *Second Part of the History of Don Quixote de la Mancha*, written not by Cid Hamete, the original author, but by an Aragonese who, by his own account, is a native of Tordesillas."

"Take it away," said the other. "Throw it into the bottomless pit so I shan't have to see it."

"Is it as bad as all that?"

"It is so bad," said the first devil, "that if I had deliberately set myself to write a worse one, I shouldn't have been able to achieve it."[67]

The play with the apocryphal sequel culminates in chapter 72, where Don Quixote and Sancho, on their way back to their village, stop at an inn,

where they run into Don Alvaro Tarfe, one of the characters invented by
Avellaneda. Don Alvaro is obliged to say that the Don Quixote and Sancho
Panza that he knew are not the ones he sees before him. The real Don
Quixote never went to Saragossa and was never locked up in a madhouse
in Toledo. Don Alvaro Tarfe swears to this before the mayor of the village
and declares "with all the legal formalities" that "he was not personally
acquainted with Don Quixote de la Mancha, also present, and it was to be
further stated that this latter person was not the individual referred to in
a history entitled *Second Part of Don Quixote de la Mancha*, composed by a
certain Avellaneda, native of Tordesillas."[68] Couched in the lexicon of legal
documents (the deposition is a *petición* and begins with the legal formula
"de que a su derecho convenia"), Don Alvaro Tarfe's statement is one of the
many devices that Cervantes uses to transform Avellaneda's "plagiarism" into
a theme of his own fiction. Perhaps he remembered Mateo Alemán, who,
in part two of the *Life of Guzmán d'Alfarache*, published in 1604, had transformed the author of a sequel that had appeared two years earlier into a
character in his book. Written (essentially) by the Valencian Juan José Martí,
this sequel was presented as having been composed by "Mateo Luján de
Sayavedra, natural vecino de Sevilla." In chapter 9 of book 2 of part 2 of
Guzmán, Mateo Alemán's Sayavedra "falls ill, lapses into a frenzy, thinks he
is Guzmán himself, and hurls himself into the sea, where he drowns."[69] Don
Alvaro Tarfe does not meet with such a sad fate, but the game is the same:
using the sequel published under a pseudonym as grist for the literary mill,
providing characters and stories. In *Don Quixote*, the reality effect produced
by the text stems not only from the fact that Cervantes, as Borges notes, set
his story amid "the dusty roads and sordid inns of Castille" rather than the
"vast and vague geography of the Amadis."[70] It comes, in the first place, from
the constant interchange between the fiction and the technical and literary
circumstances in which it was composed (in both senses of the word composed: aesthetic and typographical).

Name, History, and Enchantment

The final allusion to Avellaneda's sequel comes in the will that Don Quixote
dictates on his deathbed. The final clause is

ITEM: I entreat the aforementioned gentlemen, my executors [i.e., the curate and the
bachelor Samson Carrasco], if by good fortune they should come to know the author

who is said to have composed a history now going the rounds under the title of *Second Part of the Exploits of Don Quixote de la Mancha*, to beg his forgiveness in my behalf, as earnestly as they can, since it was I who unthinkingly led him to set down so many and such great absurdities as are to be found in it; for I leave this life with a feeling of remorse at having provided him with the occasion for putting them in writing.[71]

The ironic pardon granted to Avellaneda is intimately related to Don Quixote's return to reason, with which the final chapter of the novel begins: "My mind now is clear, unencumbered by those misty shadows of ignorance that were cast over it by my bitter and continual reading of those hateful books of chivalry."[72] The first sign of the recovery of judgment is the recovery of identity: "'I have good news for you, kind sirs,' said Don Quixote the moment he saw them. 'I am no longer Don Quixote de la Mancha but Alonso Quijano, whose mode of life won for him the name of "Good."'"[73] By reclaiming his true name, Don Quixote marks the end of the fable, a few pages before his death. He thus cancels the opening act, when the *hidalgo* Quixana (or Quijana), as he was called in the second edition of 1605 (and not Quexana, as in the original edition),[74] begins calling himself Don Quixote.[75]

At this point, the other major characters offer the reader an astonishing moment. They refuse to allow the *hidalgo* to resume his true identity, preferring to perpetuate the illusion. They want to become shepherds, as Don Quixote had decided to do after his defeat by the knight of the White Moon, when he promised to give up the life of knight-errant for a year. All the characters, and perhaps the reader as well, enticed by the prospect of reading a parody of yet another genre, dream of living in spirit in a pastoral world more pleasant than that of their everyday cares and travails. The bachelor Carrasco, Sancho, and the narrator himself persist in using the knightly appellation of the man who in his own mind is once again Alonso Quijano. Don Quixote is obliged to say a second time that he has reclaimed his authentic identity: "I was mad and now I am sane; I was Don Quixote de la Mancha, and now I am, as I have said, Alonso Quijano the Good. May my repentance and the truth I now speak restore to me the place I once held in your esteem."[76] Henceforth, "the ingenious knight of la Mancha" has a double identity. For his own time, he is "one of those gentlemen who always have a lance in the rack, an ancient buckler, a skinny nag, and a greyhound for the chase,"[77] but for posterity, thanks to his madness and Cide Hamete's pen, he will forever remain the madman to whom "it now appeared . . . fitting and necessary, in order to win a greater amount of honor for himself and serve his country at the same time, to become a knight-errant and roam the world on horseback, in a suit of armor; he would go in quest of adventures, by way of putting into practice all that he had read in his books."[78]

Don Quixote is a man of many names: the name he gave himself (Don Quixote de la Mancha), his real name (Alonso Quijano the Good), and those attributed to him by scholars: "They will try to tell you that his surname was Quijada or Quesada—there is some difference of opinion among those who have written on the subject—but according to the most likely conjectures we are to understand that it was really Quijana."[79] This amusing parody of learned debate allowed Cervantes to include in the story of the knight of La Mancha a common feature of contemporary literary texts: variability of names. This was true, as we have seen, of *Love's Labor's Lost*, and of *Lazarillo de Tormes*, in which, despite the title, the hero is named not Lazarillo but Lázaro (except in the play on words *lacerado/lazarillo*).[80] These were but two of many examples of variability in naming, for which the reasons were many: carelessness on the part of authors, who forgot or mixed up the names of their characters; errors by compositors and proofreaders; and, underlying all this, a doubt as prevalent in life as it was in literature that individuals possess a single, stable, fixed identity.[81] Cervantes' genius was to use his hero's name changes to mark the beginning and end of the period of enchantment in his story.

In the time of *Quixote*, the print shop became the key place where texts in search of readers turned into books. The technology had its detractors, who denounced the dangers and uselessness of printing and contained to place their faith in manuscript copies.[82] Unlike printed texts, manuscripts allowed their authors to maintain control over the circulation of their works and to keep ignorant readers away from texts they would be unable to understand. Judgment was not unanimous, however, and even kings honored print shops with their visits, if we believe Melchor de Cabrera, who intended to demonstrate the honorable character of printing, the "art of arts." Cabrera reminds us that Louis XIII, who had a print shop in the Louvre, was reputed to be an excellent compositor, and then he describes the visit that Philip III and his daughter, the infanta Doña Ana, paid to the print shop of the duke of Lerma, his *válido*. The young infanta stopped in front of a case and, "wanting her name written in the palm of her hand, removed letters from the boxes that were pointed out to her and placed them in the compositor."[83] Then "his Majesty entered the shop and asked the workers to stay where they were and, remaining seated, to go on with their work. When he came to a case, for as long as he stood there watching the work of composition, he allowed his hand to rest on the compositor's left shoulder."[84] With this familiar and protective gesture, the king demonstrated better than any written text the nobility and usefulness of the art of printing.

Like his sovereign, Don Quixote longed to visit a print shop. Like the king, he demonstrated respect and esteem for the work of those thanks to whom the great deeds of an illustrious prince as well as the amusing adventures of a poor knight could be conveyed to the world: "Going up to one of the cases, he inquired what was being done there, the workmen explained things for him, and, wondering at what he had observed, he passed on."[85]

Chapter 4
Handwritten Newsletters, Printed Gazettes: Cymbal and Butter

In 1631 a comedy by Ben Jonson entitled *The Staple of News* was published in London. The play was not of recent vintage: it had been performed for the Court in February of 1626, on Shrove Tuesday, and then for the city audience at Blackfriars Hall. Five years later, the printed edition, published in a folio format unusual for theatrical works, bestowed new life on the play.[1] Sold separately at first, the play was later bound with two other comedies, *Bartholomew Fair* and *The Devil Is an Ass*, and in 1640 came out as the second volume of Jonson's works, joining the 1616 Folio in which the playwright, in a bold and unprecedented move, had collected a selection of his plays and poems.[2]

The Staple of News owes its title to the fact that several of its scenes take place in what is called in the play an "office" or "staple," where news of the court, city, and world are collected, copied, and sold. Jonson first conceived the idea of bringing the news business to the stage in 1620. In a "masque" entitled *News from the New World*, the "factor" or gazetteer whose business is selling handwritten newsletters tells a printer of ephemera that

I have hope to erect a Staple for newes ere long, whither all shall be brought, and thence again vented under the name of Staple-newes; and not trusted to your printed Conundrums of the serpent in *Sussex*, or the witches bidding the Devill to dinner at *Derbie*: Newes, that when a man sends them downe to the Shieres where they are said to be done, were never there to be found.[3]

When the printer objects that the handwritten news items collected in the city or sent in by correspondents in the counties are no truer than the stories made up to please "the common people," the factor replies: "I confesse it; but it is the Printing I am offended at, I would have no newes printed; for when they are printed they leave to bee newes; while they are written, though they be false, they remaine newes still."[4] Five years later, in a radically new situation created by the circulation in England of the first printed gazettes,

Ben Jonson was to make the contrast as well as the kinship between the hand-written and the printed, the manuscript newsletter and the printed periodi-cal, one of the central themes of his comedy.

The play depicts a prodigal heir, Pennyboy Junior, who begins spend-ing outrageously on the news of his father's death. It belongs to a classic genre, the so-called "prodigal plays," which portrayed the extravagant expen-ditures of fortune-squandering heirs in such a way as to praise the virtues of economy by contrast. In 1605, for example, Nathaniel Butter published a comedy entitled *The London Prodigal*, which the title page attributed to Shakespeare, so that it was included in the third Folio of 1664. Rejected from the Shakespearean corpus in the eighteenth century, this comedy, which may have been written in whole or in part by Ben Jonson, inspired the plot of *The Staple of News*.[5] But as the title indicates, the comedy of 1626 linked the story of Pennyboy Junior and his allegorical mistress, Mistress Pecunia, to the presence of a news office in the prodigal heir's residence. What is more, the heir's prodigality is premature, since his father, who is not in fact dead, observes his activities in the guise of the beggar Pennyboy Canter, the man who informs the would-be heir of his father's purported demise.

The News Writers' Office

The spectator (and reader) first learn of the office through the description given by Thomas, Pennyboy Junior's barber, in Act One, Scene Two.[6] To the question, "And tell's what are the newes?" the barber responds, "O Sir, a sta-ple of newes Or the New Staple." Master Cymbal (an apt name for a person whose mission is to amplify public rumor) is the "master of the Office," which occupies several large rooms equipped with the tables, desks, and shelves required by his business. This business, according to Thomas, consists in the collection, examination, recording, and exclusive publication under the seal of the office of the "Staple Newes," including news of all kinds.[7]

The barber goes on to describe the personnel who work in the office under Master Cymbal's direction. The staff consists, first of all, of four cor-respondents, or "emissaries" ("a fine word," Pennyboy declares), who collect the news in four strategic locations in the capital of the kingdom, what the prodigal heir refers to as the "4. Cardinall Quarters." Master Fitton, Cymbal's cousin, is established at Court; Master Ambler at Saint Paul's Cathedral, where courtiers and businessmen gather before and after lunch;[8] and Master Hans Buz, a Dutchman, is at the Royal Exchange, where merchants trade commercial information and letters of exchange. The job of gathering news at Westminster Hall, where the courts of justice are located and booksellers have their shops, is vacant when the play opens and is sought by Master Picklock, who is also Pennyboy Junior's lawyer, thus reinforcing the link between the two elements of the comedy: the satire of the news business and the plot involving the marriage of the very wealthy Pecunia. There are four employees who work in the news office itself: the Examiner, the Register, and two clerks who "manage all at home, and sort, and file / And seale the newes, and issue them." Since one of the two clerkships is free, Pennyboy Junior promises Thomas the fifty pounds he needs to purchase it.

In the dialogues that follow the description of the workshop in which the manuscript newsletters are copied, we find two references to the culture of print. The first is to illustrated books used by artisans. Pennyboy Junior, well satisfied with the suit of clothes his tailor has made for him, makes this inquiry of him: "I pray thee tell me, *Fashioner*, what Authors / Thou read'st to help thy invention? *Italian* prints? / Or *Arras* hangings? They are Taylors *Libraries*."[9] The second allusion occurs in a figure of speech identifying print with perfection. When Pennyboy asks if his ruff collar is properly fitted, one of the tailor's assistants responds, "In print," meaning "to perfection."

Scenes four and five of Act One are situated in the news office and play satirically with both contemporary journalistic practices and the critics who attack them. Master Cymbal offers to show Pennyboy Junior around the workshop, and the latter invites Pennyboy Canter (in other words, his father, disguised as a beggar) to join him. Each item of news that arrives in the office is "examined," "registered," "dispatched," and "filed" in the "roll of the day," the record of each correspondent's daily activity. Processed by date, the news items are distributed among various "Rowles and Fyles," which are organized by theme ("under their heads") and, within each file, alphabetically.[10] In other words, "the staple of news" employed the same method as commonplace books, which arranged textual units in thematic order. Pennyboy Junior alludes directly to this when he says, "Sir, I admire/ The method o' your place; all things within't / Are so digested, fitted, and compos'd, / As it shewes *Wit* had married *Order*."[11] But unlike the "*sententiae*," the universal and eternal sayings that formed the primary content of commonplace books,[12] the news collected and classified in the journalists' office was anecdotal and frivolous.

Cymbal and Fitton, the court correspondent, who is in the office when Pennyboy visits, classify the news according to several criteria. First, the credibility attaching to each item owing to is provenance separates the "authentic" from the "apocryphal." The most doubtful items are those retailed by certain tradesmen such as barbers, tailors, water carriers, and Thames boatmen. Equally suspect is the news carried by printed gazettes, the so-called "Coranti and Gazetti" that have recently appeared on the scene. Indeed, it was in 1620 that the first English-language periodicals in the "coranto" format were published in Amsterdam and London. The term was the translation of the title of one of the first newspapers to appear in Dutch (the earliest surviving Dutch "coranto" dates from 1618), and it referred to a gazette in folio format printed on both sides of a single sheet.[13] In 1622, several London printers proposed another formula, the so-called "newsbooks," composed of two or three quarto "gatherings" arranged in series with a date and number to identify each issue.[14]

The market for printed news soon came to be dominated by Nathaniel Butter, who published many series of "newsbooks," first as a member of a syndicate of five or six booksellers and later, after that group was dissolved in the autumn of 1624, in association with Nicholas Bourne. The collaboration with Bourne continued until October 1632, when a Star Chamber edict prohibited the publication of "the ordenary Gazetts and Pamphletts of newes from foraine partes."[15] Ben Jonson's comedy was performed in 1626 and printed in 1631, at a time when the gazette market was dominated by Nathaniel Butter, whose name was the butt of numerous jokes in the play: one of Cymbal's clients is referred to as a "Butterwoman," and the falsification of the dates of printed news items is described as "buttering over." The prohibition of gazettes was lifted in 1638, and Nathaniel Butter was free to resume his trade, at first with Bourne and then alone until 1642.

Three other criteria were used in classifying the news items that arrived in Cymbal's shop. The first of these involved various times of the year: "vacation newes" for the period during which the courts of justice at Westminster Hall were in recess; "terme-newes," for the period during which they were in session, which was a very active time for business and for the publication of new books; and "Christmas-newes," for the holiday period, the twelve days from Christmas to Twelfth Night, which was a time of theatrical performances both at court and in the city. The second criterion had to do with religious and political commitments, which yielded "newes o' the faction": "Reformed newes" of the Calvinists; "Protestant newes" of the Lutherans; and "Pontificall newes" of Catholics. Finally, we hear of correspondents "of all ranks, and all Religions," who sent news from all the counties of the kingdom, leading to a distinction between "the Countrey" news and news of the capital, and we also learn of various distinctions among Cymbal's informants, who are described as "Factors," "Agents," and "Liegers" (or "ledgers").

Cymbal also explains the financial organization of his business to his visitors. The profits are divided into two halves, one for him, the other for his collaborators. The latter half is divided into seven parts: one for each of the "Emissaries," one for the "Examiner," one for the "Register," and the last to be divided between the two clerks. This type of structure, with an unequal distribution of profits among the partners or "shareholders" of an association, was common in sixteenth- and seventeenth-century England. It applied to the distribution of the profits of theater troupes as well as to the syndicate of six booksellers who joined forces to publish "newsbooks."[16]

Of the two clerk or copyist positions, one was held by Nathaniel, who had the same first name as Butter and was described as a "decay'd Stationer," that is, a member of the London community of booksellers and printers who had fallen on hard times, a characterization that makes the identification of Nathaniel with Butter more likely, since the latter, before going into the news business, had been a publisher of plays (including *King Lear* in 1608) and translations, including Chapman's Homer, the *Iliad* in 1611 and the *Odyssey* in 1614. The second clerk was Tom, the barber, whose place had been purchased by Pennyboy Junior and who is described as a "pretty Scholler" with a master of arts degree from the university. The allusion is a reminder that many university graduates were unemployed in the 1620s owing to an influx of students to Oxford and Cambridge coinciding with a decrease in the number of positions in the church, government bureaucracy, and courts to which their diplomas would previously have allowed them to aspire.[17] Thomas exemplified their frustrated careers, since despite his master of arts and being "skil'd in every liberall Science," he had become a barber. The "decayed stationer" and the involuntary barber performed the same tasks: classifying, transcribing, and if necessary inventing items of news. At least that is what Fitton says about the first clerk, Nathaniel, who, like Butter, could easily fabricate false news when necessary: "And for a need can make 'hem." It was for this ability that Pennyboy Junior praised Thomas. Blessed with a quick and agile mind, he could forge fake news on demand. Ben Jonson thus saw the new journalism as totally lacking in credibility, and he despised it.

Falsehood in Print

The news staple's first client to appear on stage is a peasant woman who has come to town to sell her wares, the "Butterwoman," and she is little interested in the authenticity of the news. What she wants is fresh news at not too high a price: "a groatsworth of any Newes," that is, the value of a "groat," a coin worth four pence. As for the subject, "I care not what," but it has to be something she can take back to the pastor of her village next Saturday. The Register asks the peasant to wait until the latest news arrives from the Royal Exchange or Saint Paul's and tells her that she needs to be patient, because the "Captain" is no longer around. The allusion is to Captain Gainsford, a retired officer who died in 1624 and who had been a prolific supplier of news to the gazettes published by the "newsbook" syndicate. Nathaniel points out to the Register that it is bad for business to publish the news too quickly. It should be held for a time in order to whet the appetite of readers: "Let them attend in name of policie."[18]

The theme of the authenticity or inauthenticity of the news becomes central to the discussion among Cymbal, Fitton, and Pennyboy Junior concerning the printed gazettes with which the Staple of News hopes to compete and even destroy. Pennyboy notes that most people believe that printing is a guarantee of truthfulness: [19] "Unto some, / The very printing of them, makes them *Newes*; / That ha' not the heart to beleeve any thing, / But what they see in print." He repeats almost word for word what the Printer proclaimed in the masque of 1620: "It is the Printing of 'hem makes 'hem news to a great many, who will indeed beleeve nothing but what's in Print."[20]

Examples of such a belief abound in the theater of the time. Thus in *The Winter's Tale*, Mopsa, convinced that print cannot deceive, says this to Autolycus, who sells dry goods and ballads to the peasants of the imaginary Boehmia of Acts Four and Five: "I love a ballad in print, alife, for then we are sure they are true."[21] The hawker says nothing to contradict this certitude and offers evidence to confirm the veracity of the extraordinary tales recounted in the ballads that he sells. The fact that a usurer's wife has given "birth" to twenty sacks of coins is attested in writing by the midwife ("Here's the midwife's name to 't") and by "five or six honest wives that were present." The story of the girl who is changed into a fish for spurning the advances of her lover has "five justices' hands at it, and witnesses more than my pack will hold." The appeal of a ballad, in other words, depends on the possibility of believing that it is true, even though the marks of authenticity, which all belong to the register of the written (affidavits and signatures), are comically contradicted by the references to oral culture of storytelling: the midwife is named Mistress Taleporter and the date of the girl's metamorphosis into a fish is "Wednesday the forescore of April."

In order to undermine this false belief in the truth of print, Cymbal and Fitton attack the lies they find in printed news. Their first target is in fact ballads and broadsides, the "pamphlets of news" that retail stories to be read, recited, and sung, stories without an ounce of authenticity despite being attested to, ostensibly, by local magistrates. Another target is tales of imaginary monsters, "the many, and most innocent Monsters, / That never came i'th' Counties, they were charg'd with."[22] Pennyboy Junior observes that there is no danger if people take pleasure in fables forged for the purpose, particularly since they are no more fraudulent than the news invented by the gazetteers of the "Staple of News."[23] Fitton's response is taken almost verbatim from the masque of 1620: "O Sir ! it is the printing we oppose." To which Cymbal responds: "We do not forbid that any *Newes*, be made / But that 't be printed."[24]

The charge against the printed news was directed at the series of "newsbooks" that Nathaniel Butter and Nicholas Bourne began publishing in December 1624 under the title *Weekly Newes* and bearing the notation "Printed for Mercurius Britannicus." The accusation bore on both the sources of information and the falsification of dates. The news published in Butter and Bourne's gazette was collected from starving soldiers and obscure publicists: "So many politique pennes going, to feed the press." They fed the press, moreover, without regard for the truth ("and dish out newes were't true o false"). At a time when the ability to pronounce or certify the truth was regarded as a privilege of the social elite,[25] the tavern drunks who informed the Mercurius Britannicus were obviously devoid of all credibility.

The editors of the broadsheets and gazettes had little better to offer. They, too, falsified the dates of news reports in order to pass off old news as recent information or to use the same item more than once. The Printer in the 1620 masque had no compunctions about admitting as much: "For those I doe keepe my Presses, and so many Pens going to bring forth wholsome relations, which once in halfe a score yeares (as the age growes forgetfull) I Print over againe with a new date, and they are of excellent use."[26] Cymbal denounces this practice, associating the name of Butter and the printers who publish foreign news with the "pamphlets of news" that relate tales of monsters and other extraordinary phenomena: "Nor shall the *Stationer* cheat upon the Time / By buttering over againe/ His *antiquated Pamphlets* with new dates."[27]

The "Staple of News" did away with such abuses by affixing its seal (the "Office Seal, Staple Commoditie") on the manuscript news it sold, thereby guaranteeing the information as fresh and never before published. "All shall come from the Mint," Cymbal asserts, and Fitton adds, "Fresh and new stamp'd." These statements allude to the idea of monopoly associated with the word "staple," which originally designated a town that had been granted an exclusive privilege to engage in a particular line of commerce.

The seal of the "Staple of News" was not enough to guarantee the authenticity of the news that it published, however. Take, for instance, the news of Pennyboy Junior's good fortune: "There is a brave young *Heire* / Is come of age this morning, Mr. *Peny-boy,*" says the clerk. "An old *Canting Beggar* / Brought him first Newes."[28] Pennyboy is delighted but also astonished to find his name already set down in Cymbal's registers: "We are in here, i'the *Newes-Office*! / In this dayes *Rowle,* already! I doe muse / How you came by us, Sirs!"[29] The mystery is dispelled when he learns that Cymbal's correspondent at Westminster is none other than Master Picklock, his own lawyer. Deceived by Pennyboy Junior's father, Picklock has spread news as false as that published in the printed gazettes.

The Superfluity of News

Ben Jonson was not the first writer to vilify the news business. In 1628, Robert Burton, in the revised edition of his *Anatomy of Melancholy,* deplored the constant flow of news, which was forgotten as quickly as it arrived: "I hear new news every day, and those ordinary rumors of war, plagues, fires, inundations, thefts, murders, massacres, meteors, comets, prodigies, apparitions, of towns taken, cities besieged in France, Germany, Turkey, Persia, Poland, etc."[30] This unremitting flow of news can only complicate the task of true judgment, which calls for privacy and quiet reflection. The superfluity of news is a source of extreme confusion; it reflects the chaos of a world in which nothing is stable, neither the course of nature nor the destiny of man:

A vast confusion of vows, wishes, actions, edicts, petitions, lawsuits, pleas, laws, proclamations, complaints, grievances are daily brought to our ears. New books, every day, pamphlets, currantoes, stories, whole catalogues of volumes of all sorts, new paradoxes, opinions, schisms, heresies, controversies in philosophy, religion, etc.[31]

For Burton, the publication of news in whatever form merely aggravated the disorder attendant upon novelty.

Three years later, Richard Braithwait published *Whimzies, Or, a New Cast of Characters,* a satire in which the "Curranto coiners," the fabricators of news, were not let off lightly.[32] The periodical publication of "newsbooks" was a way of maintaining the curiosity of readers (and the profits of publishers) by promising revelations to come on the "secrecies of state." Buyers fell readily into the trap prepared by the purveyors of news: "The vulgar do admire him, holding his Novels oracular." The only consolation of reasonable men, among whom Braithwait counted himself, was the dire fate in store for these publications, which

live not long; a weeke is the longest in the Citie, and after they arrivall, little longer in the Countrey, Which past, they melt like *Butter*, or match a pipe and so *Burne*. But indeede, most commonly it is the height of their ambition, to aspire to the imployment of stopping mustard-pots, or wrapping up pepper, pouder, staves-aker, etc. which done, they expire.[33]

Indeed, as Folke Dahl notes, to judge by the very small number of surviving copies compared with the large number that were probably printed,[34] the newsbooks published by Butter and Bourne and mocked by Braithwait were indeed frequently put to the rather inglorious purposes that Braithwait assigned them.

News of State

The first three scenes of the third act take place in Cymbal's office, where Pennyboy Junior has taken the infanta Pecunia in order to encourage her to invest in the business. She is accompanied by a retinue of three allegorical figures: Broker, her secretary, Mortgage, her nurse, and Wax, her chambermaid, along with Statute and Band, two ladies-in-waiting. "We come for *newes*," Pennyboy Junior announces, "I pray thee let my *Princesse* hear some *newes*, Good Master *Cymbal*." "What newes would she heare?" Cymbal replies. "Or of what kind, Sir?" "Any, any kind," says Pennyboy, "so it be *newes*, the newest that thou hast."[35] Jonson then avails himself of the opportunity to satirize the various types of news that were collected and circulated at the time not only by the Staple of News but also by other contemporary gazettes.

In a note "To the Readers" inserted in the 1631 edition of the play, Jonson stated his intention and corrected the misapprehensions of his audience: "The *allegory*, and purpose of the *Author* hath hitherto beene wholly mistaken, and so sinister an interpretation beene made."[36] In fact,

to consider the *Newes* here vented, to be none of his *Newes*, or any reasonable mans; but *Newes* made like the times *Newes*, (a weekly cheat to draw mony) and could not be fitter reprehended, then in raising this ridiculous *Office* of the *Sta*ple, wherin the age may see her owne folly, or hunger and thirst after publish'd pamphlets of *Newes* set out every Saturday, but made all at home, & no syllable of truth in them.[37]

Between 1626 and 1631, the vogue for "newsbooks" was such that it was necessary to warn readers against confusing the play with the fabricated news it satirized, just one more gazette filled with extravagant reports. The note to the reader was intended as a strong reaffirmation of the difference between the stage and the press, the theater and newspapers.[38]

The first news read by Thomas, the barber-turned-clerk who now signs himself Clericus, are "newes of State," as befits a princess. Three of the items supposedly come from Rome. They report that the king of Spain has become Pope and Emperor, since the former emperor is now reduced to the rank of private soldier in the army of Count Tilly; that Don Spinola has been made General of the Society of Jesus; and that his predecessor, Vittelesco, is now his cook, the man who prepares his eggs. Here the text spins a dense web of allusions to contemporary events, including episodes of the European war that helped fuel the rise of the gazettes and that no one yet knew would last for thirty years. The point is to mock the Catholic party while at the same time amusing the audience with double-entendres. The eggs prepared by Vittelesco (actually Mutio Vitelleschi) are not poached but powdered ("potch'd? no, powder'd"), an allusion to the rockets used by General Spinola in the siege of Breda, which was completed in June 1625. Spinola was not General of the Jesuits but rather of a Catholic army. The deliberate confusion, reinforced by the fact that Spinola shares the same name as one of the Jesuit martyrs of Nagasaki in 1622, affords Jonson an opportunity to denounce the ambitions of the Society, whose members were apparently "the only engineers of Christendom" in both senses of the word: the only political intriguers and the only mechanical inventors, among whose contrivances is a device, antedating that of Cyrano de Bergerac, that is supposed to allow Spinola to travel to the moon.[39] The designation of the king of Spain as Emperor repeats a charge common among English pamphleteers and members of parliament, that the Spanish king aspired to impose a universal monarchy. Cymbal echoes this accusation: "All the pretence to the fifth *Monarchy*, / Was held but vaine, until the *ecclesiastique*, / And *secular* powers, were united, thus, / Both in one person."[40]

From Florence comes another report worrisome to the Protestant party, to the effect that a "burning Glasse" has been built in Galileo's workshop and sent to Spinola. This awesome weapon is said to be capable of destroying any fleet, and there is no defense against it: "His strengths will be unresistable," Pennyboy Junior comments. He then asks whether there isn't some news less favorable to the enemy of the Protestants, now doubly "generaled": "Ha' you no Newes against him, on the contrary?" Nathaniel, the other clerk, comes up with a report that a Dutchman by the name of Cornelius-Son has built a submarine automaton in the form of a large eel capable of destroying the Catholic fleet anchored in Dunkirk harbor. This allusion to Cornelius Drebbel, a Dutch engineer employed by James I, offered a good opportunity to mock the political ambiguities of the new journalists, who published news without regard for its origin. When Pennyboy expresses surprise that Tom has not heard of this news, so favorable to the Protestant cause, Cymbal replies that this is because "he keeps the Pontificall side." Pennyboy protests that it had never been his intention that Tom should be "against ourselves," and he insists that the two clerks change places. Tom is then able to read the same news of Cornelius-Son's invention and announce the arrival of "the invisible Eele" in London, but this time from a Protestant source.

Fitton reports what might be another of Spinola's ruses: a landing in Harwich on the Essex coast with army of men, horses, and cannon all mounted on cork, to catch the English defenders by surprise. Astonished by this news, Pennyboy Junior asks, "Is't true?" And Fitton replies, "As true as the rest." When Cymbal and Fitton contrast the fraudulence of the news in the printed gazettes with the authenticity of the manuscript news, Jonson paints both as equally dubious and risible, regardless of the mode of publication. The handwritten reports received, transcribed, and certified by the Staple of News are no more worthy of belief than the ballads of Autolycus or the *Mercurius Britannicus.*

In 1620, in the masque *Newes from the New World Discover'd in the Moone*, the satire of the *corantos*, which had in fact just made their first appearance in Holland and London, had an important political dimension. The removal of Ferdinand, a Catholic prince, and his replacement on the Bohemian throne by Frederick, the Calvinist elector of the Palatinate and son-in-law of James I, marked the beginning of a time of uncertainty in England. By denouncing the news originating in or copied from Holland, Ben Jonson meant to rescue the king from the pressure of public opinion, which supported the Protestant princes and was highly critical of his attitude toward Spain, a combination of prudence, temporizing, and accommodation. Manuscript gazettes and printed *corantos* mobilized readers and sought to force the king's hand and push England toward war. The masque, which was presented several times at court and in aristocratic residences, sought to undermine the nascent authority of these media so as to preserve that of the sovereign.[41]

Six years later, the situation had changed. King James died in 1625. His son Charles succeeded him as Charles I. He married Henriette-Marie de France, the daughter of Henri IV, and went to war against Spain. Jonson's comedy included numerous allusions to these events. The title "infanta" given to Pecunia called to mind the prospect of a marriage between Charles and the Spanish infanta and his journey to Spain in 1623, which had met with the hostility of the British public to such a union. Fitton's allusion to a possible invasion of England by Spinola's fleet recalled a moment of fear in late 1625, when the Spanish had broken the Anglo-Dutch blockade of Dunkirk. And one of Cymbal's clients alludes to the coronation of Charles I, which was postponed until February 2, 1626, because of an outbreak of plague.[42] In the new situation, with England now at war on the side of the Dutch, making fun of Protestant sources no longer had the same meaning as in 1620. Yet it still served as a reminder that the king should not allow himself to be taken in by false information, no matter where it came from, and that his judgment should not be held hostage to the extravagant accounts that shaped the opinion of readers of the gazettes.

Delights and Dangers of Credulity

After listening to the political news, Pennyboy Junior wants to hear "some curious newes" about magic and alchemy. The two items that are read this time belong to a carnivalesque, satirical mode. In Leipzig, Rosicrucians have discovered a way to make corpses break wind, contradicting the proverbial saying "as soon may you get a fart out of a dead man." In London, the innkeeper of *Dancing Bears* has discovered the secret of perpetual motion. The reading of these comic reports, which provide the occasion for a number of jokes, is interrupted by arrival of several customers of the news shop. According to the Register, the news arouses the enthusiasm of "the people," "the vulgar," regardless of their humor, whether curious or negligent, scrupulous or careless, unbridled or reserved, lazy or laborious. Cymbal's Staple is thus like the House of Fame or of Rumor described by Virgil, Ovid, and Chaucer, to which each visitor comes to receive the countless true and false reports that make and unmake reputations.[43]

The series of customers who come to buy the news, to which they first listen while read aloud by one of the clerks and then take away in manuscript form, afford Jonson an opportunity to assemble an amusing catalogue of the types of information that filled the handwritten newsletters and printed newspapers. These included news of radical sects, such as the Anabaptists in Amsterdam ("the Saints at Amsterdam"), who were awaiting the arrival of Baal, the prophet of the end of time, and of the Grand Turk, converted to

Christianity; news of the Indies (in this instance, the dispatch to America of a colony of cooks for the purpose of teaching a more refined cuisine to the Cannibals there); news of the court; and theater news. In this last category, Jonson imagines a bequest to the troupe called the King's Players (which was Shakespeare's company) by Antonio de Dominis, the archbishop of Spalato. This curious personage, who tried to sell James I on the idea of establishing a universal church and who later returned to Rome, where he was condemned for heresy, had left the actors a wide variety of disguises, which, however, had ultimately not been sufficient to save his life.[44] Another theatrical item was more directly political, since it mentioned both a despised competitor, the playwright Thomas Middleton, and the former Spanish ambassador to England, the count of Gondomar, who until his departure in 1621 had attempted to persuade James I of the need for peace with Spain and the wisdom of marrying his son to the Spanish infanta. Middleton's play *A Game of Chess* was performed at the Globe by the King's Players in August 1624, and because it cast Gondomar in a bad light, it was banned after nine performances.[45] In recalling the event, Jonson killed three birds with one stone: he dismissed his rival's piece as a "poore English-play," he reminded the audience that the actor who had played Gondomar had recently died, and he made fun of the former ambassador, famous for his fistula and the special chair it required, while remarking that a rather Rabelaisian use of the text of the play had aggravated the unfortunately situated malady.[46] The reading ended with an announcement of the "pageants" planned for the coronation of the new king and with "Forest-newes," including an item about the opening of a park outside the forest of the mad and reserved for cuckolds who, on becoming widowers, were entitled to have their horns cut. The dense tissue of allusions and jokes that forms the dialogue between the journalists and their clients throughout Act Four, Scene Two, gives the spectator (and reader) a vivid sense of the disorder introduced into the world by the extravagance of the news and the credulity of the customers.

The resolution of the comedy takes the form of a twofold return to order. On the one hand, the prodigal son, despoiled and repentant, is named the heir of his uncle, Pennyboy Senior, with whom he is reunited, and he marries Pecunia. On the other hand, the news office has vanished, as Thomas declares at the beginning of the final act:

Our *Staple* is all to pieces, quite dissolv'd !/ Shiver'd, as in an earth-quake ! heard you not / The cracke and ruines? we are all blowne up ! / Soone as they heard th'*Infanta* was got from them, / Whom they had so devoured i' their hopes, / To be their *Patronesse*, and sojourne with 'them; / Our *Emissaries, Register, Examiner,* / Flew into vapor: our grave *Governour* / Into a subt'ler ayre; and is return'd / (As we doe heare) grand-*Captaine* of the *Jeerers*. / I, and my fellow melted into butter, / And spoyl'd our Inke, and so the *Office* vanish'd.[47]

Ben Jonson's play is a "morality play," but a morality play of a special kind. Its moral is aimed not solely at private vices, such as the senseless prodigality of imprudent heirs, but even more at public vices that pose a danger to sovereign authority. Uncontrolled proliferation of news reports is one of these dangers, because such reports can inflame credulous imaginations and thus expose the prince to the vagaries of public opinion, which has the potential to overwhelm *raison d'état* with the unreason of the populace.

News Sold by the Item

Why did Ben Jonson bring to the stage, first in the masque of 1620 and later in the comedy of 1626, this acerbic and raucous critique of the fledgling periodical press? One reason, perhaps, was his ambivalent relation to print. Although print was capable of bestowing dignity and permanence on poetic creations, it also had the effect of allowing absurd and dangerous texts to proliferate. The 1616 volume of his *Workes*, in which Jonson in a veritable master stroke published in the monumental folio format those of his works that he deemed worthy of such an honor, attests to the credit he attached to print. Ten years later, *The Staple of News* expressed his discomfort with the authority that print bestowed on rumors bruited about by the gazettes and his anxiety in the face of the popular passions that London booksellers stirred up in pursuit of handsome profits for themselves.[48] With his comedy, Jonson was reacting to what he perceived as a dangerous challenge to the traditional form of government, by council and in secret, which was based on the assumption that the prince enjoyed full authority and was surrounded by men of letters in a privileged position of influence.[49] According to D. F. McKenzie, Jonson was even more hostile to the usurpation by the press of a role previously reserved for the theater, which had ceased to be a forum of public discussion in which the contradictions of the age were explored. Jonson's masque and comedy thus expressed hostility to a detestable innovation and nostalgia for an earlier time, when playwrights were the sole and authentic spokesmen of their age.[50]

Based on the denunciations of Butter, Bourne, and their colleagues, the printers of gazettes, these interpretations may perhaps underestimate the importance of another aspect of the play. Cymbal's office is in fact not a

typographic workshop where pamphlets and gazettes are printed but a
"scriptorium" in which handwritten news reports are registered, classified,
copied, and sold. In this sense, the "staple" was, as the Factor in the 1620
masque insists, a new form of an old practice, namely, the trade in handwritten "newsletters" or gazettes. In *Newes from the New World*, the Factor
describes his activity thus:

> I doe write my thousand Letters a week ordinary, sometime twelve hundred, and
> maintaine the businesse at some charge, both to hold up my reputation with my
> owne ministers in Towne, and my friends of correspondence in the Countrey; I have
> friends of all rancks, and of all Religions, for which I keepe an answering Catalogue
> of dispatch; wherein I have my Puritan newes, my Protestant newes, and my Pontifi-
> call newes.[51]

The debate between the chronicler, the printer, and the factor that opens
the masque dealt with an essential reality of the written culture of the time.
As Harold Love has shown, the diffusion of handwritten news copied by
professional scribes and either distributed to a network of subscribers or
sold in London bookshops was a profitable business in seventeenth-century
England.[52] A letter written in 1647 by one of five clerks employed in Sir
Joseph Williamson's office offers a precise description of the division of labor
in these enterprises. In order to meet the needs of a hundred correspondents,
each scribe was obliged to copy, every Tuesday, sixteen letters (four long,
giving the news of the week, and twelve short, containing news of just two
days); every Thursday, thirteen letters, three long and ten short; and every
Saturday, seven long, four of which covered four days' news, as well as eight
short. Thus each copyist had to produce forty-eight pages of journalistic
writing per week.[53]

How do we explain the continuing success of handwritten news, which
did not disappear even after printed periodicals arrived and began to multi-
ply? For one thing, handwritten "newsletters," including commercial ones,
were intended primarily for a readership of subscribers of high social status
employed by the church or state. The purchasers of printed newsbooks and
gazettes were anonymous, and the practitioners of what Love calls "scribal
journalism" preferred to deal with a known and select clientele. For another,
the news in handwritten gazettes circulated more freely. In the 1620s and
1630s, the English crown did not censor them in any way, not because of the
prohibition of print publication of domestic news, but because the authorities found the elitist readership of the handwritten newsletters reassuring.[54]

In both the masque and the comedy, Jonson made use of the contrast between the manuscript and the printed, between Cymbal's business and Butter's. As we have seen, however, his mockery and scorn were directed at both. His condemnation applies to both methods of news distribution, hence it is wrong to contrast the two too sharply. Despite differences in the way the news was sold and in the nature of the clientele in each case, the press runs of the printed gazettes were not very different from the number of copies made of each handwritten newsletter. Estimated at 200 to 400, the print runs of the *corantos* and *newsbooks* were in fact roughly the same as the number of newsletter copies, which in many cases reached into the hundreds.[55]

Furthermore, it was often the same men who produced and sold both printed periodicals and handwritten news. One such was John Pory, who replaced Gainsford as the publisher of the gazettes printed by Butter after 1624 and who also distributed a handwritten newsletter and copies of political speeches, which were sold in Butter's own shop.[56] Thus the two lines of business were closely related, and that is why Ben Jonson criticized the news in all its forms, each as corrupt and corrupting as the next.[57]

As if to demonstrate this point, Cymbal's "staple" is a fictional composite of all the journalistic practices of his time and does not correspond exactly to any of the places where news was published.[58] Although some scholars want to see Cymbal as a satirical incarnation of Butter, the staple is not one of the typographic shops where *corantos* and *newsbooks* were printed. Nor is it a shop of the sort in which handwritten newsletters were published. News items are not copied one after another into a single "letter," nor are they reproduced in a certain number of copies to be sent to subscribers, as in Williamson's office. Instead, they are sold one by one to clients who come to the "staple." Excerpted from the office registers and files, each report is read to its purchaser, who then leaves the office with a written copy of what he or she has just heard. Thus at the end of Act Three, Scene Two, each client who enters the "staple" purchases the news he is after and pays on the way out for the desired excerpt. The Anabaptist woman (designated "she Anabaptist" or "Dopper," the later being a Dutch word meaning "dipper," an allusion to the practice of baptism by immersion) pays six pence for the announcement of the coming of the prophet Baal and, after refusing to pay a shilling, nine pence for the announcement of the Grand Turk's impending visit to the church in Amsterdam.[59] The cost of news sold by the item was not insignificant: the price of a ballad was a penny,[60] whereas that of a printed *coranto* was two pence.[61] Note, by the way, that the daily wage of a construction worker was only eight pence, that a copyist was paid two or three pence for four pages of writing,[62] and that in the 1620s and 1630s a subscription to a handwritten weekly gazette varied in price from five to twenty pounds, or one to four shillings per four-page issue.[63] Cymbal's business thus turned a tidy profit, but it was not that of a "newsletter scriptorium,"[64] since the staple did not publish any gazette.

In *News from the New World*, Ben Jonson imagines that two heralds receive news from the moon. That news bears little resemblance to the errors of the chronicler, the inventions of the printer of pamphlets, or the falsifications of the factor with whom the heralds converse. The reports from the moon are true because they have been transmitted by the power of poetry in a language that does not deceive. That language consists not of lying words but of pure and soothing melodies: "They have no articulate voyces there, but certaine motions to musicke: all the discourse there is harmonie."[65] For the amusement of King James and his court, Ben Jonson imagined that the language of the moon was a perfect tongue, unblemished by the treachery and confusion of earthly language in general, and not just that of newsmongers. On the other side of the Channel, a few years later, Cyrano de Bergerac was to conceive a quite similar fantasy.

Chapter 5

Talking Books and Clandestine Manuscripts: The Travels of Dyrcona

Why are young moon dwellers better informed than earthlings? Dyrcona, who wanders the moon in the company of Socrates' *daimon*, finds out when his guide, before leaving him, gives him two books. These turn out to be quite unfamiliar objects: they have no pages, are not bound, and are not written with the letters of the alphabet. An entire "book" fits into a tiny box the size of a diamond or large pearl. Thanks to a mechanism of springs similar to that of a clock, these miraculous books produce sound: they are made for the ear, not for the eye. The "readers" of the Other World have only to rewind the mechanism and place the needle on the desired chapter to listen to their talking books.[1]

In this passage from *States and Empires of the Moon*, Cyrano de Bergerac played with a number of common themes from the written culture of his time. First, he bestowed literal reality on the tired metaphor of *voces paginarum*, vanished voices nevertheless present on the page. Lope de Vega was one of many authors to make use of this very ancient trope,[2] when he said that he had reduced to silence the voices of ancient playwrights irritated by the innovations of his "*comedias*": "And if I must compose a comedy, / According to the rules of the art I turn the key six times, / And kick Terence and Plautus out of my study, / In order to spare me their cries, for frequently one sees / Truth proclaimed in silent books."[3]

The metaphor usually referred to the elimination of voice and ear in favor of silent reading, but Cyrano restored its original force by imagining lunar books that could read themselves, out loud: "So you have all the great men, all the dead and living, around you eternally, conversing with you in their actual voices." Thus it comes as no surprise that the young moon people are very well informed: "Because they can read as soon as they can speak, they are never without reading material: in the bedroom, while strolling, in town, while traveling, on foot, on horseback, they can carry thirty books in their pockets or tied to their saddle horns, and all they have to do is wind

a spring to hear a chapter or even several chapters, if they're in a mood to listen to an entire book."[4]

Cyrano thus anticipated the triumph of small-format books, which
came to dominate Parisian publishing in the second half of the seventeenth
century[5]: the books of the Other World, no larger than a nutshell, are but an
extreme form of this miniaturization of the book. The moon traveler makes
good use of these devices: having penetrated the mystery of the talking book,
he goes walking with those that Socrates' *daimon* has given him "attached to
his ear like earrings."

The Perfect Language

The moon books naturally speak the local idiom, which does without syllables or words. It consists of tones, which can be emitted either by the human
voice or by a musical instrument. This language, which is spoken by the
moon's upper class, offers many advantages:

Certainly it is an invention altogether useful and agreeable, for when they are tired
of speaking, or when they disdain to prostitute their throats to this usage, they take a
lute or some other instrument with whose aid they communicate their thought as
easily as by the voice, so that sometimes fifteen or twenty of them may be met with
debating a point of theology or the difficulties of a law case in the most harmonious
concert that could tickle one's ears.[6]

Borrowed from *The Man in the Moon* by Francis Godwin, a text published in English in 1638 and translated into French ten years later,[7] the word-
less language spoken, performed, and listened to by the moon people was
Cyrano's fantastic response to two of the preoccupations of his time. First,
because this perfect language involved only tonal differences, like music
without words, it offered a most elegant solution to the search for indicators
of intensity by all who remained dissatisfied with sixteenth-century norms of
punctuation, which indicated only pauses of unequal length.[8] For evidence of
these efforts to make the voice more clearly present in written and printed
texts, witness the nonstandard uses of ordinary punctuation marks, which
were transformed into a kind of musical notation, such as the exclamation
point in Ronsard or the question mark in Racine;[9] or the use of initial capi-
tals to mark words intended to be pronounced more forcefully, according to
Moxon's indications and La Bruyère's practice.[10] Musical by nature, the language of the moon people had no need of such artifices.

Second, the ancient idea of music as a perfect and universal language, comparable to geometry because both are based on proportions, movements, and harmonies, figured in the programs of late sixteenth-century academies.[11] By Cyrano's time, such ideas were no longer in vogue, and the Académie Française, founded by Richelieu, made no place for music. Only in the states of the moon did the language of tones grant access to the most subtle forms of knowledge. Hence it could not be the language of everyone. The moon's lower orders did not speak with their mouths or with musical instruments, as the men of letters did, but rather by "movements of the limbs" and other body parts: "For example, the movement of a finger, of a hand, of an ear, of a lip, of an arm, of a cheek will make singly a discourse or a sentence; others are only used to designate words, such as a wrinkle in the forehead, different shiverings of the muscles, turnings of the hands, stampings of the foot, contortions of the arm." The distinction between the learned and the simple, the knowledgeable and the ignorant, was fundamental with Cyrano, and the two moon languages reflect this quite immediately. The sonorous harmonies of upper-class language stand in contrast to the gestures of the vulgar, which could take extreme forms that Cyrano did not shrink from describing: "When they talk, their limbs, which are accustomed to gesticulate their ideas, move so briskly that it does not seem a man talking but a body trembling."[12]

While the narrator of the moon journey can listen to the books given him in Paris, in the first world, by Socrates' *daimon*, Cyrano wrote for a knowing reader, who would encounter his work in various printed editions (such as the *Œuvres diverses* published by the Parisian bookseller Charles de Sercy in 1654 or the *États et empires de la Lune* published by the same Sercy in 1657, two years after Cyrano's death on July 28, 1655[13]) or in one of the manuscript copies that had earlier enabled the text to circulate in a form less subject to the censor's scrutiny. This dual mode of transmission is one reason why Cyrano deserves a place in this book, one of whose purposes is to point out that in the early modern period print was far from being the only form of inscription and publication of the written. But there is also another reason to travel with him to the moon and, later, the sun. Indeed, the account of the narrator's tribulations is filled with the presence of books, and not only musical ones. What Jacques Prévot[14] has nicely termed the "bookish tissue" of Cyrano's work means that the entire narrative is organized, in its articulations and themes, in terms of a multifarious appropriation of the written world.

I will not choose among the various interpretations of what René Pintard has called Cyrano's "flamboyant libertinage."[15] Should it be understood as a form of vitalism, in which the endless metamorphoses of matter become the basis for denying the existence of a divine creator, because the universe is eternal, and of the individual soul, because each being plays its part in the unbroken chain of transformations?[16] Or, as Cyrano's polyphonic writing suggests, should we refrain from assigning a definite philosophical position to the author and, assuming that Dyrcona is not Cyrano despite the near anagram of the two names, see his work as a skeptical rejection of all systems and all beliefs?[17] Madeleine Alcover moves closer to the latter view in her recent edition, because, although she persists in the notion that the irreducible core of Cyrano's thought lies in "the recurrence of monism, of matter as the *alpha* and *omega*, of its endless and proteiform recycling," she also identifies an "eclectic attitude" in the work, which presents contradictory philosophical discourses and therefore demonstrates "the impossibility of adhering completely to any system at all."[18] My goal is not to choose among these different interpretations but simply to look at what Dyrcona and Cyrano do with books, both their own and those of others.

In the Beginning Was the Book

The adventure begins with a book: "I returned home and scarcely had I entered my room to rest after the journey when I found on my table an open book which I had not put there. . . . It was the works of Cardan [Girolamo Cardano]."[19] In other words, the narrator, upon returning from a meeting of learned friends in the course of which he had argued that the moon, like the earth, constitutes a world, he finds Cardano's work fortuitously open on his table to confirm his opinion. The book, which was no doubt *On Subtlety and Subtle Inventions*, published in 1550, revised in 1554, and translated into French in 1556,[20] had mysteriously found its way from the narrator's shelves to his table. It lay open to the page on which (according to Cyrano, not the original book) Cardano recounted a visit he had received from two "important elderly" moon people. No doubt it is the same two visitors who "force" the narrator to read this story, which ultimately leads him to plan a journey to the moon and, after overcoming several obstacles, to set out for this other world: "I took this whole train of events to be an inspiration of God urging me to make known to men that the Moon is a world."[21]

Cardano, a mathematician and astrologer whose *De Subtilitate* was one of the "bestsellers" of the sixteenth century,[22] appears a second time in the story. When Socrates' *daimon* draws up the—short—list of "considerable individuals" he met during his second stay on earth, "over the past hundred years," he places Cardano in the front rank: "One day I appeared to Cardan as he was reading. I instructed him in many things, and in recompense he promised me that he would bear witness to posterity that I was the person from whom he obtained knowledge of the miracles he proposed to write."[23] Among those "miracles," Cyrano may have read of the seven men whose bodies were made of air and who had appeared to Cardano's father and transformed them into the two old men from the moon who set his own narrative in motion.

In the beginning was the book. The two books that Socrates' *daimon* gives the narrator confirm this. Both were written in a third world, from which the *daimon* comes: "I was born in the Sun; but because our world is sometimes overpeopled on account of the long life of its inhabitants and the fact that it is practically free from wars and diseases, our rulers from time to time send out colonies to the surrounding worlds."[24] In the *daimon*'s case, this meant first the Earth, then the moon. One of the two talking books is the *Great Work of the Philosophers*, "written by one of the sun's most powerful minds." The title, which was not printed as such in the 1657 edition, can be understood in more than one way: as a generic expression, without reference to a particular work; as an allusion to an actual work bearing that title; or as an implicit citation of the philosophy of Giordano Bruno, which is adequately described by what the *daimon* says about the solar book, which

proves . . . that all things are true, and shows the way to unite physically the truths of each contradiction; for example, that white is black and black is white, that you can be and not be at the same time, that there can be a mountain without a valley, that nothingness is something, and that all things which exist do not exist.[25]

The other book is entitled *States and Empires of the Sun*, in other words, the same title as the work that would be published five years after *States and Empires of the Moon*, and which was no doubt already in the works in 1650.[26] Was Cyrano already thinking of possibly continuing the philosophical and moon-exploring adventures of Dyrcona in yet another world? If so, he may have alluded to it in the earlier narrative, just as if Cervantes had evoked the second part of *Don Quixote* in 1605 and Mateo Alemán the second part of *Guzmán de Alfarache* in 1599. That may be, even if the title, *States and Empires of the Sun*, which parodied the titles of two books by Pierre Davity (*The States, Empires, Kingdoms, and Principalities of the World*, published in 1625, and *The World, or the General Description of Its Four Parts, with all its empires, kingdoms, estates, and republics*, published in 1643), can be understood generically, so that Cyrano need not have written or conceived of such a work at the time he finished the story of the trip to the moon.[27]

Readings and Copies

Clinging to the Devil, who is dragging off to Hell a lunar blasphemer with the face of the Antichrist, the traveler from the other world lands near Vesuvius, embarks for Provence, and, at the beginning of *States and Empires of the Sun*, finds hospitality in Toulouse with one of his friends, a Monsieur de Colignac. Colignac is eager to hear of Dyrcona's adventures on the moon. This is the first point at which we learn Dyrcona's name, because in the first novel he remained an anonymous "I," upon whom we have retrospectively bestowed the name "Dyrcona." Colignac urges him to recount his wanderings and then begs him to "write them down." In a *mise en abyme* opposite that of the first novel, where one of the books Dyrcona was given to read may have been the account of a journey he had not yet taken, here, in the second novel, the text recounts in the present tense the writing and diffusion of a work that the reader may already have read.[28]

As with Cervantes and Don Quixote's visit to the print shop in Barcelona, Cyrano transformed the very conditions in which his work was published into a theme of his fiction. But there is an important difference: the story here does not involve printing. *The States and Empires of the Moon* circulated in a different form. At first M. de Colignac reads it out loud to small groups of friends and scholars in Toulouse: "As soon as I finished a quire he went to Toulouse to vaunt it in the best company, for he was more anxious for my reputation than his own; he was considered one of the greatest minds of his century and by making himself the indefatigable echo of my praises he made me known to everyone."[29]

This first form of publication put the author's autograph manuscript into circulation in its material reality, quire after quire, rather than according to the divisions of the text itself. This nevertheless afforded the work a first form of public existence, as it became first an object of favorable judgment and later of criticism in literary circles, as well as sufficiently well known to lead to the sale of engravings of the author's portrait: "Already, without having seen me, the engravers had cut my portrait and from every square the town echoed with peddlers shouting at the top of their voices from hoarse throats: 'Portrait of the author of *The Voyage to the Moon*.'"[30]

The portrait offered to the citizens of Toulouse was presumably the print inserted in some but not all copies of the edition of the *Œuvres diverses* in 1654, with a caption that mentioned two of Cyrano's oldest friends, Henri Le Bret and Jean Le Royer de Prade.[31]

The second mode of circulation of Dyrcona's work refers, in Harold

Love's typology, not to an "authorial publication" based on the author's manuscript but to a commercial enterprise or "entrepreneurial publication" based on handwritten copies of the work.[32] What ensures the success of the work is the controversy that takes place in select societies between those who praise it and those who condemn it as "a potpourri of ridiculous fables, a farrago of disconnected snippets, a collection of fairy tales good for putting the children to sleep."[33] The difference of opinion stirs up dispute: "The contrasting opinions of the clever and the idiotic enhanced the work's renown. Soon copies of the manuscript were being sold under the table. Everyone in society and out, from the nobleman to the monk, bought the play. Even women took sides. Families divided, and interest in the dispute ran so high that the city was divided into two factions, the lunar and the anti-lunar."[34] For the "anti-lunar" side, the work was doubly discredited: as a fairy tale for children and "idiots," it was full of extravagant, incredible stories, and as a clumsy text that made rudimentary use of the technique of commonplaces, it juxtaposed fragments in a disorderly, incoherent way. For the "lunar" side, on the other hand, the work contained profound but dangerous truths, so that it had to circulate discreetly in the form of manuscripts sold "under the table" rather than that of printed books displayed in bookstore stalls.

As the story continues, we learn that this caution proved insufficient to protect Dyrcona from the wrath of the censors. The first obstacle is raised by the "long-robed beards" of the Parlement of Toulouse, who accuse the author of sorcery and magic, since he could not have visited the moon without making a pact with the devil. The judges, who are either relatives or friends of Colignac, assure him that his protégé will receive a very discreet punishment: "You have only to put him in our hands, and because we love you, we pledge on our honor to burn him without provoking a scandal."[35] This is clearly an allusion to the trial of the libertine Vanini, who was condemned to the stake by the Parlement of Toulouse in 1619,[36] but it also pokes fun at the judges who remained faithful to the descriptions of the old treatises on demonology at the very moment when certitudes about the reality of sorcery were fading and thus doubts about trying people for the crime of sorcery were on the rise.[37]

Dyrcona's second censor is the parish priest, Messire Jean, who, in the aftermath of a failed lawsuit involving the tithe, is embittered with hatred of the local lord, M. de Colignac, against whom he intends to seek vengeance. To that end, he adopts a twofold strategy: to denounce Dyrcona in Toulouse so as to compel officials of the Parlement to launch an investigation, and to manipulate the superstitious beliefs of the peasants so as to lure him into a

trap. An opportunity presents itself when Dyrcona heads out alone for residence of the marquis de Cussan, a friend and neighbor of Colignac's, where
he hopes he will be safe from arrest by the Parlement. Once again, a book
plays an essential role in the structure of the story. For his stay with the
marquis, Dyrcona has prepared "a bundle of volumes that I did not expect to
find in Cussan's library, and loaded them onto a mule." Among these books
is Descartes's *Physique*, that is, the *Principia Philosophiae* of 1644, which was
translated into French in 1647. When the narrator is attacked and taken pris-
oner by villagers spurred on by the priest, who is on the scene, this is the first
volume they open:

When they perceived all the circles by which this philosopher has traced the movement of each planet, they all with one voice bawled out that these were the magic
circles I drew to call up Beelzebub. The man who held the book dropped it in terror
and unfortunately as it fell it opened at the page on which the action of the magnet
is explained; I say unfortunately, because at the place I speak of there is a drawing of
this metallic stone where the little bodies which detach themselves from its mass to
seize the iron are represented as arms. Hardly had one of these fellows perceived it
when I heard him roar that this was the toad they found in the trough in his cousin
Fiacre's stable when his horses died.[38]

The terrified peasants become even more frightened at what they take
to be the spells cast by this sorcerer, who has made a pact with the Devil, but,
encouraged by their priest, who shouts "at the top of his lungs that no one
should touch anything, that all the books are filled with black magic and the
mule is a Satan,"[39] they turn Dyrcona over to the jailer in a town on the road
to Toulouse. After a series of escapes and further arrests, he is imprisoned in
the Grosse Tour, where, with the help of Colignac and Cussan, he has enough
space and materials to start building the flying machine that will take him to
the States and Empires of the Sun.

The Gullible and the Disabused

Twice, a book opened by chance, without any intention of the reader, triggers
a "sequence" of events that takes the narrator to another world. The page
in Cardano, which persuades him that the moon is another world and that
he must prove it by traveling to the great orb, and then, as if in response, the
page in Descartes that convinces the credulous villagers that he is a sorcerer
who deserves to be punished by the judges in Toulouse. The icosahedron that
he builds in his gilded prison is beyond his wildest dreams of escape, because

it takes him from orb to orb until at last he approaches the "great glowing plains" of the sun.

The scene in which Descartes' book is mistaken for a book of sorcery is not only a narrative device for moving the narrator and his reader from Toulouse to the sun but also a forceful representation of the divide that exists in Cyrano's mind between the disabused "philosophers" and the ignorant "populace," maintained in its superstitions by the manipulations of clerics and the credulity of judges. The written word does not have the same significance for these two groups. Like the rebels led by Jack Cade in Shakespeare's *Henry VI*, the villagers fear the evil power that books give to those who know how to make and decipher the signs found in them.[40] The only recourse against diabolical writing is another magical power, that of Christian writing, not read but carried on the body as a talisman capable of warding off evil spells. On the road to Cussan, the first peasant to block Dyrcona's way and shout "*Satanus Diabolas!* . . . I conjure you by the great living God," is clad in writing: "A long gown made from the leaves of a book of plainsong covered him down to his nails, and his face was hidden by a card on which was written *In principio* [the first words of the Gospel of John]."[41]

In contrast to these superstitious fears of the written word, literary societies made gentle commerce in the written word the very basis of friendly intellectual collaboration. Listen to Dyrcona's description of the time of *otium* that he spends with Colignac and Cussan:

Those innocent pleasures of which the body are only a slight part of those the mind takes in study and conversation, whereof we lacked none; and our libraries, united like our minds, brought all the learned into our society. We mingled reading with conversation, conversation with good cheer, and that with fishing or hunting, when we went out; in a word, we enjoyed, so to speak, both ourselves and all that is most agreeably produced by Nature for our use; we placed no limits on our desire save those of reason.[42]

The exercise of reason as opposed to fanaticism, familiarity with the written word as opposed to its magical uses, conversation as opposed to superstition: these were for Cyrano the fundamental oppositions that defined the sociability of the erudite.

The erudite thrived, moreover, on common references: Cardano, whose *De Subtilitate* inspired the journey and the novel, and Campanella, who accompanies Dyrcona to the sun and the "province of Philosophers" and along the way signs the praises of Descartes' *Physique* (or *Principia*), the book that had so frightened the peasants of Colignac. The fictional Campanella invented by

Cyrano, who both is and is not the Calabrese philosopher, plays in *States and Empires of the Sun* the role played by Socrates' *daimon* in *States and Empires of the Moon*. Moreover, the *daimon* says that he has met him and helped him out during his imprisonment in Rome:

> I knew Campanella also. When he was in the Inquisition at Rome, it was I who advised him to conform his face and body to the usual grimaces and postures of those whose inner mind he needed to know, so that he might excite in himself by a similar position the thoughts which this same situation had called up in his adversaries; because he would treat better with their soul when he knew it.[43]

Cyrano's Campanella uses this talent when he meets Dyrcona, telling him that "by matching my body to yours and becoming as it were your twin, a given movement of matter must inevitably cause both of us to experience an identical movement of mind."[44] Socrates' *daimon* concludes his brief portrait of Campanella with these words: "He began, at my urging, a book that we entitled *De sensu rerum*." Indeed, this book, which was reprinted in Paris in 1637, is more present in the story than *Civitas Solis*, whose rigid utopia Cyrano rejected, although the philosophy of the former, harshly judged in intellectual circles, was not entirely accepted.[45]

The company of Socrates' *daimon* and of Campanella gives rise to a narrative filled with "philosophical" dialogues, creating a "farrago of disconnected snippets" according to the learned judges of Toulouse. As in Baudri de Bourgueil, but for a different purpose, spoken exchanges form the basis of the social bond. Thus the *daimon* remembers his conversations with Gassendi (whom Cyrano may have met in the early 1640s, after his return from the army, when he was a student in the Parisian *collège* of Lisieux), La Mothe Le Vayer, and Tristan l'Hermite, whom he sets apart from "so many others, whom your century treats as divine, but in whom I found nothing but a lot of babble and pride."[46]

Masculine Amours

Along with a shared taste for metaphysical speculation, natural philosophy, and a more or less materialist form of skepticism, the erudite sociability of libertine circles also had, in Cyrano's case, at any rate, a significant homosexual dimension. As Madeleine Alcover has shown, there is ample and convincing evidence of this.[47] In the Preface to the printed edition of *States and Empires of the Moon* in 1657, Henri Le Bret, Cyrano's childhood friend, sketched the first biography of the writer, laying down the themes that would eventually inspire the verse of Edmond Rostand[48]: rural childhood, joining the company of M. de Carbon Castel-Jaloux, panache in duels, the fight of a hundred against one at the Porte de Nesles, the wound received at the siege of Arras, the hatred of dependence and the refusal of any patron (apart from the duc d'Arpajon at the very end of the author's life), the taste for study and poetry (which he wrote even in the guardroom), and the blow to the head that ultimately did him in.[49]

In Le Bret's account, however, no one in skirts figures in the hero's life other than the devout women who accompany him in his final months, when his ailing body is taken under the protection of a family ally, Tanneguy Renault de Boisclairs, a counselor of the king and Grand Provost of Burgundy and Bresse. These fervent Christian ladies are identified by name in the preface: Mother Marguerite de Jésus, the founder of the community of Daughters of the Cross, "who particularly admired him," and her cousin, Madeleine Robineau, baroness of Neuvillette, who was "wholeheartedly pious, wholeheartedly charitable, and wholeheartedly for her fellow man, because she was wholeheartedly for God."[50]

On the other hand, we find two allusions to Cyrano's sexual preference that suggest that no Roxane would have tempted him. Le Bret indicates that it was to protect Cyrano that he encouraged his friend to make a career of the military:

Being of an age when nature is more easily corrupted, and of a temperament that claimed the greatest liberty to do only what it pleases, he had a certain dangerous penchant, from which I dare say I rescued him, because when I finished my studies and confronted my father's wish that I serve in the Guards, I obliged him to join M. de Carbon Castel-Jaloux's company along with me.

Later, in praising his friend's moderation in drinking wine very seldom and eating very little, he adds ironically that "to these two qualities he joined that of a reserve in regard to the fair sex so great that it can be said he never failed to demonstrate the respect we owe it."[51]

Homosexual amours are not absent from the two journeys. On the moon they take a rather amusing turn. Because Dyrcona walks on two feet, rather than four like the natives, he is mistaken for an animal, namely, "the female of the queen's little pet." The queen's pet turns out to be a Spaniard, who has been condemned by the Inquisition for asserting the existence of natural vacuums and the unity of matter. Birds brought him to the moon, where the queen mistook him for an ape, "because it happens they dress their monkeys in Spanish clothes [i.e., ruffs and breeches], and . . . when she found him dressed in this manner on his arrival, she had not doubted he belonged to the species." The mockery of the Spanish does not preclude sympathy, however:

> The King commanded his monkey keeper to take us away, with strict orders to make the Spaniard and me lie together to multiply our species in the kingdom. The Prince's command was carried out in every point, and I was very glad of it because of the pleasure I took in having someone to converse with during the solitude of my brutification.[52]

Here we see coupling of a sort not imagined by Dr. García in his *Antipathy of the French and Spanish.*[53]

On the sun, the tone is different, more poetic and antique. The oak of Dodone recounts the fable of two trees that fall in love, offering an apologia for same-sex love that draws on numerous mythological and historical examples, using the technique of composing a story around quotes and allusions. Here the narrative proceeds from the love of Pylades and Orestes to the twin shrubs that are born from their entwined bodies to the irresistible love engendered by the miraculous fruits of those shrubs in couples who bite into them: "No sooner did you eat the fruit of one than you fell passionately in love with whoever had eaten the fruit of the other."[54]

There are numerous, and in some cases peculiar, examples of similar passions: thus, Artaxerxes falls in love with a plane tree that has received a graft from Orestes' tree; Salmacis and Hermaphrodite are joined as one, neither male nor female; and Narcissus falls madly in love with himself. The heterosexual loves are no less bizarre, linking daughter to father, Pasiphae to the Minotaur, and the marble Venus to Pygmalion. But the finest fruits borne by the shrubs that were once Orestes and Pylades are of another order: they unite "a Hercules with a Theseus, an Achilles with a Patroclus, a Nisus with an Euryales" and achieve their consummate form in the "sacred band" of Thebes, that "amorous company" or "troop of lovers" of unrivaled brilliance, for "each of these brave warriors, to protect his lover or to prove himself worthy of his love, ventured efforts more incredible than any Antiquity had ever seen."[55] Cyrano thus summoned up his schoolboy memories, his reading of the Ancients, and perhaps his notebook of commonplaces to celebrate the most authentic of virile friendships, those that link lovers.

Scribal Publication

States and Empires of the Sun was not published during its author's lifetime. According to Le Bret's 1657 Preface, the text was probably among a chest full of manuscripts that was stolen from Cyrano while he lay ill after the accident, attempted murder, or attack on the carriage of his protector, the duc d'Arpajon, in which he suffered a grave injury to the head.[56] The recovered manuscript was printed by Charles de Sercy in 1662 with the approval of Cyrano's brother, Abel II, his residual legatee. This edition is the only known version of a work of which no manuscript has survived.

The same cannot be said of *States and Empires of the Moon.* The 1657 edition was a highly censored print version of a text that had previously circulated in manuscript, exactly as described in the opening narrative of the second novel. The three surviving manuscripts, known as the Sydney, Munich, and Paris versions, have given rise to sharp controversy as to which is more faithful to Cyrano's autograph.[57] Each seems to correspond to a particular type of handwritten text. The Sydney manuscript, on paper whose watermark fixes its date as between 1646 and 1652, might have been copied by someone close to Chapelain and Gassendi to allow clandestine circulation of the work among libertine scholars. The Munich manuscript, which is poorly transcribed and full of errors, might have been a copy intended for private use. The Paris manuscript was copied by a professional scribe, no doubt trained by a master-writer, who transcribed the text mechanically, as can be seen in the way he cuts off words and the total lack of punctuation. This text, written in a regular hand and featuring "catchwords" (words printed at the bottom of each page that duplicate the first words of the following page) to ensure assembly of the quires in the proper order, may have been intended for reproduction and (possibly commercial) circulation but probably not for printing, since there is no evidence that Cyrano wished to have the work set in type (whether out of caution or for some other reason).[58]

The existence of these three manuscripts—and only these three—leaves us uncertain as to the extent to which Cyrano's first novel circulated. Must we assume, as Margaret Sankey does, that a "large number" of intermediate manuscripts must once have existed but not survived in order to explain "the number, variety, and configuration of the variants" that have come down to us?[59] Or must we share Madeleine Alcover's conclusion that neither the manuscript of *The Other World* nor those of Cyrano's other works "circulated much or was much reproduced?"[60] Comparison with the number of surviving manuscripts of other works scarcely resolves the issue. To be sure, the work of some authors who preceded Cyrano have survived in far greater abundance, including the *Colloquium heptapiomeres* attributed to Jean Bodin, of which a hundred or so manuscripts remain, and Machiavelli's *Prince,* of which forty copies are extant in Italian, French, and English. By contrast, compared with the works of other erudite libertines of the early seventeenth century, Cyrano's fared rather well.[61]

One should be careful not to be misled by the relative scarcity of copies. In the seventeenth century, manuscript publication in various forms was still one of the fundamental ways in which texts circulated. There were numerous reasons for this, and not all had to do with a desire to circumvent the rigors of censorship as they applied to works at odds with religious orthodoxy, political authority, or common standards of morality. As we saw in the previous chapter in regard to seventeenth-century England, some genres that had nothing subversive about them relied primarily on the manuscript medium: not only handwritten news reports and copies of parliamentary speeches but also anthologies of poetry intended for limited circulation in aristocratic or literary circles, as well as musical scores, of which printed and engraved editions were more costly than manuscript copies.[62] In Golden Age Castille, the same was true of books of instructions that nobles prepared for their sons, family histories, accounts of political events and battles, defamatory lampoons, and books of magic.[63] The invention of the printing press did not put an end to the circulation of manuscripts, not by a long shot.

Compared with the books that came out of print shops, manuscripts offered many advantages.[64] For one thing, it allowed for controlled and limited diffusion of texts without the risk that they might fall into the hands of ignorant readers, since they circulated within a distinct social milieu defined by family ties, similar social status, or shared sociability. For another, the very form of the manuscript book left it open to correction, deletion, and insertion at all stages of production, from composition to copying to binding, so that the writing could proceed in successive stages (as when nobles made additions to their instructions to their offspring with each new generation) or by several hands (as in the case of poetry anthologies, to which readers often became contributors). Finally, manuscript publication was a response to corruptions introduced by printing: it rescued the commerce of letters from economic interests (except when it took a commercial form itself, as with handwritten newsletters), and it protected works from the alterations introduced by clumsy compositors and ignorant proofreaders.

Censored Print

Thus clandestine literature was the only source of hand-copied texts in circulation, but there is no doubt that it was better suited than print for evading the censure of those to whom the Spaniard who becomes the queen's monkey refers as "doctors in pall," some of whom wore the "square bonnet" of the judge, others the "hood" of the university doctor, and still others the "cassock" of the priest.[65] When the censors' wrath fell on a printed edition, all or nearly all copies of the work could be destroyed (this was the fate of the anonymous and pornographic 1655 edition of the *Ecole des filles*[66]) or censored (only three copies of the 1682 edition of the works of Molière, the first to include the text of *Dom Juan*, seem to have escaped the drastic cuts demanded by the Lieutenant Général de Police[67]).

The publication of Cyrano's works also attests to the vulnerability of print to various forms of censorship and self-censorship. When *States and Empires of the Moon* appeared in bookshops in 1657, 561 lines present in the Paris manuscript, or nearly a fifth of the work, had been eliminated from the text.[68] The cuts seriously affected the episode in which Dyrcona visits Paradise, the first phase of his sojourn on the moon. His dialogue with old Elijah, one of six humans to have been admitted (after Adam, Eve, and Enoch and before Saint John the Baptist and Dyrcona himself), was of course by no means orthodox. Burlesque and licentious parodies of Scripture abound, including the following observation by the narrator after Elijah informs him that the serpent's punishment for tempting Eve was to have been confined inside the male body:

"Truly," said I, interrupting him, "I have observed that since this serpent is always trying to escape from man's body, his head and neck may be seen projecting from the lower part of our bellies. But God did not permit man alone to be tormented by it; he willed that it should rise up against woman to cast its venom upon her and that the swelling should last nine months after she had been bitten. And to prove to you that I speak according to the word of the Lord, he said to the serpent (to curse it) that thought it might make woman fall by rising up against her, she would make it lower its head."[69]

The other omissions involved statements denying aspects of Christian morality or dogma, including, at the end of the novel, the young blasphemer's denials of the immorality of the soul, miracles, the resurrection of the body, and even the existence of God. The attribution of these "diabolical and ridiculous opinions" to the Antichrist, who can be recognized by his "small, deep-set eyes, dark complexion, large mouth, hairy chin, and black nails" as well as his abduction by "a large, very hairy black man," was not enough to save the passage from the censors. The conclusion of the printed text no longer discusses the resurrection or the bet on the existence of God. And Dyrcona enters the clouds and begins his journey back to earth in the arms of Socrates' *daimon* rather than clinging to the hairy man and the blaspheming moon dweller.[70]

Beyond these spectacular cuts, the differences between the printed and manuscript editions reveal a meticulous rewriting of the text involving changes in the characters to whom various statements are attributed so as to portray the narrator as a more staunch and sincere defender of Christian orthodoxy. It is difficult to know who was responsible for these changes. Was it Cyrano himself? In the devout circle that took care of him after his accident, he supposedly underwent a "great change," as Le Bret put it in his preface to the 1657 edition, adding "that at last the libertinage of which most young people are suspected came to seem monstrous to him, and I can attest that from then on he felt all the aversion toward it that anyone who wishes to lead a Christian life should have."[71]

Yet, as Madeleine Alcover asks, "Can anyone seriously believe that an authentic convert would not have simply taken a match to the work rather than a pair of scissors?"[72] Should we therefore attribute the cuts and rewriting to Le Bret because he says of the book, "I took it upon myself to see it through the press?" Or should we impute responsibility to an editor, who on the final page invents a story of the publication quite different from that proposed in *States and Empires of the Sun* and who is apparently unaware of the existence of this second novel? Indeed, there Cyrano reveals himself behind the mask of the narrator. He indicates that he has spent two weeks in Rome with his cousin (in fact Cyrano would spend the last days of his life with his cousin Pierre in Sannois) and declares of the story of his trip to the moon that he "put it in order as much as the illness that keeps [him] in bed allows."

The text ends with the request to Le Bret to "give the public" not only the *States and Empires of the Moon* but also the works that were stolen from him, *The History of the Republic of the Sun* and *The Spark*, both titles cited by Le Bret in his preface.[73] Even though we do not know who was responsible, the censorship to which Cyrano's text was subjected shows clearly that it was possible to take risks in a text intended to circulate—though not without danger—in manuscript, but that it was absolutely necessary to tone down such provocations before putting the book on sale to readers of printed books.

Stop-Press Corrections and Cancels

Yet even when a manuscript was sedulously purged prior to going into print, the work still remained subject to further alterations. Under the old typographic regime, there were two ways of revising texts in the course of printing.[74] The first was to make "stop-press corrections," that is, to modify the work as it was being printed. If the text of certain pages already set in type, imposed in forms, and printed was still deemed unacceptably heterodox or indecent, it could be corrected and reset before printing resumed. The new printed sheets coming off the press therefore contained a version of the text different from that in the pages printed originally, which the printer, for economic reasons, did not wish to destroy. When such changes were made at different times on different pages, the result was that the copies of the same edition were different, since the sheets with corrected and uncorrected pages could be assembled in a variety of different ways. This occurred with the 1662 edition of the *Nouvelles Œuvres de Monsieur Cyrano de Bergerac*, which contained the *States and Empires of the Sun*. The surviving copies are all different, no doubt because Cyrano's brother corrected the forms in the course of printing so as to tone down the cruder language and modify certain passages concerning Descartes.[75]

The second procedure was still more drastic: the use of "cancels" (*cartons* in French), that is, pasting new pages in place of old ones. These allowed for more fundamental changes in the text, which could even go so far as to substitute one entire gathering for another. This is what the censors did to the 1682 edition of *Dom Juan* and to Cyrano's letters as published in the 1654 edition of his *Œuvres diverses*. The purpose of this was to eliminate impieties and remove the names of individuals who were attacked, or, in the case of Scarron, of an entire letter vilifying him.[76] The 1657 edition of *States and Empires of the Moon* was also canceled. We know this because Le Bret's preliminary texts, the epistle dedicatory to Tanneguy Renault de Boisclairs and the preface, occur in two different versions in the three surviving copies. Two copies (the one in Houghton Library at Harvard and the one that belonged to Flaubert) contain violent accusations against Abel, alleging that he mistreated his brother by holding him hostage "out of lust for his property" and that this "inhumanity" aggravated his illness, whereas the third copy (in the French Bibliothèque Nationale) makes no mention of this, the text having been corrected, presumably, at the insistence of Abel himself.[77]

Cyrano's case shows that it is not easy to give a general diagnosis of the effects of censorship, no matter who was responsible. On the one hand, the censors were unable to prevent the circulation of works at odds with orthodox dogma and Christian morality. On the other hand, they were not entirely without power, including that exercised by encouraging self-censorship on the part of writers. The omnipresent threat of censorship led prudent authors to choose clandestine circulation over printing, and the threat was serious enough that printed texts differed substantially from manuscript copies, where bolder expression was possible. Before *States and Empires of the Moon*, this was already the case with the comedy entitled *Le Pédant joué*, which Cyrano wrote in 1645 and of which the publication in the *Œuvres diverses* of 1654 yielded a text that drastically toned down the more audacious statements found in a manuscript copy that dates from 1650 or 1651.[78]

Eaten Poems

In *States of the Moon*, clever men are never in want. Dyrcona, invited to lunch by Socrates' *daimon*, is surprised to see him pay the innkeeper with a piece of paper: "I asked him if it was a promissory note for the value of the bill. He replied in the negative, indicating that he no longer owed anything and that the paper had contained verse."[79]

Poems are currency on the moon, and those who are starving rhymesters in this world are saved from penury by their talent in the other. There, moreover, bad money cannot drive out good, because the "poet jurors" of the lunar Court of Currency appraise and certify the verse submitted to their expert judgment: "There, official versifiers submit their coinage for appraisal, and if they are deemed to be of sterling quality, they are stamped not according to their weight but according to their wit."[80] Unlike the metal coins used by earthlings, whose value depends on the quantity of gold, silver, or copper that they contain, the poetic paper money of the moon is gauged by its lightness. Once stamped by the authorities, a poem can only be used once. Anyone who copies a poem will suffer the sad fate reserved for counterfeiters.

Socrates' *daimon* has a well-stocked purse, or, rather, a purse full of poems. The lunch cost him a *sixain*, or six-line stanza, but, as he puts it, "I'm not afraid of running out, because when we have a feast here that lasts a week, we spend no more than a sonnet, and I have four on me, along with nine epigrams, two odes, and an eclogue."[81]

In the manuscript version, Cyrano acknowledges his debt to Sorel, but he stands it ironically on its head and pokes fun at Sorel's mother: "Ha! I said to myself, that's what Sorel has Hortensius use for money in *Francion*, as I recall. He probably stole the idea from the moon world. But who the devil could he have heard it from? It must be his mother, because I've heard that she was a lunatic."[82] In the *Histoire comique de Francion*, Hortensius says that in his kingdom "poems will be worth whatever their value is set at."[83] This allusion is missing from the printed edition, from which insults to individuals were banished. The new text does not acknowledge the borrowing: "May it please God, I said to him, that it be the same in our world! I know many respectable poets who are dying of hunger there and who would eat well if grocers were paid in this currency."[84]

As in any number of works of spirituality, the monetary reference was transformed into a metaphor for the economy of salvation. Indeed, certain lunar innkeepers ask for payment not in the soft but sonorous cash of poetry but rather in the form of "a receipt for the Other World." The formula they copy down in a large ledger labeled "God's Accounts" parodies the indulgences that promised a reduction of the soul's time of suffering in Purgatory in exchange for coin of the realm. Like the *cedula* that Don Quixote gives Sancho to persuade her niece to give him the three ass-colts that are to compensate him for the theft of his ass, the text of the receipt reads like a comical burlesque of a letter of exchange: "*Item*, the value of so many lines of poetry, delivered on such and such a day, to such and such a person, for which God is to reimburse me on demand from the first available funds."[85] The printed text toned down the blaspheming irony: "God's Accounts" become merely "Accounts of the Great Day," and the name of God is eliminated from the text of the receipt: "*Item*, the value of so many lines of poetry, delivered to such and such a person on such and such a day. And for which I am to be reimbursed on demand from the first available funds."[86]

Socrates' *daimon* concludes his conversation with the observation that "when they feel ill, in danger of dying, they chop these ledgers into pieces and swallow them, because they believe that if the books were not digested in this way, God would not be able to read them."[87] The parody here works on a number of different levels. First, there is the allusion to the methods of commonplace books, both anthologies published by compilers as well as handwritten notebooks kept by readers, where the assumption was that texts were "digested" in the form of citations and references classified by theme and topic.[88] Cyrano no longer believed in the value of such a practice (even if people who heard his novel read in Toulouse accused him of it), and it is not surprising that innkeepers on the moon, who belong to the vulgar masses, prefer their "digested" receipts to the sublime verses of the poets.

The allusion to swallowed texts also had a religious significance. As Madeleine Alcover notes, it may have been a reference to communion, which was necessary for indulgences to be effective. But it also evokes the eating of the biblical text, as in Ezekiel 3:3: "And he said unto me, Son of man, cause thy belly to eat, and fill thy bowels with this roll that I give thee. Then did I eat it; and it was in my mouth as honey for sweetness." This is echoed by Revelation 10:10: "And I took the little book out of the angel's hand, and ate it up; and it was in my mouth sweet as honey: and as soon as I had eaten it, my belly was bitter."[89] Once again, this parody of Scripture proved unacceptable to the editors of the printed text. The sick innkeepers swallow the pages of the "Accounts of the Great Day" not so that God can read them but "because they believe that if they were not digested in this way, they would not derive any profit from them."[90]

In what language and with what characters are the poems of the moon people written? Neither Socrates' *daimon* nor Dyrcona is clear about this, but the reader can imagine, because he knows that on the moon, the idiom of important people "is none other than a non-articulated difference of tones, rather similar to our music when no words are added."[91] Later in the novel, in both the Paris and Sydney manuscripts as well as in the edition of 1657, we come across five proper names transcribed in a fairly clear and legible musical notation: the names of a great king on whom the moon people have declared war, of a river and a brook, of one of the queen's ladies-in-waiting, who is in love with Dyrcona, and of a wicked individual who is sent to earth for his misfortune rather than burned like all the good people of the Other World.[92]

The first language spoken by the small naked man who is the first person Dyrcona meets on the sun is the perfected form of the universal language of which the musical idiom of the moon people is but an approximation. The solar language expresses in a fully adequate, precisely accurate way the conceptions of the mind and the reality of things. It is universal by nature. Even people who, like Dyrcona, are not familiar with it can understand it immediately: "He discoursed to me for three long hours in a language which I know I had never heard before, which bore no relation to any in this world, yet which I understood more quickly and more intelligibly than my nurse's."[93] This language, which one knows without having learned it, is "the instinct or voice of nature," which enables all creatures—men and beasts, sun people and earthlings—to exchange thoughts with one another. Preserved in the States of the Sun, this original language is lost forever to Cyrano's readers. It is only by virtue of having been captured in a work capable of imagining it that they are able to glimpse its perfection.

Chapter 6
Text and Fabric:
Anzoletto and Philomela

Late in the year 1761, Count Baschi, the French ambassador in Venice, conveyed to Goldoni a letter from Francesco Antonio Zanuzzi inviting the playwright to join the troupe of Comédiens Italiens at the former Hôtel de Bourgogne in Paris. Goldoni, who had already written a hundred comedies, responded favorably and signed a two-year contract guaranteeing him an income of six thousand *livres*. In Paris he was to write new plays that would rejuvenate the repertoire of the Théâtre Italien. Goldoni arrived in the French capital on August 28, 1762, but while he was en route, the situation had changed considerably. Because the Comédie Italienne had merged with the Opéra Comique, priority would now go to musical theater, which was more to the taste of the Parisian public: "The new genre won out over the old, and the Italians, who had been the centerpiece of the theater, were merely auxiliaries in the new type of show," as Goldoni recounted in his memoirs, written in French between 1783 and 1787, when they were published by the Widow Duchesne.[1] He was therefore obliged to return to writing mere sketches for *commedia dell'arte* so as to allow for improvisation by the actors, despite the fact that since 1743, when *La Donna di garbo* was first performed, he had been writing comedies in which the parts were fully written out.[2]

By way of farewell to Venice, where he had been born in 1707 and pursued his entire career as playwright to that point, moving from theater to theater with each new contract, Goldoni staged *Una delle ultime sere di carnovale* on Shrove Tuesday, February 23, 1762.[3] Sixteen years later, in a "note to the reader" ("L'autore a chi legge") that preceded the text in vol. 16 of the Venetian edition of his works published by Pasquali,[4] he explained the allegory on which the plot was based, which would have been immediately clear to the audience in the Teatro San Luca in 1762 but may have been lost on readers in 1778:

Underlying this comedy there is an allegory that needs to be explained. I had been called to France that year, and having decided to stay for at least two years, I conceived the idea of bidding the audience of Venice farewell with a comedy. And since it seemed inappropriate for me to speak impudently and unambiguously of myself and my affairs, I turned my actors into a society of weavers, or fabricators of fabrics, and I concealed my identity by assuming the title of designer. The allegory was not ill chosen; actors perform the works of authors, and weavers work on patterns conceived by their designer.[5]

In the comedy, Anzoletto, the fabric designer, is called to Moscow to exercise his talents and must leave the Venetian weavers to whom he has been supplying patterns. In Moscow he is awaited by Italian colleagues of those weavers, who have settled there previously and now wish to make original designs available to their customers. The allegory was obvious, and as Goldoni wrote in his 1778 note to his readers, it was "well understood and appreciated" (*ben compressa, e gustata*).

In chapter 45 of part two of his *Memoirs*, Goldoni looked back at the play he called "a Venetian and allegorical Comedy." He says:

The play enjoyed a good deal of success. It closed out the theatrical calendar of 1761 [according to the Venetian calendar, the new year began after Carnival], and the Evening of Shrove Tuesday was for me the most dazzling, because the Hall resounded with applause, in the midst of which could be heard distinctive shouts of, "Bon voyage! Come back! Don't fail us!" I confess that I was moved to tears.[6]

Goldoni never returned to Venice. He remained in Paris, dividing his time between the City, where his new sketches and comedies were performed, and the Court, where he served as Italian tutor to Mesdames de France, the daughters of Louis XV and sisters of Louis XVI. Later, half-blind and ignored by the Revolution, he died in Paris on February 6, 1793, the day before the Convention reinstated the pension of 3,600 *livres* that the king had granted him in 1769 and the Legislative Assembly had taken away in 1792.

An Allegorical and Venetian Comedy

In the *Memoirs*, two epithets are applied to the comedy. On the one hand it was "allegorical," and Goldoni reveals the key (just as he had done in his note to his readers)—a key so transparent, moreover, that in an amusing *lapsus calami*, he drops the Muscovite mask: "A French Embroiderer called Madame Gatteau finds herself in Venice on business. She knows Anzoletto, and is as fond of the man as of his designs. She engages him and prepares to take him off to *Paris*: this riddle was not difficult to unravel."[7] On the other hand, he also characterizes the play as "Venetian," which referred to the language in which it was written and performed on the stage of the Teatro San Luca.

In the *Memoirs*, Goldoni justifies the use of the language of his native city for theatrical purposes by referring to its use in the *Putta onorata* in 1749:

> The Venetian language is incontrovertibly the sweetest and most agreeable of all the dialects of Italy. The pronunciation is clear, delicate, and easy; the words are abundant and expressive; the sentences are harmonious and clever; and just as the basis of the character of the Venetian Nation is gaiety, the basis of the Venetian language is wit. This does not mean that the language is not capable of dealing grandly with the most serious and interesting subjects. Lawyers plead in Venetian, and Senators deliver orations in the same tongue. But without diminishing the majesty of the Throne or the Dignity of the Bar, our Orators have the happy natural ability to couple the most sublime eloquence with the most agreeable and interesting turns of phrase.

Goldoni concludes that "the success of my first Venetian Plays encouraged me to do others," including *Una delle ultime sere di carnovale*.[8]

In that play, Venetian is the language spoken by the weavers (*fabriccatori di stoffi*), sior Zamaria, sior Lazaro, and sior Agustin, their wives, their workers, and the calendrer (*manganaro*), sior Momolo. None of them is really at ease with Tuscan, which makes it that much more difficult for them to understand the mixture of Tuscan, French, and Gallicisms spoken by the embroideress, Madame Gatteau. They invariably speak and respond to her in Venetian. When Anzoletto uses an obscure word, he is upbraided by Marta, the wife of Bastian, the silk merchant (*mercante da seta*), as if he were already speaking a foreign tongue:

Anzoletto: Ma xe vero *altresì* . . .
Marta: Belo quel *altresì*; el scomenza a parlar forestier.
Anzoletto: Tutto quelo che la comanda. Parlerò venezian.

[Anzoletto: But it is true notwithstanding . . .
Marta: Splendid, this "notwithstanding." He's already starting to sound a little foreign.
Anzoletto: As you wish, I shall speak Venetian . . .][9]

Even rudimentary knowledge of another language was a sign of social elevation in the world of Venetian craftsmen as represented on stage. Bastian, the merchant, is able to answer Madame Gatteau in French, and, what is more, in a highly impolite manner:

Madama: Pardonnez-moi, monsieur. Je n'ai pas de mauvaises odeurs.
Bastian: Pardonnez, madame; vous avez des odeurs détestables.

[Madama: Pardon me, sir, I have no bad odors.
Bastian: Pardon me, Madame, you have detestable odors.][10]

And Anzoletto is the only character who understands the French spoken by the old embroideress (*vecchia francese ricamatrice*) and who, unlike the other characters, is not obliged to ask her in their Venetian dialect to please "parlar italian":

Madama: J'ai quelque chose à vous dire. [I have something to say to you.]
Anzoletto: Avé da dirme qualcossa. [You have something to say to me.]
Madama: Oui, mon cher ami. [Yes, my dear friend.]
Anzoletto: E ben, cossa voléu dirme? [So what do you want to tell me?][11]

Play with dialects[12] and manners of address (formal or informal second person, polite form of the third person) is of course a way of indicating cultural differences among the characters as well as the nature of their relationship, which can be more or less familiar and more or less unequal.[13]

Using the analogy between the fabrication of textiles and the production of works for the theater, Goldoni offers any number of variations on the theme of text and textile. Both plays and fabrics are the result of collaboration between those who compose the themes and those who put all the elements together and make them available to the public. The comedy thus echoes the etymological evolution of the Latin verb *texere*, which by the first century B.C.E. no longer meant simply to weave or braid but could also mean to compose a work. From the first century C.E. on, the word *textus* took on its modern sense of "written text," yet it remained common in the lexicon of weaving: *textor* (weaver), *textrinum* (workshop), *textum* or *textura* (fabric or textile).[14]

In order for the metaphor to work properly, the distinction between "weavers," who perform plays, and "designers," who write or compose them, has to make sense. Here is Anzoletto's account of the success of Italian fabrics abroad:

Our designs have long since found favor and been appreciated everywhere. Whether credit belongs to the designers of the weavers, our fabrics have enjoyed success. Some workers have gone abroad and received a warm welcome. We've sent them designs, and they have been accepted, but that was not enough for them. They want to see if an Italian hand designing in the taste and style of the Muscovites can concoct a mixture pleasing to both nations.[15]

The "weavers" in need of a designer are obviously the Italian actors who settled in Paris in the seventeenth century and performed plays improvised on the basis of traditional sketches. By going to Paris and producing comedies written "by an Italian hand" but in "the taste and style of the Muscovites," Goldoni hoped to succeed in France with the "mixture" that had inspired his reform of the comic theater and created a new Italian repertoire on the basis of an inventive appropriation of the French model.

In his *Memoirs*, he described the composition of *Momolo Cortesan*, his earliest character comedy, first performed in 1739, as follows:

The only written part was that of the principal Actor [Antonio Sacchi]. All the rest was merely sketched: "Well, then," I continued my reflections. "Perhaps the time has come to try the reform that I have had in mind for so long. Yes, subjects dealing with character must be attempted. That is the source of good Comedy. That is how the great Molière began his career and attained a degree of perfection merely suggested by the Ancients and yet to be equaled by the Moderns.[16]

As he departs for "Moscow," Anzoletto is convinced that the public will be satisfied when it recognizes familiar themes executed in an original manner by a foreign hand. His disillusionment matched his outsized expectations:

Most of the Comédiens Italiens wanted nothing more from me than sketches. The Public was used to them, the Court suffered them. Why should I refuse to give them what they wanted? . . . I was more successful than I thought I would be, but no matter how successful my Plays were, I seldom went to see them. I liked good Comedy, and I went to the Théâtre Français for pleasure and instruction.[17]

Reforming the Italian Theater

In *Il Teatro comico*, a comedy performed in Milan in 1750 and published in the first volume of the Paperini edition in 1753, Goldoni brought the principles of his theatrical reform to the stage. In his note to the reader, "L'autore a chi legge," Goldoni presented the play as "piuttoso che una Commedia, Prefazione può dirse alle mie Commedie" ("Rather than a comedy, this play, which I have entitled 'The Comic Theater,' might be called the Preface to my comedies").[18] In his memoirs, he refers to this play as "a Poetics in action"[19] because, like Molière's *Impromptu de Versailles*, it portrays the rehearsals of a comedy entitled *Il padre rivale del figlio* performed by the troupe led by Orazio.

The first break with the past, without which the allegory of *Una delle ultime sere di carnovale* would not have been possible, was to move from plays performed *all'improviso* or *a soggetto*—that is, based on an unwritten or barely written sketch (*canovaccio, scenario, soggetto*)—to a fully written dialogue in verse or prose. The change was not easy for actors accustomed to a different kind of performance. In *Il Teatro comico*, Tonino is frank about his embarrassment at having to learn Pantalone's text:

A poor player who has learned his craft in the *commedia dell'arte* and who is used to spilling out whatever pops into his head, now he finds himself forced to study books and say what somebody else has thought up; if he has a reputation to worry about, he must wear his brains out memorizing, and every time a new comedy comes along he's afraid that either he won't know it well enough or he won't play his part as he's supposed to.[20]

After arriving in Paris, Goldoni met the same difficulty with the Comédiens Italiens, or at any rate with some of them, when he presented them with fully written comedies:

I shared my ideas with my players. Some encourage me to stick with my plan, while others wanted nothing but farces. In the first group were the Lovers, who wanted written Plays. The latter were the comic Actors, who were not accustomed to learning anything by heart and whose ambition was to perform brilliantly without taking the trouble to study.[21]

Despite the playwright's prudence, which led him to "limit my ideas and remain within the bounds of mediocre subjects so as not to risk a work that might demand a more exacting performance" by "actors who had lost the habit of learning their roles,"[22] the first comedy that Goldoni wrote for the Théâtre Italien in Paris, *L'Amore paterno o sia la serva riconoscento*, ended in failure, closing after only four performances.

Molière's name was invoked to justify a second change. It was to Molière that Goldoni dedicated a comedy in five acts, written in rhymed verse (a rhymed double septenary, or "Martellian" verse, so-called for its inventor Pier Jacopo Martello), first performed in Turin and later in Venice during the 1750–1751 season. The play was conceived as a thoroughgoing transformation of the traditional "masks" of the *commedia dell'arte*: Pantalone, the Doctor, Brighella, Harlequin. To have eliminated them would have been maladroit and offensive to the audience: "Woe unto us if we hoped to embark on such a novel course: the time was not yet ripe." But like the other characters with whom they now appeared on stage, they were obliged to repeat a written text, so that despite their traditional names they became singular individuals, marked by the various virtues and foibles of the human condition. For Orazio, "it was appropriate to look for a good way to use them and establish them properly in their ridiculous characters, even alongside the clearest and most agreeable of serious themes."[23]

Comedy writing therefore had to adopt an easy, familiar, plausible style, and the actors had to respect the naturalness of the text both in the way they spoke it and in the way they performed on stage. This is what the director of *Il Teatro comico* tries to teach them:

Be careful, above all, not to fall into sing-song or decalamation, but utter your words naturally as if you were speaking. Drama is an imitation of nature, and in it one should do only what is plausible. And as for gestures, they too should be natural. Move your hands according to the sense of the words.[24]

Thus reformed, comedy demanded a new attitude of its audience, which was asked to give up its traditional raucousness and agitation, characteristics mentioned, not without bitterness, by two of the actors of *Il Teatro comico*. Eugenio, the *secondo amoroso*, says that improving decorum in the theater ("il buon ordine de'teatri") will require "the people in the loges not to make so much noise" ("nei palchetti non facciano tanto romore"). And Placida, the *prima donna*, laments that "to be blunt, it's really tiresome for those of us on stage to act when there's a racket in the audience" ("Per dirla, è un gran pena per noi altri comici recitare, allora quando si fa strepito nell'udienza").[25]

To capture the attention of the crowd, theater had to represent the daily life and travails of ordinary people. In the preface to *Baruffe chiozzotte*, published in vol. 15 of the Pasquali edition, Goldoni justifies the new theatrical dignity accorded to the *popolo minuto*, the *gente volgare* who are the centerpiece of that play, first performed in the final days of January 1762:

The theaters of Italy are frequented by all classes of society, and the price of seats is so low that merchants, servants, and poor fishermen can take part in this public diversion. In French theaters, by contrast, one pays around twelve *paoli* for one of the better seats and two *paoli* to stand in the pit. I deprived the lower class of the people of Harlequin, to whom they were accustomed. They heard talk about reforming comedy. They were eager to find out what this meant. But not all the characters were within their grasp. And it was only fair that in order please people of this sort, who pay just as the noble and wealthy do, I wrote comedies in which they saw not only their own customs and foibles but also, I might add, their virtues.[26]

Thus at the Teatro San Luca, the neighbors of *Il Campiello* (performed in the final days of the Carnival of 1756), the fishermen and boatmen of *Le Baruffe Chiozzotte*, and the weavers of *Una delle ultime sere di carnovale* were mirror images of the humblest members of the audience.[27]

Designers, Workers, and Merchants

At several points in *Una delle ultime sere di carnovale,* Anzoletto promises that
his departure for Moscow will not prevent him from sending new designs to
the weavers of Venice. But Bastian the merchant worries that in the absence
of the designer the execution may not be of the same quality and that customers may come away disappointed: "If you are not present at the loom
yourself, do you think that our weavers will be able to weave the pattern
as you wish?"[28] Anzoletto's response shows that the allegory underlying the
comedy cannot be reduced to a single, fixed relation between designer and
weavers or author and actors: "I'll take more care and draw more detailed
designs, with all the highlights and shadows. I'll polish my cartoons and put
all the colors in. Don't worry. I have every hope that the customers will be
happy and that your servant Anzoletto will not prove useless, even though he
is far away."[29]

Note, first, that "cartoons" can be more or less detailed—and under the
new arrangement, where dialogues are completely written out, Goldoni
would add all the directions essential to a proper performance. Second, more
people are involved in the production than just the artist who composes
and the workers who execute his design. The comedy depicts a whole chain
of dependencies, in which the masters are neither the designer nor the
weavers. All work for the merchant, who, as Zamaria says, "sells the silk and
gives me work throughout the year."[30] We are thus reminded of the hierarchy
of crafts in the silk trade in all cities where this was a central activity, such
as Venice and Lyon, and allegorically we are also reminded of the organization of the Venetian theater. Each theater was owned by an entrepreneur,
often a noble, who rented it to a troupe of actors, and authors generally
signed contracts with the director of the troupe agreeing to deliver a certain
number of sketches or comedies in return for a fixed remuneration.[31] This
was Goldoni's situation at the Teatro San Samuele, which was owned by the
noble Michele Grimani and rented to the Imer troupe, for which he wrote
from 1734 to 1743. In 1747 it once again became his situation at the Teatro
Sant'Angelo, which was owned by a senator, Antonio Codulmer, and directed
by Girolamo Medebach. The contract he signed with the latter stipulated that,
in return for the sum of 450 ducats annually, he would provide eight comedies, two operas, and adaptations of old sketches.

After 1753 the situation changed, because his new contract with the Teatro
San Luca was signed directly with the theater's owner, Antonio Vendramin,
who paid him 600 ducats annually for eight comedies and various other

compositions. Goldoni had this to say in his memoirs about the change of theater and status:

I moved from the Teatro Sant'Angelo to the San Luca, where there was no Director. The Actors shared the receipts, and the owner of the hall, who took the profit on the loges, paid them pensions on the basis of merit or seniority. It was with this Patrician that I had to deal. It was to him that I submitted my Plays, for which I was paid on the spot and before they were read. My emoluments were nearly doubled. I was completely free to have my Works printed [Medebach had allowed Goldoni only to print one volume of his comedies each year] and under no obligation to follow the Troupe to Terra Firma [which was the custom when Venetian theaters were closed from Shrove Tuesday until the first Monday in October]. My condition had become much more lucrative and infinitely more honorable.[32]

In the world of the theater, both the "designer" and the "weavers" were dependent on "merchants," that is, on the owners of theaters. But the owners were in turn dependent on their suppliers, as Bastian's wife Marta observes: "So what? We merchants need the weavers, and they in turn need a designer."[33]

The reciprocal relations among merchant, workers, and designer do not exhaust the complexity of the allegory. Other characters in the comedy also have equivalents in both worlds, theater and textile production. Zamaria's young workers (*garzoni lavoranti*) are equivalent to apprentice actors; siora Polonia, the gold spinner (*che fila oro*), and Momolo, the calenderer, give the fabrics their finishing touches, like those who make costumes and scenery for the theater. Even the audience is represented in the form of customers who are hard to satisfy and eager for novelty. Deploring Anzoletto's impending departure, Marta worries that her customers may not be happy: "This really upsets me too, because, you know, every year there's a need for new styles of fabric. And as far as our shop was concerned, he always came up with ideas that pleased everybody."[34]

In an exchange with Zamaria, Anzoletto tempers this overly enthusiastic appreciation of his talents by pointing out that his compositions were not always to the taste of the Venetian clientele: "Of the hundred or more designs I've done, some did not go over well, and on occasion you threw away silk, gold, and silver on my account." Zamaria then reminds him that the items scorned in Venice found favor in other Italian cities: "That's not what I say. When I couldn't sell fabric woven to your designs in Venice, I sold them on Terra Firma. If some were not successful, I more than made up for them with the ones that did well."[35]

One of the keys to the clients' ambiguous response has to do with ambivalence in their relation to French fashions. French models constituted the standard against which Venetian products were judged. For Momolo, there is no better way to praise Anzoletto's designs than to compare them with their French counterparts: "I am telling you that I saw one of these fabrics on a loom there! Never have I seen one more beautiful! A design of Sior Anzoletto, a magical piece in no way inferior to the finest French models."[36] And for Bastian, certain fabrics woven in Lazaro's shop were successful because customers thought they were French: "Lazaro: What say you, Sior Bastian, about the fabrics that came from my looms this year? / Bastian: Splendid, they sold like hotcakes. Do you remember that satin with the imitation sable? Everybody thought it was French. They were even prepared to bet on it." But as a good Venetian patriot, an adept of protectionist mercantilism, he added: "But thank God, no foreign merchandise comes into my shop."[37]

Contracts, Subscriptions, Pensions

Writing comedies, like designing textiles, is at once an art and a business, situated, according to an old dichotomy already present in *Don Quixote*, between honor and profit. On two occasions, the reasons for Anzoletto's departure for Moscow hover between these two poles, *onor* and *danari*. In the second act, when all the characters come together in the game of the *Meneghella*, Domenica, who is in love with Anzoletto, accuses him of leaving for money, on account of "those wretched deniers, which are the reason for your departure." Anzoletto responds: "Not only the deniers but also, a little, the honor."[38] At the end of the act, Domenica, left alone on stage, acknowledges the sincerity of the man she loves while criticizing as vainglory his desire for recognition outside his own country:

He's going more on a whim than for profit. It isn't, I think, that he wants to put money aside. I know him, he's a decent man. If he makes a lot or a little, at the end of the year it's all the same. He says that he is going for honor. What more does he want than he already has here? Haven't there been times when four or five looms were working on his designs? Aren't the shops full of his fabrics? Does he want them to put up a statue of him with drums and trumpets? It might be better for him and for me if he stayed. For every ten unhappy people, a hundred would be happy to keep him with us.[39]

Thus the comedy takes metaphorical aim at the fundamental contradiction of all literary activity in early modern European societies: how to reconcile an aristocratic model of honor, based on liberty and disinterested motives, with the need to live (at least in part) by the pen? This tension is evident in Goldoni's career: he tried to free himself from the mercenary dependency of the contracts he signed with Medebach in 1749 and Antonio Vendramin in 1752. The latter was revised in 1756 by a new agreement with Francesco Vendramin, who offered terms more favorable to Goldoni, who was now required to supply only six comedies per year, each of which was to yield 200 ducats, with a bonus of 200 additional ducats. In his memoirs, however, Goldoni indicates a retrospective awareness of the subaltern status implied by such contracts. Although he remembered having been pleased with the 1749 contract ("I was very happy with my status and my terms with Medebach"), he had this comment from Paris:

So my muse and my pen were subject to the orders of an individual. A French Author might find this agreement peculiar. Some will say that a man of letters ought to be free, ought to be contemptuous of servitude and constraint. If that Author is a man of private means, as Voltaire was, or cynical, as Rousseau was, I have nothing to say to him. But if he is one who does not shrink from sharing the house receipts and the profits from printing, I beg that he listen to my justification.

He then gives two reasons for his decision: first, in Italy, the author's share of the house receipts is inevitably small, because the income from the loges goes to the theater owner and tickets for the pit are very cheap; and second, unlike French authors, Italians receive no "rewards from the Court or pensions or favors from the King."[40]

Like other authors of the time who could not live on their rents or emoluments, Goldoni tried to loosen somewhat the constraints imposed on him by his contracts with acting companies and theater owners by selling his works through booksellers and seeking subventions from patrons. His first goal was the "profit from printing."[41] His first experience was not a happy one. His contract with Medebach allowed him to print only one volume of comedies each year. What is more, after the publication of the first two volumes of his plays beginning in 1759, the Venetian bookseller Betinelli said "that he could no longer take my originals from me, that he had them from Medebach, and that it was for that Comedian's account that he was going to continue the Edition."[42] Preferring to avoid a lawsuit "against the Director who disputed ownership of my Plays and against the Bookseller who was in possession of the faculty to publish them," the privilege having been drawn in his name, Goldoni asked the Florentine Paperini, "a most esteemed Printer and a very honorable man," to publish a new edition of his plays with "changes and corrections." This edition, paid for by subscription, was issued in a run of 1,700 copies, of which 500 went to Venetian subscribers despite the fact that its importation into the territory of the Republic had been banned at the behest of Bettinelli and the community of booksellers. Ten volumes were published between 1753 and 1757.[43]

In 1760, Goldoni envisioned a third edition of his plays: "When I saw that after my first Florence edition, my Theater was being plundered everywhere and that people had printed fifteen editions without my consent, without informing me, and, worse still, all very badly printed, I conceived the plan of producing a second edition at my own expense." Subscribers were solicited, and the edition was entrusted to the "honorable and esteemed" Florentine bookseller-printer Pasquali. Seventeen volumes (and two supplements) were published between 1760 and 1778. The original feature of this edition was the inclusion of autobiographical capsules by the author: "I conceived the plan . . . of including in each volume, instead of a Preface, a part of my life, imagining that by the end of the Work, the history of my Person and that of my Theater might be complete." Goldoni's definitive departure for Paris seriously disrupted the regular pace of publication, and in the preface to his memoirs Goldoni conceded "that a Work that was supposed to run to thirty volumes and be finished in eight years is still after twenty years only at volume XVII, and I will not live long enough to see it finished."[44] The "historical prefaces" to the seventeen volumes would serve as raw material for the writing of the memoirs, at least for the period "up to the beginning of what the Italians call the reform of the Italian Theater."[45]

Disappointed by publishing, Goldoni also failed to find satisfaction in the protection of the powerful. To be sure, the duke of Parma remained loyal to him and maintained, along with the title of "Poet and servant of His Royal Highness," the annual pension of 2,200 lira of Parma that Goldoni had been awarded after his residence in the city and performances of three comic operas in 1756. The much-admired Court of France was not so generous. It was only after three years of service, in 1769, that his teaching of Italian to the daughters of Louis XV was compensated with an annual pension of 3,600 livres. When he left Versailles a second time in 1780, having resumed his function as Italian tutor to the sisters of Louis XVI, the "king's kindness" (a special bonus of 6,000 *livres* and an annual stipend of 1,200) was not enough to allow to repay debts he had incurred to maintain himself while living at court. He was obliged to sell part of his library to Gradenigo, the Venetian ambassador in Paris.[46]

When he left for the Parisian "Moscow" in 1762, Goldoni hoped to shore up his financial situation. But he was also obliged to defend his honor and reputation against Gozzi's jibes. The polemic, which began in 1756 with the publication of *La Tartana degl'influssi*, which made fun of both Goldoni and his rival Chiari, flared up again in 1760 and 1761 with the performance at the Teatro San Samuele of *L'amore delle tre melarance* and then of two other *fiabe* by Gozzi, *Il corvo* and *Il re cervo*.[47] In a dialogue with Momolo, to whom he promises to send news of himself frequently, Anzoletto alludes to these cruel and unjustified attacks but says that they are unworthy of reply. Momolo asks what he should do in regard to the plays that Anzoletto will send to Venice from Moscow: "And if there is criticism, do you want me to send it to you?" Anzoletto responds:

If it is criticism, yes, but satire, no. Today it seems hard to criticize without satirizing, so don't bother sending it to me. I don't like it, either for myself or for others. If someone attacks me, too bad. To reply is no use, because if you're wrong, it's worse to speak, and if you're right, sooner or later the world will recognize it.[48]

Leaving Venice breaks Anzoletto's heart, and he begins to feel the pangs of separation even before embarking on his journey. But the hoped-for recognition far from his "beloved fatherland" is his best chance of restoring in the eyes of all the honor that has been besmirched by hostile satire.

Quite melancholy in its gaiety, *Una delle ultime sere di carnovale* is "a comedy of farewell and nostalgia, an autobiographical metaphor for a painful departure, but also an uncertain assessment of the reform."[49] Its allegory can be understood in a biographical register, with Goldoni concealed beneath the mask of Anzoletto and perhaps Momolo as well, and it can also be understood in a theatrical register, with the equivalence between Italian designs in the French style and reformed comedy exported from Venice. More profoundly, however, it is rooted in the metaphorical and material similarities between texts and textiles, between the trades of fabric making and writing.[50]

Poetic Metaphors, Material Similarities

Bear in mind, first, that this metaphor has no transhistorical value. John Scheid and Jesper Svenbro have shown that it appears in Homer only to designate the confrontation of arguments and verbal duels. In order for the poem itself to be considered a fabric and the poet a weaver, two conditions need to be met, and these were not satisfied before the sixth or perhaps fifth century B.C.E.: first, the poetic composition had to be recognized as the work of a craftsman rather than the inspiration of a muse invading the bard, and, second, a creative situation had to exist in which the subject proposed by the patron intersected with the manner provided by the poet. First used by lyric poets (Pindar, Bacchylides) to compare the labor of the poet with the activity of the weaver, the metaphor shifted to the discourse itself, understood as the result of combining the warp, the canvas of the work, with the woof, or readerly voice, which weaves it all together.[51]

We should be careful, however, not to be misled by the artisanal metaphor as it appeared in ancient Greece. Unlike the modern notion of labor, it assumed "a gap between the productive operation and the product," as Jean-Pierre Vernant has written: "Between the labor of the artisan and the essence of the work defined by its use, there was no common measure."[52] As great as the poet-artisan's excellence might be, it lay in the audience's judgment of the achieved form, not in the labor of the poet. Thus the status of poetic creation in the metaphor was ambiguous, because even though the work was assigned to its author rather than to the external inspiration of the muse, it left him dependent on the demands and judgments of his patrons and audience.

With the Latins, the metaphor became commonplace, as the etymology suggests, and it was applied to all genres of writing: letters, poems, histories, and works of philosophy. There were two reasons for this. One was material, because papyrus was itself a "woven" material, composed of intersecting horizontal and vertical fibers. The other was cultural, since the Roman appropriation of Greek culture was often conceived as a Latin warp woven onto a Hellenic woof. In Rome the metaphor became fundamentally scriptural, referring not to the weaving of poetic language as in fifth-century Greece but rather to the warp of words inscribed on papyrus.[53]

In ancient society, the kinship between writing and fabric was not only metaphorical. It was also evident in the material proximity of the products of writing and sewing or embroidery. Take, for instance, the hawker's bundle, as we see in *The Winter's Tale*, where Shakespeare shows us the hawker Autolycus.[54] His stock in trade includes both printed songs and the instruments as well as the products of needlework. Along with ballads recounting happy and unhappy loves, he brings the peasants of a fantastic Bohemia all the milliners' goods that seventeenth-century English peddlers carried in their packs.[55] The servant enumerates them: "He hath ribbon of all the colours i'th' rainbow [. . .] inkles, caddises, cambrics, lawns."[56] In the songs that he sings himself, Autolycus completes the inventory:

Lawn as white as driven snow,
Cypress black as e'er was crow,
Gloves as sweet as damask roses,
Masks for faces, and for noses ;
Bugle-bracelet, necklace amber,
Perfume for a lady's chamber ;
Golden coifs, and stomachers
For my lads to give their dears ;
Pins and pocking-sticks of steel,
What maids lack from head to heel.[57]

And later:

Will you buy any tape,
Or lace for your cape,
My dainty duck, my dear-a?
Any silk, any thread,
And toys for your head,
Of the new'st and fin'st wear-a?[58]

After leaving his customers, Autolycus totes up his profits:

I have sold all my trumpery; not a counterfeit stone, not a ribbon, glass, pomander, brooch, table-book, ballad, knife, tape, glove, shoe-tie, bracelet, horn-ring to keep my pack from fasting.[59]

Thus in the peddler's pack dry goods are jumbled together with printed texts and songs and writing objects such as "table-books," which are no doubt the very "tables" that Hamlet carried and that enabled him, as we have seen, to record instead of useless notes the only words that mattered to him, those of his father's ghost: "Remember me."

In the plot lines that weave around Autolycus, a strong link was thus established between ballads, which were mostly love songs, and a variety of objects associated with sewing and embroidery, which young men offered to young women for purposes of seduction. But the peddler's bundle was not the only object in Elizabethan England that brought texts and fabrics together. Well-to-do young women often owned caskets covered with embroidered silk or satin in which they kept, along with jewelry and perfumes, writing implements. Surviving examples feature biblical imagery depicting the stories of Jael and the queen of Sheba.[60]

Arachne, Philomela, and Lavinia

Autolycus's bundle and the caskets of young Englishwomen "feminized" the relation between texts and textiles that Goldoni would locate in the masculine world of craftsmen and merchants. Nevertheless, the Venetian playwright's allegory, which is set in the world of textile manufacturing and production for the market, should not be allowed to obscure representations and practices that featured embroidery and tapestry as female forms of writing and took weaving as a possible metaphor for sexual intercourse and procreation. In the hands of girls and women, the needle and shuttle could be transformed into pens and thread into ink, despite pedagogical models that denied women the ability to write.

This theme, which found wide application during the Renaissance, had an ancient source: the story of Philomela recounted by Ovid in Book VI of *Metamorphoses*.[61] The book begins with a textile competition between Arachne and Pallas after Arachne claimed to have outstripped the goddess in the art of weaving wool.[62] Against Pallas, who chooses to portray her victory over Neptune for the prize of Athens and who adds in the corners of her composition depictions of the punishments inflicted on mortals who dare to defy the gods, Arachne enters a tapestry that combines movement with sensuality in the depiction of gods who change into animals, objects, or human beings for the purpose of seducing or deceiving mortals:

Neither Pallas nor Envy itself could fault that work. The golden-haired warrior goddess was grieved by its success, and tore the tapestry, embroidered with the crimes of the gods.[63]

Then she struck Arachne with her shuttle for having achieved an excellence forbidden to mortals. Arachne cannot bear the indignity and "out of spite slips a noose around her neck."[64] Pallas spares her life but condemns her to a metamorphosis symbolic of weaving: Arachne becomes a spider which "spins a thread and . . . weaves her ancient web."[65]

The beginning of Book VI of *Metamorphoses* can be compared with the contest in Book V between the Muses and Pierides, in which the Nymphs serve as judges.[66] The daughters of King Pieros challenge the Muses to see who is best in the art of song. The competition is won by Calliope with a lengthy song recounting the history of Ceres, and it is lost by the Pierides, who, like Arachne, have chosen to mock the gods, whom she depicts as having been vanquished by the Giants and transformed into animals in order to escape them. Sore losers, Pieros's daughters are punished by being turned into magpies: "Even now, as birds, their former eloquence remains, their raucous garrulity, and their monstrous capacity for chatter."[67]

From the parallel between the song of the Pierides and the tapestry woven by Arachne, Jesper Svenbro and John Scheid conclude that the sequence of two challenges was Ovid's way of proposing a double metaphor: poetic song into fabric, and woven fabric into song.[68]

It is possible, however, to read (or hear) the contest between Pallas and Arachne as heralding another story, also in Book VI, which links weaving, vengeance, and metamorphoses. Philomela has been ravished by Tereus, king of Thrace and husband of her sister Procne. To ensure that she will not tell anyone of his dreadful crime, which violated the laws of hospitality, family, and marriage, Tereus "severed her tongue with his savage blade."[69] Imprisoned in the sheepfold made of massive stones where she was violated, held under strict watch, and incapable of speech, "what should Philomela do?"[70]

But suffering sharpens the wits and misfortune makes one resourceful. / She craftily strung a warp on a primitive Thracian loom, / and into the pure white threads she wove a message in purple / letters revealing the crime. When the pieces was completed, she handed it / over to one of her sister's women and gestured her orders / to put it at once in her mistress' hands. The woman then took it / to Procne as bidden, with no idea of what it contained.[71]

Dressed in the garb of the Bacchantes, Procne rescues Philomela and imagines vengeance of the most dreaful sort. She strikes Itys, her son by Tereus, and then slits his throat. After dismembering his corpse, the two sisters boil some of the parts "in bronze cauldrons, [while others] hiss on the spit: and the distant rooms drip with grease."[72] Then they serve it to the king: "Tereus eats by himself, seated in his tall ancestral chair, and fills his belly with his own child."[73] Punishment for these abominations is immediate: Procne is transformed into a swallow, Philomela into a nightingale, and Tereus into a hoopoe.

Allusions to Philomela's misfortune were common from the Middle Ages to the seventeenth century. Baudri, in many of his poems, recalled if not the work then at least the lamentations of the martyred young woman.[74] Five centuries later, Shakespeare revisited the ancient fable in *Titus Andronicus*, first performed in 1594 and printed in several quarto editions (in 1594, 1600, and 1611) before appearing in the Folio of 1623.[75] Lavinia, the daughter of Titus, raped and mutilated by Chiron and Demetrius, the two sons of Princess Tamora, who reigns over the emperor Saturninus and over Rome, is another Philomela but even more unfortunate than the original. In scene four of Act II, the stage directions of the Quarto read: "Enter the Empress' sons, Chiron and Demetrius, with Lavinia, her hands cut off and her tongue cut out, and ravished." Upon seeing her, Marcus Andronicus, her uncle, recalls the tragic tale told by Ovid:

But, sure, some Tereus hath deflower'd thee,
And lest thou shouldst detect him, cut thy tongue.

Without hands, Lavinia cannot respond as Philomela did. She cannot write her misfortune, not even in purple thread:

Fair Philomela, why she but lost her tongue
And in a tedious sampler sew'd her mind.
But, lovely niece, that mean is cut from thee.
A craftier Tereus, cousin, hast thou met,
And he hath cut those pretty fingers off
That could have better sew'd than Philomel.[76]

In the first scene of Act IV, the comparison is reversed. Lavinia's misfortune is no longer measured against Philomela's; rather, Philomela's story makes it possible to reveal the crime of which Titus's daughter has been the victim. Lavinia searches for a book among those that young Lucius has dropped on the ground and when she finds it begins turning the pages in feverish haste. It is Ovid's *Metamorphoses*, in which she finds the lines describing the place where Philomela was tortured: "The king took her to a high-walled building, hidden in an ancient forest."[77] This forest, described in the poem and embroidered on the fabric that Philomela sends to her sister (and perhaps depicted in an engraving in the book Lavinia has opened), is where Titus hunted and his daughter was raped:

Lavinia, wert thou thus surpris'd, sweet girl,
Ravish'd and wrong'd as Philomela was?
Forc'd in the ruthless, vast and gloomy woods?
See, see. Ay, such a place there is where we did hunt
(O had we never, never hunted there!)
Pattern'd by that the poet here describes
By nature made for murders and for rapes.[78]

Lavinia cannot write the names of her torturers with needle on fabric, but, following her uncle's example ("He writes his name with his staff and guides it with his feet and mouth"), she uses a staff for a pen and the sand for a page:

Heaven guides thy pen to print thy sorrows plain,
That we may know the traitors and the truth.[79]

Then "she takes the staff in her mouth, and guides it with her stumps, and writes: '*Stuprum.* Chiron, Demetrius.'"[80]

The tragedy thus offers an extreme image of the ability of women to invent instruments and media to overcome all the usual and terrifyingly unusual obstacles placed in the way of their ability to write. As in Ovid with Procne, but even more as in Seneca's tragedy *Thyestes* with Atreus,[81] Titus's vengeance is terrifying, culinary, and sacrificial:

For worse than Philomel you us'd my daughter,
And worse than Procne I will be reveng'd.[82]

After killing Tamora's two sons, he bakes them into a pie, which he serves to their mother:

They are, both baked in this pie,
Whereof their mother daintily hath fed,
Eating the flesh she herself hath bred.[83]

"Samplers" and Marks

Philomela's sad story was a common theme in Elizabethan embroidery on canvas, no doubt because, as Ann Rosalind Jones and Peter Stallybrass note, it illustrated the fundamental tension between two roles ascribed to needlework: on the one hand, it confined women to the private space of the home and thus subjected them to male domination, but, on the other hand, it allowed them to transgress those boundaries thanks to the "voice of the shuttle" (as Aristotle put it, alluding to the way in which Sophocles used Philomela's tapestry in his tragedy *Tereus*[84]), or the language of the needle in which they wrote their works.[85] Fortunately, not all the fabrics embroidered by Englishwomen in the eighteenth century were as tragic as the one that denounced Tereus' crime. Girls made "samplers," on which they wrote in needlepoint the letters of the alphabet, numbers, prayers, and occasionally a short text, such as this one, which mingled capital letters with small as in the clumsy handwriting that was common at the time:

I AM A MAID BUY YOUNG SKILL / IS YeT BVT SMALL BVT GOD / I HOP WILL
BLes Me SO I MAY LIVE / TO MeND THIS ALL RACHEL LOADer / WROVGHT
THIS SAMPLeR BeING / TWeLVE YEARS OVLD THE THENTH / DAY DeSeMBeR
1666 HL.[86]

Samplers generally included the name of the person doing the embroidering, the date of the work, and in some cases the name of the person to whom the work was dedicated: a mother, aunt, or friend. It was an opportunity to express a female identity not recognized in many other places but important to the relationships among girls who did needlework together. Helena reminds Hermia of this happy time while accusing her of betrayal:

We, Hermia, like two artificial gods
Have with our needles created both one flower,
Both on one sampler, sitting on one cushion,
Both warbling of one song, both in one key,
As if our hands, our sides, voices, and minds
Had been incorporated.[87]

In addition to samplers, many other objects (tapestries, canvas, covers, handkerchiefs, etc.) carried embroidered "writing."[88] This "writing" sometimes took the form of pictorial images, but it could also appear in more literally textual form as legends or quotations accompanying such images and usually borrowed from the Bible or mythology or even, in England after the Revolution, from current political events. The iconographic matrices drew on numerous sources: books of emblems, plates from works of natural philosophy, illustrated travel narratives, and engravings used as political or religious propaganda. Some of this work was based on printed collections of models, many of which were reprinted and translated. In England, for example, there was Richard Shorleyker's *A Schole-house for the Needle*, which came out in 1624,[89] as well as *The Needles Excellency* by John Taylor, the popular "Water Poet," published in 1631,[90] while all of Europe read *La Corona delle nobili e virtuose Donne* by Cesare Vecellio, published in Venice in 1591.[91] In France, these collections belonged to the genre known as "*pourtraicts*," and they were used in commercial workshops, as we know from inventories of the libraries of merchants and artisans in the city of Amiens in the sixteenth century.[92] They also found their way into homes, as is shown by the engraving on the title page of the *Fleur des patrons de lingerie*, published in Lyon by Pierre de Sainte-Lucie in 1549. The image depicts two girls working on small looms quite different from those used by weavers.[93]

The link between feminine identity, embroidery work, and writing with the needle was a fundamental trait of traditional societies, as Yvonne Verdier has shown in her splendid study of Minot, a village in northern Burgundy.[94] The range of functions ascribed to apprenticeship in sewing and embroidery revolved around the lexicon of the "mark." In order to "mark" her wedding trousseau, that is, to embroider her name or monogram on it, a future bride was expected to complete a first project, or "marquette," on which she would embroider, as on English and American samplers, in needlepoint with red cotton thread (red was the color of the thread that Philomela used), the letters of the alphabet, the series of numerals, her name, her age, and the year of the work. This exercise was a rite of passage coinciding with the onset of puberty and the young woman's first period, which was also denoted by the verb "to mark." It also symbolized the specifically female role of maintaining the linen and involved a specific female figure, the village seamstress, who "trained" young girls by introducing them to the world of finery and fashion. The seamstress remained with her girls right up to the wedding ceremony, in which she played a role as the costumer of the bride.

When women and girls embroidered writing and wove texts, they conformed to social norms that assigned them specific tasks and types of training. Yet even they were supposed to be obedient readers and nothing more, writing with needle and quill enabled them to construct a different image of themselves and created the possibility of a life less completely subject to the male order. The proximity of text and fabric may thus be seen as providing an option for women to loosen traditional constraints and engage in writing.[95]

Mirandolina

Ten years before his departure for Paris, ten years before the allegory that brought to the stage the masculine world of the workshops, in which, as in the theater, each person has a task and a role to play, Goldoni imagined a liberated female character who demonstrated mastery of a variety of skills. In order to seduce the Knight, who claims to hold women in contempt and whom she does not love, Mirandolina, the "*locandiera*," arranges to meet him by personally delivering a fine set of linen sheets to his bedroom: "I made this linen for persons of importance—people who appreciate it."[96] In other words, Mirandolina, like other young women, has learned the skills appropriate to her sex, not only in embroidery but also in cooking, which allows her to prepare a delicious stew that will lure the Knight into her net. But she has also conquered the very masculine power of writing. Eager to leave the inn in order to escape Mirandolina's dangerous charms, the Knight asks for his bill. Fabrizio, the valet whom she will eventually marry, says: "The landlady is making it out now." When the Knight expresses surprise: "Does she make out the bills!" the valet answers, "Always, even in her father's. She writes and draws up a bill better than any young merchant."[97] "Amiable and intelligent, industrious and witty,"[98] the delightful, flirtatious, but ultimately wise Mirandolina can not only embroider but also write, sew, and keep the books. Set against the masculine world of the Venetian weavers, she is the very embodiment of an independent woman, as clever as she is reasonable, who works the needle but also holds the pen.

Chapter 7

Commerce in the Novel: Damilaville's Tears and the Impatient Reader

As the lead article in its January 1762 issue, the *Journal étranger* published an *Éloge de Richardson* (In Praise of Richardson).[1] The text, which came out a few months after the English novelist's death on July 4, 1761, was written by Diderot, probably between September and November of 1761. The periodical in which it appeared, devoted to literary news from abroad, had been edited for the previous two years by abbé Arnaud.[2] Although it enjoyed a good international reputation as well as the support of Suard and Turgot, it was destined to cease publication after its September 1762 issue— yet another example of the vulnerability of early newspapers, whose existence was often ephemeral.

Later in 1762, the *Éloge* appeared again in Lyon, where the Périsse brothers added it to the *Supplément aux Lettres anglaises, ou Histoire de Miss Clarisse Harlowe* that they published that year. After 1766, it appeared in all the reprints of abbé Prévost's translation of *Clarissa*, which included fragments missing from the first edition of 1751, namely, Morden's account of Clarissa's burial, the reading of her last will and testament, and eight posthumous letters. The text was republished in 1768 and then again in 1770 in anthology compiled by Arnaud and Suard, *Les Variétés littéraires, ou Recueil de pièces tant originales que traduites, concernant la Philosophie, la Littérature et les Arts*, and then in 1784 and 1810 in Prévost's *Œuvres choisies*, which were published in Amsterdam and Paris.[3] In Germany it was reprinted in February 1766 by a periodical in Hamburg entitled *Unterhaltungen*, in a translation that Herder praised enthusiastically in the *Königsbergsche gelehrte und politische Zeitungen* in August of the following year.[4]

Pictures and Words

In the *Salons*, Diderot faced a formidable challenge, summed up as follows by Louis Marin: "How to paint pictures with words," or,

To put it another way, what powers of language should be summoned up and mobilized so that when read, whether out loud, in a low voice, or silently, an image would appear, vague at first, wandering like an Elysean shade, then insistent, obsessive, and before long enchanting, invading the soul, occupying the mind, shaping meaning, working on the senses, and ready to penetrate the boundary between interior and exterior on the way to becoming a vision or hallucination?[5]

The point of the *Éloge de Richardson* was the opposite of that of the *Salons.* It was not to summon up, in and through narration, the real but absent image of the exhibited work but rather to convert the scenes of the novel or of the reading of the novel into a series of pictures in writing. The editor of the *Journal étranger* was not mistaken when he chose to precede Diderot's text with an introductory portrait of the author-reader as painter: "The author allows his pen to be guided by his imagination. But beyond the disorderly strokes and delightful negligence of the freely wielded brush, one easily recognizes the sure and disciplined hand of a great painter."[6] The critic of the *Salons,* whose task was to represent a representation in writing, is here obliged to do the reverse: to play the role of a "painter," who must transform words into images.

To understand what is going on here, we must first recall that Diderot's essay was born of the disputes that swirled around Richardson's novels, which were known in France by way of translation. The French translation of *Pamela* came out in 1742, probably owing to the work of Protestant refugees, possibly under the oversight of Jean-Frédéric Bernard. This was followed by translations of *Clarissa* in 1751 and of the first three volumes of *Sir Charles Grandisson* in 1755, all by abbé Prévost (who was very quickly but erroneously credited with the translation of *Pamela* as well).[7] The French translations appeared shortly after the publication of the novels in English: respectively, two years, three years, and one year later.[8] In Diderot's correspondence with Sophie Volland, there are nine letters written between 1760 and 1762 in which Richardson's work is quoted or commented on, and two allusions to literary debates concerning him. The first took place at the home of the baron d'Holbach in Le Grandval in October 1760, with Galiani, Grimm, and Diderot in attendance. The second, which came a year later in September 1761, at the Vollands' château in Isle-sur-Marne, and pitted Madame Volland, who did not like *Clarissa,* against her two daughters, who defended the novel.

Some time between the allusions to these two debates, one by Diderot, the other by Sophie, Diderot became a convert to Richardson. On October 20, 1760, he wrote: "There was much dispute about Clarissa. Those who despised the work despised it utterly. Those who admired it, and who were as extravagant in their esteem as the former in their scorn, regarded it as one of the *tours de force* of the human spirit."[9] A neutral observer, Diderot remained above the fray and, to judge by what he wrote, took no part in it. A year later, in his response to Sophie on September 17, 1761, his feelings had changed completely: "What you are telling me about Clarissa's burial and will I had felt. This is just one more proof of the resemblance of our souls."[10]

Two facts explain this change.[11] First, in late August 1761, Madame d'Epinay sent Diderot a manuscript of Prévost's translation of the episodes that he had cut out of the 1751 edition and whose suppression Grimm had criticized in August 1758 in the *Correspondance littéraire*. Before lending the manuscript to Sophie, Diderot read them with the greatest emotion, as he mentions in the letter of September 17:

> But my eyes again filled with tears. I could no longer read. I stood and began to wail, to address the brother, the sister, the father, the mother, and the uncles, to speak out loud, to the great astonishment of Damilaville, who understood nothing of either my emotion or my speech and who asked what was troubling me.[12]

Second, in September and October 1761, Diderot read the original text, made notes on it, and discovered the power of a work that Prévost's translations had deformed, weakened, and watered down.

Reading Richardson

The emotion produced by these readings of *Clarissa* led to the writing of the *Éloge*. The text is a representation of the effects caused by the reading of the novel. In Diderot's recounting, several traits characterize the modalities and effects of this reading, whereby the real reader identifies with what Louis Marin calls the "simulacrum-reader" as constructed in and by the work. First, the reading is described as a "re-reading," as the repetition of an already completed reading, as if the work had always been there, inescapable and eternal. The idea is expressed through the reader's imagining of a forced sale of his library:

> O, Richardson, Richardson, to my eyes incomparable! You shall be my reading in all ages. Should I be forced by pressing needs, should my friend fall into want, should my fortune be insufficient to afford my children the care their upbringing requires, I would sell my books, but you would remain with me. You would remain on the same shelf as Moses, Homer, Euripides, and Sophocles, and I would read you one after the other.

[O Richardson, Richardson, homme unique à mes yeux! tu seras ma lecture dans tous les temps. Forcé par des besoins pressants, si mon ami tombe dans l'indigence, si la médiocrité de ma fortune ne suffit pas pour donner à mes enfants les soins nécessaires à leur éducation, je vendrai mes livres, mais tu me resteras; tu me resteras sur le même rayon avec Moyse, Homere, Euripide et Sophocle, et je vous lirai tour à tour.]

This same insistence underlies the repeated injunctions to readers: "Re-read him, my friends" ["Mes amis, relisez-le"] or "Painters, poets, people of taste, good people, read Richardson, read him continually" ["Peintres, poètes, gens de goût, gens de bien, lisez Richardson, lisez-le sans cesse"]. This is a novel to be revisited frequently, as the Bible is, among Protestants. By virtue of constant re-reading, the work becomes the reader's companion in his travails and everyday life; it inhabits his memory and becomes a guide to life. The reader's own writing plays a part in this intimate appropriation; it seeks out the text on the printed page. Thus Diderot read the 1759 English edition with pen or pencil in hand: "I penciled into my copy the hundred-twenty-fourth letter, which is from Lovelace to his accomplice Léman" [J'ai crayonné dans mon exemplaire la cent vingt-quatrième lettre qui est de Lovelace à son complice Léman"].

The second characteristic of reading Richardson is that it can be done either alone or in company. According to the *Éloge*, several people can read the text "in common," with each member of the company taking turns, but it can also be done "separately," that is, by each person privately, for the purpose of conversation:

I remarked that, in a society in which Richardson was read in common or separately, conversation became more lively and interesting. Whenever this text was read, I heard discussion in depth of the most important issues of morality and taste.

[J'ai remarqué que, dans une société où la lecture de Richardson se faisait en commun ou séparément, la conversation en devenait plus intéressante et plus vive. J'ai entendu, à l'occasion, de cette lecture, les points les plus importants de la morale et du goût, discutés et approfondis.]

Yet an authentic reading of Richardson, the kind of reading the novel expected and deserved, assumed a reader freed from worldly exigencies:

The details in Richardson are and must inevitably be disagreeable to a frivolous and dissipated man, but it was not for such a man that he wrote; it was for the tranquil and solitary man, who has known the vanity of the world's buzz and amusements and who loves to dwell in the shadows of some retreat and to be moved usefully in silence.

[Les détails de Richardson déplaisent et doivent déplaire à un homme frivole et dissipé; mais ce n'est pas pour cet homme-là qu'il écrivait, c'est pour l'homme tranquille et solitaire, qui a connu la vanité du bruit et des amusements du monde, et qui aime à habiter l'ombre d'une retraite, et à s'attendrir utilement dans le silence.]

The vocabulary—"solitary," "retreat," "silence"—is indicative of the transference of an older model, that of spiritual reading, onto the text of the novel. It also indicates that only a select few are fully susceptible to the influence of that text: "The works of Richardson will to some degree please everyone in all times and places, but the number of readers who will appreciate their full value will never be large" ["Les ouvrages de Richardson plairont plus ou moins à tout homme, dans tous les temps et dans tous les lieux; mais le nombre des lecteurs qui en sentiront tout le prix ne sera jamais grand"].

For impatient, hurried readers put off by the number of characters, the complexity of the plot, or the length of the novel, a concession could be made: they might read an abridged version. In an age when publishers were quick to publish "excerpts," "digests," samplers, and anthologies, Diderot with disabused irony gave his seal of approval to such treatment of this "man of genius, who broke the barriers that custom and time imposed on artistic production and brushed aside protocol and its proprieties" ["homme de génie qui franchit les barrières que l'usage et le temps ont prescrites aux productions des arts, et qui foule au pied le protocole et ses formules"]:

Let us be fair, however. In a nation diverted by a thousand distractions, where the twenty-four hours of the day are not enough to accommodate the amusements with which people have become accustomed to filling them, Richardson's books will inevitably seem long. That is why this nation has already ceased to produce operas, and before long other theaters will limit their performances to selected scenes of comedy and tragedy. My fellow citizens, if Richardson's novels seem long to you, why not abridge them?

[Cependant soyons équitables. Chez un peuple entraîné par mille distractions, où le jour n'a pas assez de ses 24 heures pour les amusements dont il s'est accoutumé de les remplir, les livres de Richardson doivent paraître longs. C'est par la même raison que ce peuple n'a déjà plus d'opéra, et qu'incessamment on ne jouera sur ses théâtres que des scènes détachées de comédie et de tragédie. Mes chers concitoyens, si les romans de Richardson vous paraissent longs, que ne les abrégez-vous pas?]

In the second half of the eighteenth century Richardson's lengthy novels were indeed published in abridged forms, which substituted continuous, impersonal narration for the epistolary form, and also in anthologies, which presented excerpts from the novelist's work in alphabetical order. Diderot was wrong, however, to think that such abridgements were solely the work of publishers anxious about the public's impatience. They were inaugurated by the author himself. To be sure, after mentioning and rejecting the possibility of abridgment in the preface to *Clarissa*, Richardson condemned certain abridged versions of his novel, such as *The Path of Virtue Delineated: or, the History in Miniature of the Celebrated Pamela, Clarissa Harlowe, and Sir Charles Grandisson, Familiarised and Adapted to the Capacities of Youth*, published in London in 1756 and reprinted many times either in its entirety or in separate volumes.

Yet Richardson himself brought out anthologies containing moral lessons drawn from his stories. In 1749 he added a table of contents summarizing each letter in the second edition of *Clarissa*, and then, in 1751, he published a *Collection of such of the Moral and Instructive Sentiments, Cautions, Aphorisms, Reflections and Observations contained in the History* [Clarissa], *as presumed to be of general Use and Service, Digested under Proper Heads.* In 1755 he brought out a *Collection of the Moral and Instructive Sentiments, Maxims, Cautions, and Reflections, Contained in the Histories of Pamela, Clarissa, and Sir Charles Grandisson.* Five years later, the maxims of the *Collection* were presented in the form of a deck of cards engraved on copper "*Consisting of moral and diverting Sentiments, extracted wholly from the much admired Histories of Pamela, Clarissa, and Sir Charles Grandisson.*"[13] As in the old collections of commonplaces, which were also "digested under proper heads," the novels' teachings were detached from the narrative framework and formulated as sentences and aphorisms that could be found easily thanks to their neat classification under heads ranging from "Absence" to "Zeal." For Diderot, however, the particular twists of the plot were inseparable from the universality of the sentiments they revealed. Only the frivolity of the age could explain why readers found Richardson's books too long, with the unfortunate consequence of separating readers who simply found the stories pleasant from those capable of understanding the moral lessons they contained.

Reading Richardson, whether "solitary" or "in common," engaged the entire sensibility, agitated the heart and body, and elicited cries and tears. In the *Éloge*, Diderot ascribed to Damilaville reactions that he described as his own in a letter to Sophie Volland dated September 17, 1761. Here is his description of the effects of the most moving passages in *Clarissa* on the reader:

I was with a friend when someone gave me the scenes of Clarissa's burial and her last will and testament, two pieces that the French translator had left out for reasons that are difficult to understand. This friend is one of the most sensitive men I know and one of Richardson's most ardent fans, hardly less than I am. He grabbed the quires, went off into a corner, and read. I watched him. First I saw tears flow. Then before long he began to gasp and sob. Suddenly he stood up and began to walk about aimlessly, uttering cries as if upset, and he reproached the entire Harlowe family in the bitterest of terms.

[J'étais avec un ami lorsqu'on me remit l'enterrement et le testament de Clarisse, deux morceaux que le traducteur français a supprimés, sans qu'on sache trop pourquoi. Cet ami est un des hommes les plus sensibles que je connaisse et un des plus ardents fanatiques de Richardson: peu s'en faut qu'il le soit autant que moi. Le voilà qui s'empare des cahiers, qui se retire dans un coin et qui lit. Je l'examinais: d'abord je vois couler des pleurs, bientôt il s'interrompt, il sanglote; tout à coup il se lève, il marche sans savoir où il va, il pousse des cris comme un homme désolé et il adresse les reproches les plus amers à toute la famille des Harloves.]

The reader is overcome by increasingly violent reactions of body and soul: tears, sobs, agitation, cries, and finally curses. Later in the *Éloge*, the emotion provoked by reading (a scene from *Pamela* in this instance) ends in "the most violent flailing" ["les plus violentes secousses"].

The final characteristic of reading Richardson's novels is that it abolishes every distinction between the world of the book and the world of the reader. The reader, who is often a woman, is projected into the narrative, and, conversely, the hero of the fiction becomes someone just like the reader him- or herself: "I heard arguments about the behavior of his characters just like arguments about actual events. Readers praised or blamed Pamela, Clarissa, and Grandisson as if they were living individuals whom they had known and in whom they took the greatest interest" ["J'ai entendu disputer sur la conduite de ses personnages, comme sur des événements réels; louer, blâmer Pamela, Clarice, Grandisson, comme des personnages vivants qu'on aurait connu et auxquels on aurait pris le plus grand intérêt"]. For some, the reality effect was greater still, engendering belief in the actual existence of the protagonists:

One day, a woman of uncommon taste and sensibility, and much preoccupied with the story of Grandisson, which she had just read, said to one of her friends, who was about to leave for London: "Please pay my respects to Miss Emily, Mr. Belford, and especially Miss Howe, if she is still alive."

[Un jour une femme d'un goût et d'une sensibilité peu commune, fortement préoccupée de l'histoire de Grandisson qu'elle venait de lire, dit à un de ses amis qui partait pour Londres: "Je vous prie de voir de ma part Miss Emilie, M. Belford et surtout Miss Howe, si elle vit encore."]

What imparted such substantial reality to the novel was its universality. As Diderot explained, Richardson's works were unlike historical narratives that "encompass only a portion of time or a point on the surface of the globe" ["n'embrasse qu'une portion de la durée, qu'un point de la surface du globe"], because they show us the very essence of humanity, revealing a higher truth that is valid in all times and all places: "the human heart, which was, is, and always will be the same, is the model you copy" ["le cœur humain qui a été, est et sera toujours le même, est le modèle d'après lequel tu copies"]. Thus the usual distinction between the universal truth of history and the singular narratives of novels was stood on its head.[14] Resolved as well was the contradiction between the infinite variety of character portrayed by Richardson and the revelation of the constants of the human heart, which allowed flesh-and-blood readers to recognize themselves in the heroes of fiction.[15] Thus the community of Richardson readers was based on shared gestures, emotions, and commitments. It is an admirable symbol of all that is best in man.

A Reading Revolution?

Diderot's account of how novels were read enables us to take a fresh look at the question of the "reading revolution" of the eighteenth century. There are two aspects to the question. The first is historical and bears on contemporary diagnoses of the morally beneficial or physically disastrous effects of the captivation of readers by fiction. Using categories drawn from sensualist psychology, these diagnoses reformulated old denunciations of the perils faced by readers of works of the imagination. In Golden Age Castille, for example, three elements were strongly linked: repeated mentions of Plato's expulsion of poets from the Republic; use of the vocabulary of rapture (*embelesar, maravillar, encantar*) to characterize the fable reader's neglect of the real world; and the idea that the turn to silent, solitary reading rather than reading out loud to others or to oneself encouraged confusion between the world of the text and the world of the reader.[16]

   In the eighteenth century, the discourse was medicalized: a pathology was constructed in which "excessive reading" figured as an individual malady or collective epidemic. Uncontrolled reading was considered dangerous, because it combined physical immobility with stimulation of the imagination. This led to ills of the worst sort: engorgement of the stomach and intestines, derangement of the nerves, physical exhaustion. Professional readers, namely men of letters, were the most vulnerable to such disorders, all of which could lead to their characteristic affliction, hypochondria.[17] Furthermore, solitary reading could lead to corruption of the imagination, rejection of reality, and a preference for the chimerical. Thus excessive reading was linked to solitary pleasures. Both practices resulted in the same symptoms: pallor, anxiety, prostration.[18] The danger was most severe when the reading was of a novel and the reader a woman withdrawn into solitude. It might be objected that the generous emotion spurred by the reading of Richardson had nothing in common with the lascivious rapture denounced by physicians. Quite so, and yet in both cases reading was conceived in terms of its physical effects. This somatization of a practice traditionally described in terms of intellectual or moral categories was perhaps the first sign of a major mutation, if not of behavior then at least of representations.

A second aspect of the eighteenth-century "revolution in reading" question is historiographic in nature. It is connected with the hypothetical opposition between a traditional form of reading, dubbed "intensive," and a modern form, characterized as "extensive." According to this dichotomy, first proposed by Rolf Engelsing,[19] the intensive reader faced a limited corpus of texts, which were read and re-read, memorized and recited, heard and learned by heart, and transmitted from generation to generation. This type of reading was deeply imbued with a sacred character and subjected the reader to the authority of the text. The "extensive" reader, who first appeared in the second half of the eighteenth century, was quite different: he read numerous printed texts, many of them new and ephemeral, and consumed them avidly and rapidly. His gaze was detached and critical. Thus a communal and respectful relation to the written supposedly gave way to a more irreverent and casual mode of reading.

Historians' reactions to this thesis have varied. Without a doubt Robert Darnton has been the most skeptical that such a revolution ever took place:

Although tastes changed and the reading public expanded, the experience of reading was not transformed. It became more secular and more varied, but not less intense. It did not undergo a revolution. Historians have discovered and dismissed so many hidden revolutions of the past that the "reading revolution" might be safely ignored.[20]

Wary of the expression but sensitive to the mutations in practice, Hans Erich Bödeker offers a nuanced judgment: "Although it is possible to doubt aspects of the 'revolution in reading' hypothesis, a transformation of reading habits did indeed take place at the end of the eighteenth century."[21] Reinhart Wittmann is more categorical: "Was there a reading revolution at the end of the eighteenth century? . . . In spite of all the limitations, the answer to the question is yes."[22] Thus it would seem worthwhile to return once more to this debate in order to clarify the issues and perhaps to shift the ground somewhat.

The reading of Richardson, as practiced by Diderot and other adepts of the English novelist, radically undermines Engelsing's proposed chronology. The eighteenth-century novel took hold of its reader, captivated him, governed his thoughts and actions. It was read and re-read, studied, quoted, and recited. The reader was invaded by the text, which came to dwell within him, and through identification with the heroes of the story he began to decipher his own life in the mirror of fiction. This particularly intense and "intensive" form of reading engaged the entire sensibility of readers, male and female alike, who could not restrain their emotion or tears. This was true not only of Richardson but also of Rousseau's *Nouvelle Héloïse*, which came out in 1761 and was implicitly present in Diderot's text. This leads us to question the validity of a sharp opposition between two styles of reading, the one supposedly following and supplanting the other.

Is that enough, however, to invalidate the idea of a "revolution in reading?" Perhaps not. Throughout enlightened Europe, profound changes transformed the production of print and the conditions of access to books despite the stability of typographic technology and labor. Everywhere, the growing supply of books, the secularization of the titles on offer, the circulation of banned books, the proliferation of periodicals, the triumph of small formats, and the mushrooming of literary *cabinets* and reading societies where one could read books without buying them both allowed and imposed new ways of reading. For the most literate readers of both sexes, the possibilities of reading seemed to expand, opening the way to a variety of practices associated with different times, places, and genres. Each reader was thus at one time or another either "intensive" or "extensive," absorbed or casual, studious or amused. Why not assume that the eighteenth-century "revolution in reading" consisted precisely in this newfound capacity to read in a variety of ways? Such a formulation has the advantage of making clear the limitations of the notion, since that possibility was not available to everyone but limited to the most expert and affluent of both sexes. It also explains the complex nature of the revolution, which is characterized not by the general adoption of a new hegemonic and distinctive style but rather in the recourse to a variety of practices, some of which were old, others new.[23] An "intensive" reader of Richardson, Diderot was also a learned, avid, and ironic reader—and many other things besides.

This diversity suggests that any fully historical approach to literary texts should avoid the temptation to universalize any particular mode of reading and should rather seek to identify the specific skills and practices of each community of readers and the specific codes and conventions associated with each genre. Against the assumption that the reading remains invariant regardless of the text involved or the circumstances in which it is read, Pierre Bourdieu's comment should be borne in mind:

> To ask about the conditions under which reading is possible is to ask about the social conditions under which the situation in which one reads is possible . . . and also about the social conditions governing the production of *lectores* [in the medieval sense of learned readers]. One of the illusions of the *lector* is to forget his own social conditions of production, unconsciously to universalize the conditions under which his reading is possible.[24]

One of the principal tasks of combining textual criticism with cultural history is precisely to dispel this illusion.

Converting Narrative to Image

Diderot's *Éloge de Richardson* is more than just a staging of the effects produced by reading the novel. It is also an elucidation of the aesthetic devices that produce those effects. The expression "without my noticing" occurs twice in the text, where its role is paradoxically to indicate acute awareness of the omnipotence of certain narrative traps.[25] The first occurrence involves the obligatory imposition of feeling:

> People, come learn from him how to reconcile yourselves with life's woes. Come, let us weep together over the unfortunate characters in his fiction, and then if we find ourselves overwhelmed by fate, we can say, "At least good people will weep for us too." In whom did Richardson seek to arouse our interest, if not the unfortunate? In his work, as in the world, men are divided into two classes: those who enjoy and those who suffer. He always brings me closer to the latter, and *without my noticing*, the feeling of commiseration comes into play and is strengthened. (my italics)

> [Hommes, venez apprendre de lui à vous réconcilier avec les maux de la vie; venez, nous pleurerons ensemble sur les personnages malheureux de ses fictions, et nous dirons, si le sort nous accable: "Du moins les honnêtes gens pleureront aussi sur nous." Si Richardson s'est proposé d'intéresser, c'est pour les malheureux. Dans son ouvrage, comme dans ce monde, les hommes sont partagés en deux classes: ceux qui jouissent et ceux qui souffrent. C'est toujours à ceux-ci qu'il m'associe; et, sans que je m'en aperçoive, le sentiment de la commisération s'exerce et se fortifie.]

Later we find judgments and actions being dictated by the text with absolute if invisible force, in the manner of the "spiritual directors" of an earlier time:

He directs me to good people and diverts from bad. He teaches me to recognize them by swift and subtle signs. He guides me at times *without my noticing*. (my italics)

[Il m'adresse aux honnêtes gens, il m'écarte des méchants; il m'a appris à les reconnaître à des signes prompts et délicats. Il me guide quelquefois sans que je m'en aperçoive.]

For Diderot, the text's hold on its reader is ensured by a double mechanism. First, a fragment of the narrative is transformed into a pictorial or theatrical scene, so that the reader is transformed into a spectator or beholder and the reading into a visual and aural event. Not all such conversions are equally effective. The effectiveness varies from novel to novel: "*Grandisson* and *Pamela* are also beautiful works, but I prefer *Clarissa*. In that book the author's every step is marked by genius" ["*Grandisson* et *Pamela* sont aussi de beaux ouvrages, mais je leur préfère *Clarisse*. Ici l'auteur ne fait pas un pas qui ne soit de génie"]. It also depends on language. Prévost's translations deformed the novels. Even more fundamentally, they lacked the power to produce this reverse ekphrasis: not the restoration of a pre-existing scene or image by means of words but the production by means of language of a scene intended to spur the imagination: "You who have read Richardson's works only in your elegant French translations and think you know them are mistaken" ["Vous qui n'avez lu les ouvrages de Richardson que dans votre élégante traduction française et qui croyez les connaître, vous vous trompez"]. Elegance of style is of no avail where the transformation of the narrative into image requires violence of feeling.

Diderot thus sees the novel in terms of a paradoxical and problematic aesthetic, according to which the effect of a work depends on "the constitution of a new sort of beholder—a new 'subject'—whose innermost nature would consist precisely in the conviction of his absence from the scene of representation."[26] The production of this absence by and in the work itself, whatever it might be, is the condition of its power. It is the common basis of Diderot's theatrical aesthetic, his "dramatic" conception of painting, and the preference of many contemporary painters for depicting characters who, by virtue of their status or condition, are unaware of being looked at: for instance, people who are absorbed, asleep, or blind.

Richardson's novels enjoyed considerable success at the booksellers. *Pamela*, for example, went through eight editions between 1740 and Richardson's death, and the novel was read in the American colonies, although the edition published by Benjamin Franklin in Philadelphia in 1742 brought him only a mediocre profit, so that American booksellers preferred either to import English editions or publish abridged narratives.[27] The novel was also brought to the stage in any number of adaptations, including one by Voltaire (*Nanine ou le Préjugé vaincu*, 1749) and two by Goldoni (*La Pamela*, 1750, and *La Pamela maritata*, 1760, written in response to a play of the same title by Pietro Chiari that was produced in 1753).[28] In London, in the very year the novel appeared, the *Daily Advertiser* carried this advertisement in its April 28, 1741, issue: "For the entertainment of the Ladies, more especially for those who have the Book, Pamela, a new Fan; representing the principal adventures of her Life, in Servitude, Love, and Marriage." That same year, two episodes of the story ("Pamela revealing to Mr. B. her desire to return home" and "Pamela escaping from Lady Davers' home") were painted on the walls of garden bowers in Vauxhall for the intimate dinners of well-to-do clients. The paintings were commissioned by Jonathan Tyers, the official in charge of the gardens, from the painter Francis Hayman, who illustrated the octavo edition of the novel that came out in 1742. For a wider audience, scenes from the novel were depicted in wax figurines, which according to the *Daily Advertiser* of August 8, 1745, were installed "at the corner of Shoe Lane, facing Salisbury Court Fleet-Street."[29] The novel was thus transformed into images, which presented to a variety of audiences (women of "quality," elegant strollers in Vauxhall, the common people of the London street) various interpretations of the story as a depiction of feminine virtue, nobility of the heart, or social hierarchy.[30] Painters also took possession of the text and filled their canvases with tender and sensuous scenes from the novel, turning the beholder into a voyeur: for instance, John Highmore, in a series of twelve paintings done in 1743–44, or, in a somewhat more suggestive vein, Philip Mercier, who produced twelve images of Pamela in a variety of intimate settings.[31]

Erotic parodies of the novel, such as Fielding's *Apology for the Life of Mrs. Shamela Andrews* (1742), as well as moral condemnations, such as the anonymous and ambiguous *Pamela Censured*, which presented a convenient anthology of all the (allegedly) licentious passages, made good use of the aesthetics of painting. The reader became a voyeuristic spectator, who, even without the help of a painted or engraved image, was projected into the licentious scene depicted for him. This sort of device transposed what Richardson's writing itself demanded into an unexpected register.[32] The reader whom the novelist produced, whether that novelist was the Richardson of *Clarissa* or the Diderot of *La Religieuse*, was negated by the narrative only to become all the more deeply implicated in it[33]:

O, Richardson! No matter how we feel about it, we play a role in your works, we take part in the conversation, we approve, we criticize, we admire, we become irritated or angry. How often have I caught myself shouting like a child attending a play for the first time, "Don't believe him, he's deceiving you [. . .] if you go there, you're lost!" My soul was in a state of perpetual agitation.

[O Richardson! on prend, malgré qu'on en ait, un rôle dans tes ouvrages, on se mêle à la conversation, on approuve, on blâme, on admire, on s'irrite, on s'indigne. Combien de fois ne me suis-je pas surpris, comme il est arrivé à des enfants qu'on avait menés aux spectacles pour la première fois, criant: Ne le croyez pas, il vous trompe . . . si vous allez là, vous êtes perdu. Mon âme était tenue dans une agitation perpétuelle.]

The Reality of Fiction

The second device that was supposed to involve the reader automatically in the narrative was the elimination of all distance between the fiction and the social world, or, rather, the establishment of the certainty that the literary fiction was truer than the empirical reality. We see this in the process of composition. To begin with, Richardson claimed only to be the editor of letters he happened to stumble upon, thus refusing the position of author. In addition, in the case of *Pamela*, at any rate, he solicited epistolary reactions from his male and female readers, in some instances by sending them copies of his novel with blank pages inserted into the text. Preserved in bound volumes, some of these letters were later published in reprints of the work as if they were part of the epistolary fiction.[34] This procedure, which had been used for medical texts at the beginning of the century (e.g., Dr. Bekker's *Onania*, published in 1710), would later be applied in a way to Diderot's text, which appeared in reprints of Prévost's translation of *Clarissa*.

In the *Éloge*, the theme of letters found by chance was shifted from the "author-editor" to the reader himself, the supposed discoverer of letters written by Richardson's heroines:

An idea that has occurred to me several times while dreaming about Richardson's works is that I had bought an old castle and, while visiting its apartments one day, noticed in a corner an armoire that had not been opened for a long time, and that, on opening it, I had found a pile of letters from Clarissa and Pamela. After reading some of them, how eagerly I arranged them by date! How vexed I would have been if I had found one missing! Do you suppose I would have suffered if so much as a line had been erased by a rash (I almost said a sacrilegious) hand?

[Une idée m'est venue quelquefois en rêvant aux ouvrages de Richardson, c'est que j'avais acheté un vieux château, qu'en visitant un jour ses appartements, j'avais aperçu dans un angle une armoire qu'on n'avait pas ouverte depuis longtemps, et que l'ayant enfoncée, j'y trouvais pêle-mêle les lettres de Clarice et de Pamela. Après en avoir lu quelques-unes, avec quel empressement ne les aurais-je pas rangées par ordre de dates! Quel chagrin n'aurais-je pas ressenti, s'il y avait eu quelque lacune entre elles! Croit-on que j'eusse souffert qu'une main téméraire (j'ai presque dit sacrilège) en eût supprimé une ligne?]

Though directed at the cuts made by Prévost, the unfaithful translator, the reverie says more. It puts the reader in the position of "author" of a book that nevertheless denies that it has an author and creates the illusion that the printed pages of novels are in fact handwritten texts.[35] It thus proposed an extreme version of the role attributed to the reader as interpreter by works that paradoxically but effectively associated moral intent with textual indeterminacy, didactic lessons with self-effacing writers.[36] Diderot understood better than anyone else the new place that Richardson's ambiguities and ellipses created for the reader, who was led to judge and to approve or disapprove of the behavior of fictional heroes in the same way he or she would judge the behavior of real-life contemporaries.

The reader's creative freedom of interpretation was not altogether unfettered, however. The text worked on him "without his noticing." In this sense, Richardson's novels are perfect examples of the kinds of textual machinery that Louis Marin has described for a very different genre, the historical narrative: "What is not represented by the narrator in the narrative is represented by the reader in the reading as narrative effect."[37] As Marin was well aware, however, the result could not be taken for granted. Minute deconstruction of the textual mechanisms that produce the reader as an effect of the text does not oblige us to assume that all readers necessarily identify with the "simulacrum-reader" of the discourse. On the contrary. A gap is always possible, and always to be feared. Indeed, it is the reason why writers resort to such subtle methods, why they employ any number of ruses and stratagems in order to persuade the reader of his freedom and make him feel or imagine spontaneously whatever vision the writer wants to impose on him.[38]

The Malicious Reader

In the *Éloge de Richardson*, the figure of an impatient female reader, restive and resistant to emotion, exemplifies the way in which the text fails when its reader lacks the proper disposition to understand it correctly. Diderot draws the portrait of this malicious reader by telling the story of two female friends who quarrel "because one despised the story of Clarissa, while the other prostrated herself before it" ["parce que l'une méprisait l'histoire de Clarisse, devant laquelle l'autre était prosternée]. He quotes at length from a letter that the second woman is supposed to have sent him, a letter that is an outraged response to the reactions of the first woman. This short fiction may have been constructed from an authentic letter, perhaps from Sophie Volland describing her mother's reaction to the book, or, more likely, from Madame d'Epinay. But Diderot transforms the situation by attributing his own sentiments to his imagined female correspondent and by ascribing, as he does elsewhere, a female identity to his indignation in the face of criticism of Richardson.[39]

The bad reader is insensitive and indifferent. She laughs where others cry and is cold where others' hearts break. Each paragraph of the letter Diderot claims to have received begins with an italicized statement of this malicious woman's reactions:

Clarissa's piety makes her impatient! . . . She laughs when she sees the child in despair at her father's curse! . . . She finds it extraordinary that reading this brings tears to my eyes! . . . In her opinion, Clarissa's intelligence amounts to nothing more than making phrases, and when she has made a few, she feels consoled.

[La piété de Clarisse l'impatiente . . . Elle rit, quand elle voit cette enfant désespérée de la malédiction de son père . . . Elle trouve extraordinaire que cette lecture m'arrache des larmes . . . À son avis, l'esprit de Clarisse consiste à faire des phrases, et lorsqu'elle en a pu faire quelques-unes, la voilà consolée.]

The good reader cannot find words harsh enough to denounce the bad reader's attitude. She renounces her old friendship: "I say that this woman can never be my friend; I blush to think that she once was" ["Je vous dis que cette femme ne peut jamais être mon amie: je rougis qu'elle l'ait été"]. She rejects the person whose heart is so vile: "I confess, it's a great curse to feel and think that way, so great that I would rather my daughter die in my arms than to know her so afflicted. My daughter! Yes, I've had this thought, and I will not retract it" ["C'est, je vous l'avoue, une grande malédiction que de sentir et penser ainsi; mais si grande, que j'aimerais mieux tout à l'heure que ma fille mourût entre mes bras que de l'en savoir frappée. Ma fille! Oui, j'y ai pensé, et je ne m'en dédis pas"]. And she urges Diderot to read the most moving passages of *Clarissa* to this person to bring out the baseness of her soul: "Read her those two passages [the burial and the will], and be sure to let me know if her laughter accompanies Clarissa to her final resting place, so that my aversion for may be complete" ["Lisez-lui même ces deux morceaux, et ne manquez pas de m'apprendre que ses ris ont accompagné Clarisse jusque dans sa dernière demeure, afin que mon aversion pour elle soit parfaite"].

What we learn from this episode is, first, that the community of readers of Richardson was not open to everyone, male or female. Only the good and tender-hearted, who recognized the virtuous characters in the novel as kindred spirits, could join this harmonious society, whose members hearts beat as one and who were all bent on self-improvement. But we also learn that reading could go awry, that a text could be appropriated without order or rule. The discourse might contain explicit or hidden constraints, but these could not prevent them from being misappropriated. The history of reading must learn to take advantage of evidence of such misreadings and must recognize that if the reader is an effect of the text, he is also its creator.[40]

Merchandise and the Sacred

As the *Éloge* suggests, it was with Richardson that the reader's relation to the novelistic genre was transformed. To be sure, Diderot's language is entirely traditional, even conventional and banal, when he celebrates the ethical orientation of the English novelist's work.[41] Beyond the call for a redefinition of genres, what is in fact praised, in a very classical manner, is the dramatization of moral lessons:

What "novel" has meant until now was a tissue of fanciful and frivolous events, the reading of which was dangerous to taste and mores. I wish there were another name for Richardson's works, which ennoble the spirit, touch the soul, invariably breathe love of the good, and which also go by the name "novel." All that Montaigne, Charon, La Rochefoucault, and Nicole put into maxims, Richardson has put into action.

[Par roman, on a entendu jusqu'à ce jour un tissu d'événements chimériques et frivoles, dont la lecture était dangereuse pour le goût et pour les mœurs. Je voudrais bien qu'on trouvât un autre nom pour les ouvrages de Richardson, qui élèvent l'esprit, qui touchent l'âme, qui respirent partout l'amour du bien, et qu'on appelle aussi des romans. Tout ce que Montaigne, Charon, La Rochefoucault et Nicole ont mis en maximes, Richardson l'a mis en action.]

But beyond the "obsolete problematic" of the novel, as Sgard calls it, what Diderot sensed and anticipated was a radical novelty, namely, the presence of literary fiction beyond the text itself. This came about, first, because of the commercial exploitation of literary works and their transformation into commonly used objects. As we have seen, Richardson's novels, especially *Pamela*, entered the familiar world of readers in a variety of ways: through the advertising campaigns that preceded their publication, through numerous adaptations, translations, sequels, and parodies, and also through engravings, wax figurines, fans, and playing cards, which gave an everyday reality to the heroes and heroines of fiction.[42] After Pamela, Julie, Paul and Virginie, and young Werther would be subject to similar "commodification."

In Diderot's text this new conception of the reader's relation to the work went hand in hand with a new critical position, of which Jean Starobinski has given a masterful analysis.[43] With the *Éloge*, the principles of aesthetic judgment that had classically applied to comedies and novels were stood on their head. In the classical tradition, the projection of the reader (or beholder) into the work of fiction and his identification with imaginary heroes were denounced as terrible dangers, but Diderot transformed these practices into criteria of aesthetic and therefore moral excellence in works of art. The reader's participation in the text, his recognition of good and abhorrence of evil, counted as an essential mediation on the road to better behavior: "Hence the proof of the novel's beauty, goodness, and truth was to be given not by a critique (even a critique full of praise) of the novel itself but by the claim that the work was a source of energy that could all be channeled back into real life."[44]

Furthermore, the reader's identification of the text was not restricted to the time of reading: it was "unlimited." Because the action and heroes in fiction were more intensely real than reality itself, reading imparted pragmatic and critical knowledge of people and things. Consequently, the novel enabled its readers to internalize the deepest truths about the world and thus, for those capable of perceiving it by the light of their own feelings, the difference between good and evil:

I have formed images of the characters whom the author included in his story. Their faces are there. I recognize them in the street, in public places, in people's homes. They inspire affection or aversion in me. One of the advantages of [Richardson's] work is that it takes in a vast field, so that some portion of his canvas remains always before my eyes. Seldom do I find six people together without attaching some of his names to them. He points me toward decent people and steers me away from wicked ones. He has taught me to recognize them by swift and subtle signs.

[Je me suis fait une image des personnages que l'auteur a mis en scène; leurs physionomies sont là: je les reconnais dans les rues, dans les places publiques, dans les maisons; elles m'inspirent du penchant ou de l'aversion. Un des avantages de son travail, c'est qu'ayant embrassé un champ immense, il subsiste sans cesse sous mes yeux quelque portion de son tableau. Il est rare que j'aie trouvé six personnes rassemblées, sans leur attacher quelques-uns de ses noms. Il m'adresse aux honnêtes gens, il m'écarte des méchants; il m'a appris à les reconnaître à des signes prompts et délicats.]

The distinction between the righteous and the wicked forms the basis of the comparison, so often commented on, with the Bible: "Then I compared Richardson's work to a still more sacred book" ["Alors, je comparais l'ouvrage de Richardson à un livre plus sacré encore"]. Like the Gospel, the novel unites the pure of heart and sets them apart from those who are incapable of hearing the call of virtue and goodness. Like the Gospel, it gives meaning and beauty to the universe, transfiguring it into a great open book inhabited by its own word.[45]

The Divine Richardson

Finally, the quasi-religious status ascribed to the work sustained a new figure of the author. This expressed itself, first, in reiterated professions of desire to meet the writer, whose person now became the guarantor of his text's authenticity and authority.[46] In two places in the *Éloge*, Diderot expresses regret that a visit to the writer is now impossible:

Who has read Richardson's works without wishing to know this man, to have him for a brother or friend?

[Qui est-ce qui a lu les ouvrages de Richardson sans désirer de connaître cet homme, de l'avoir pour frère ou pour ami?]

And later:

Richardson is no more. What a loss for letters and for humanity! This loss touched me as if he had been my brother. I carried him in my heart though I had never met him, though I knew him only through his works. I have never encountered one of his countrymen, or one of mine who had traveled in England, without asking, "Have you seen the poet Richardson?" And then, "Have you seen the philosopher Hume?"

[Richardson n'est plus. Quelle perte pour les lettres et l'humanité! Cette perte m'a touché comme s'il eût été mon frère. Je le portais en mon cœur sans l'avoir vu, sans le connaître que par ses ouvrages. Je n'ai jamais rencontré un de ses compatriotes, un des miens qui eût voyagé en Angleterre, sans lui demander: "Avez-vous vu le poète Richardson? ensuite: avez-vous vu le philosophe Hume?"]

Thus the author's self-effacement behind his characters led, paradoxically, to the celebration of his person.

For Diderot, Richardson's writing was first of all a "labor." Such a definition made it possible to assimilate literary compositions to the other products of human labor and to justify the author's right of ownership. One year after the publication of the *Éloge de Richardson*, Diderot, writing at the behest of the community of booksellers and printers of Paris, prepared a *Lettre sur le commerce de la librairie* (Letter on the Book Trade), in which a defense of perpetuity of the *privilège*, or right to sell a book, underlay the assertion of the author's inalienable right to the work he produced.[47] This preoccupation echoes the question posed by the very form of Richardson's works, since the author presented himself as merely the "editor" of the letters that went into his novels: "How to claim ownership of texts while disclaiming authorship of their contents."[48] Indeed, it was not easy to reconcile the myth of a correspondence stumbled upon by chance, which cast the characters of the fiction as its true authors, with the writer's categorical assertion of ownership of the text—and in the case of Richardson, the writer was also the printer and publisher. Denying the fiction, Diderot praised Richardson as the creator of a work that was all his own but in which anyone could and should recognize himself as in a mirror.

To describe the peculiar force of such writing, he compared it with creations that were not the work of man: "In this immortal book, as in nature during springtime, no two leaves are the same color green. What immensely subtle variety!" ["Dans ce livre immortel, comme dans la nature au printemps, on ne trouve point deux feuilles d'un même vert. Quelle immense variété de nuances"]. The work of "an omnipotent hand and infinitely wise intelligence" ["d'une main toute-puissante et d'une intelligence infiniment sage"] was animated by a vital energy, from which it derived its inexhaustible, shimmering force. In 1759 Edward Young used an identical image in his *Conjectures on Original Composition in a Letter to the Author of Sir Charles Grandison*, when he maintained that an original work "may be said [to be] of a vegetable nature; it rises spontaneously from the vital root of Genius, it grows, it is not made."[49]

This brings us to the last of the vocabularies Diderot employed: the very religious vocabulary associated with his invocation of "the divine Richardson."

O, Richardson! If you did not enjoy quite the reputation you deserved during your lifetime, how great you will be in the eyes of our offspring when they see you from the distance from which we see Homer! Who then would dare strike a line of your sublime work? Among us you have even more admirers than in your native land, and I rejoice in this. Centuries, pass quickly and bring with you the honors Richardson is due! I vouch for them to all who hear me: I have not waited for others to pay you homage. Today I bowed down at the feet of your statue, I worshipped you, searching the depths of my soul for expressions adequate to the extent of my admiration for you, and I found none.

[O Richardson! si tu n'as pas joui de ton vivant de toute la réputation que tu méritais, combien tu seras grand chez nos neveux, lorsqu'ils te verront à la distance d'où nous voyons Homère! Alors, qui est-ce qui osera arracher une ligne de ton sublime ouvrage? Tu as eu plus d'admirateurs encore parmi nous que dans ta patrie, et je m'en réjouis. Siècles, hâtez-vous de couler et d'amener avec vous les honneurs qui sont dus à Richardson! J'en atteste tous ceux qui m'écoutent: je n'ai point attendu l'exemple des autres pour te rendre hommage; dès aujourd'hui j'étais incliné au pied de ta statue, je t'adorais, cherchant au fond de mon âme des expressions qui répondissent à l'étendue de l'admiration que je te portais, et je n'en trouvais point.]

Immortality through posterity, silent veneration, adoration: Diderot here employs words and images to effect a transfer of sacrality to the writer and to inaugurate literature's "sacred calling."[50] Literature now found itself invested with religious expectations somewhat remote from traditional Christian expressions. This change accounts for the novelty of the *Éloge* and perhaps also for the most essential feature of the eighteenth-century "reading revolution."

Epilogue: Diderot and His Pirates

In the fall of 1763, Diderot drafted a brief (*mémoire*) to which he gave several successive titles. On the manuscript that he revised in the first months of 1764, he settled on *Lettre historique et politique adressée à un magistrat sur le commerce de librairie, son état ancien et actuel, ses règlements, ses privilèges, les permissions tacites, les censeurs, les colporteurs, le passage des ponts et autres objets relatifs à la police littéraire* (Historical and Political Letter to a Magistrate on the Book Trade, Its Past and Present State, Its Regulations, Its Privileges, Tacit Permissions, Censors, Peddlers, Bridgeways, and Other Matters Concerning the Regulation of Literature). This long title, in the form of a summary, reminds us that the brief was addressed to a "magistrate," Antoine Gabriel de Sartine, who was both Lieutenant General of Police for the City of Paris, a post to which he was nominated in 1759, and Director of the Book Trade, in which position he succeeded Malesherbes in October 1763.[1] A few years later, in a letter addressed to Madame de Meaux (probably in 1775), Diderot discussed plans to bring out an anthology of miscellaneous works in which he would publish his letter, to which he now referred as "a piece on the freedom of the press, in which I discuss the history of regulations pertaining to the book trade, the circumstances in which they developed, which ones should be preserved and which eliminated" ["un morceau sur la liberté de la presse, où j'expose l'histoire des règlements de la librairie, les circonstances qui les ont fait naître, ce qu'il faut en conserver et ce qu'il faut en supprimer"]. *Freedom of the press*: with these words, Diderot indicated what for him was the fundamental significance of a text initially presented as nothing more than a "historical and political" brief examining the regulations around which literary commerce was organized.[2]

Tacit Permissions and Freedom of the Press

The occasion was indeed an excellent one for presenting the Director of the Book Trade with a pointed critique of censorship and its disastrous effects.

In broaching "this rather delicate subject" ["un peu plus délicat "], Diderot sought to show that banning books was ineffective because it not only failed to keep the banned books out of circulation but actually encouraged their sale. His irony turned mordant, as, for example, in his use of the word "consequently" ["par conséquent"] in the following characterization of Montesquieu's *Lettres persanes*:

What book is more contrary to good morals, to religion, to conventional ideas of philosophy and administration, in a word, to all vulgar prejudices, and, consequently, more dangerous than *Les Lettres persanes*? Is there anything worse? Yet there are a hundred editions of *Les Lettres persanes*, and there is not a single student of the Quatre Nations who can't find a copy on the quay for twelve sous. (p. 549)

[Quel livre plus contraire aux bonnes mœurs, à la religion, aux idées reçues de philosophie & d'administration, en un mot à tous les préjugés vulgaires & par conséquent plus dangereux , que les Lettres persanes? que nous reste-t-il à faire de pis? Cependant il y a cent éditions des Lettres persanes, & il n'y a pas un écolier des Quatre-Nations qui n'en trouve un exemplaire sur le quai pour douze sols.]

Not only was it pointless to ban books, it was also ruinous for French booksellers, profiting only the foreign publishers who printed the banned titles and smuggled them into France.[3] The truly dangerous books were not the ones so designated by the censors:

I shall tell you, sir, straight out: the books that are truly illicit, condemnable, and pernicious for a magistrate who sees straight, who is not preoccupied with false, pusillanimous, and petty ideas and who trusts in experience, are the ones printed in other countries, which we buy abroad when we could get them from our own manufacturers; there are no others. (pp. 546–47)

[Je vous dirais d'abord: Monsieur, Monsieur, les vrais livres illicites, prohibés, pernicieux, pour un magistrat qui voit juste, qui n'est pas préoccupé de petites idées fausses & pusillanimes, & qui s'en tient à l'expérience, ce sont les livres qu'on imprime ailleurs que dans notre pays, & que nous achetons à l'étranger tandis que nous pourrions les prendre chez nos manufacturiers; &et il n'y en a point d'autres.]

Thus the needs of commerce and the search for truth conspire to require freedom of the press. To achieve this, it is not necessary to abolish prior censorship altogether, even if the English example might inspire such action: the Licensing Act of 1662, which required permission from the authorities for all printed publication, had been abolished in 1695. But as Diderot wrote, ironically: "I should be quite upset if such a regime were established here. It would soon have us behaving all too well" ["Je serais bien fâché que cette police s'établit ici. Bientôt elle nous rendrait trop sages" (p. 559).

To guarantee the freedom of the press, it would suffice to issue an un-limited number of tacit permissions, that is, to use an existing method that had in fact been invented by the Directorate of the Book Trade. "Tacit per-missions," at first purely verbal but later registered as if the books involved were foreign works being authorized for sale in France, differed from "pub-lic permissions" in that they did not imply approval by the Chancellor.[4] Tacit permissions were instituted to allow works to be printed in France that could not be approved officially yet were not dangerous enough to be prohibited and thus left to foreign booksellers. In Diderot's conception they became an instrument for dismantling prior censorship. In fact, "it is almost impossible to imagine a hypothetical case in which a tacit permission would have to be refused" ["il est presque impossible d'imaginer un supposition où il faille refuser une permission tacite"], since the authors of "infamous works" ["pro-ductions infâmes"] would certainly not venture to request authorization of any kind, tacit or otherwise (p. 547). To establish the freedom to print within the regime of monarchical censorship, indeed with its assistance: that was the first paradoxical aspect of Diderot's brief.

Privileges and Literary Property

It was not the only one. The Letter was in fact a commissioned work, which Diderot was asked to write on behalf of the Communauté des Libraires Parisiens, or Community of Parisian Booksellers, by its syndic, Le Breton, the principal publisher of the *Encyclopédie*. The Paris booksellers were worried about the possible elimination of so-called *privilèges de librairie*, which they believed should grant them an exclusive and renewable right to publish works acquired from their authors. They were greatly alarmed by a decision of the King's Council in 1761 granting the *privilège* for the publication of the *Fables* of La Fontaine to the descendants of the author, thereby abrogating the rights of booksellers who had obtained that *privilège* in the past. The council deci-sion "undermined the very foundation of the booksellers' estate and spread the most acute alarm throughout the corporation of book dealers" ["qui sapait l'état des libraires par ses fondements répandit les plus vives alarmes dans tout le corps des commerçants"], since it affirmed the primacy of successory rights in the granting of privileges and maintained a right of patrimonial ownership in works even after cession to a bookseller.[5] The booksellers there-fore commissioned Diderot to write a brief justifying the "unalterable per-manence" ["permanence inaltérable"] of *privilèges de librairie* (p. 503).

His willingness to accept this commission might seem surprising. To begin with, his relations with the booksellers of Paris were far from idyllic. With each contract he signed with the publishers of the *Encyclopédie* (in 1747, 1754, 1759, and 1762), it was an uphill battle to win the slightest concession on terms from publishers who treated him as a salaried employee—employers to whom he referred as "my pirates" (*mes corsaires*).[6] In 1764, relations grew even worse when he learned that Le Breton had secretly tampered with certain articles of the dictionary after the proofs had been corrected. What is more, one scarcely expects to find this determined adversary of corporations and monopolies—alleged to be harmful impediments to commerce—defending the need for *privilèges de librairie*. Diderot's embarrassment in the face of this "paradox" (a word that he himself used) is apparent throughout his brief and, in fact, clearly enunciated at the outset:

Hence I shall begin by saying that the question here is not simply one of the interests of a community. What does it matter to me if there is one community more or less? Can this possibly concern me, one of the most zealous proponents of liberty in the broadest sense; who suffers if even the least talented of men is prevented from employing what talent he has; who sees an industry of arms bestowed by nature and bound by convention; who has always been convinced that corporations were unjust & catastrophic, & who would look upon their utter and absolute abolition as a step toward wiser government? (pp. 479–80)

[Je vous dirai donc d'abord qu'il ne s'agit pas simplement ici des intérêts d'une communauté. Et que m'importe qu'il y ait une communauté de plus ou de moins, à moi qui suis un des plus zélés partisans de la liberté prise sous l'acception la plus étendue; qui souffre avec chagrin de voir le dernier des talents, gêné dans son exercice; une industrie, des bras donnés par la nature, & liés par des conventions; — qui ai de tout temps été convaincu que les corporations étaient injustes & funestes, & qui en regarderais l'abolissement entier et absolu comme un pas vers un gouvernement plus sage.]

Why, then, defend the traditional claims of the community of booksellers, who were asking not only that *privilèges de librairie* be maintained but also that their renewal be made automatic and, ultimately, that they be granted in perpetuity?

The answer can be given in a few words:

I repeat, either the author is master of his work or no one in society is master of his property. The bookseller owns the work as the author owned it. He has the incontestable right to benefit as he sees fit from repeated editions. It would be as senseless to prevent him from doing so as it would be to condemn a farmer to let his field lie fallow or a landlord to leave his apartments empty. (p. 510)

[Je le répète, l'auteur est maître de son ouvrage, ou personne dans la société n'est maître de son bien. Le libraire le possède comme il était possédé par l'auteur. Il a le droit incontestable d'en tirer tel parti qui lui conviendra par des éditions réitérées. Il serait aussi insensé de l'en empêcher que de condamner un agriculteur à laisser son terrain en friche, ou un propriétaire de maison à laisser ses appartements vides.]

The irrevocability of the *privilège de librairie* is thus the basis of all literary property. There are several steps to Diderot's argument in favor of this proposition. First, the *privilège* has to be defined not as a royal favor that can be granted, refused, or revoked by the sovereign at will but rather as the "guarantee" or "safeguard" ["garantie"; "sauvegarde"] of a private contract whereby the author freely cedes to the bookseller his right to his manuscript. The property right acquired by the bookseller is similar to that obtained by the buyer of a piece of land or a house. It is perpetual, irrevocable, and transmissible and cannot be transferred or shared without the agreement of the person who holds it. Such a property right does no harm to either the general interest or the progress of knowledge because it pertains only to specific titles. It establishes no monopoly over

the inalienable right to print books in general or books on a particular subject, such as theology, medicine, jurisprudence, or history; or works on a specific subject, such as the history of a prince, a treatise on the eye, the liver, or some other disease, the translation of a particular author, a science, or an art.

[le droit inaliénable d'imprimer des livres en général ou des livres sur une matière particulière, comme la théologie, la médecine, la jurisprudence ou l'histoire; ou des ouvrages sur un objet déterminé, tels que l'histoire d'un prince, le traité de l'œil, du foie ou d'une autre maladie, la traduction d'un auteur spécifié, une science, un art.]

Thus *privilèges de librairie* leave open the possibility of "writing and publishing endlessly on the same subject" ["d'en composer & d'en publier à l'infini sur les mêmes objets"] (p. 512).

Diderot's plea on behalf of the *privilège de librairie* actually subverts the traditional definition, reducing the *privilège* to nothing more than the official sanction of a contract that is in itself sufficient to establish the right of ownership. The *privilège* thus becomes a title of ownership, and as such it must be respected by the public authorities because it constitutes one of the fundamental rights of all "citizens" ["citoyens"]. Only a tyrant would dare confiscate the property of private individuals, thereby reducing them to the condition of serfs, and "it is a truism for anyone who thinks that he who has no property in the State or who has only a precarious property in it can never be a good citizen. Indeed, what would attach him to one glebe more than to another?" ["il est constant pour tout homme qui pense que celui qui n'a nulle propriété dans l'État ou qui n'y a qu'une propriété précaire n'en peut jamais être bon citoyen. En effet qu'est-ce qui l'attacherait à une glèbe plutôt qu'à une autre?"] (p. 509).

Consequently, the protection associated with the *privilège* has to be extended to published works with a tacit permission, which also needs to be defended against counterfeits:

I think that if a book is acquired by a bookseller, who has paid for the manuscript, & who has published it with a tacit permission; that tacit permission is equivalent to a privilege. The counterfeiter commits a theft, which the magistrate in charge of regulating the book trade must punish all the more severely because it cannot be prosecuted under the law. The nature of the work, which prevents legal action, changes nothing as to its ownership. (p. 557)

[Je pense que si un livre est acquis par un libraire, qui en a payé le manuscrit, & qui l'a publié sur une permission tacite; cette permission tacite équivaut à un privilège. Le contrefacteur fait un vol que le magistrat préposé à la police de la librairie doit châtier d'autant plus sévèrement qu'il ne peut être poursuivi par les lois. La nature de l'ouvrage qui empêche une action juridique ne fait rien à la propriété.]

By subsuming the *privilège* under the logic of contract, Diderot implicitly dissociated the bookseller's title of ownership, whose legitimacy was based entirely on a private contract between two free individuals, from the corporate and state regulations governing the book trade. Hence those regulations could disappear without abrogating the property rights of the bookseller:

The prejudice comes from confusing the estate of bookseller, the community of booksellers, the corporation, with the *privilège* and the *privilège* with the title of ownership, all things which have nothing in common—no, sir, nothing! So, then, destroy all communities, restore to all citizens the freedom to use their faculties as their tastes and interests dictate, abolish all privileges, including those of the bookseller—I grant you this; all will be well, so long as the laws pertaining to contracts of purchase and sale subsist. (p. 509)

[Le préjugé vient de ce qu'on confond l'état de libraire, la communauté des libraires, la corporation avec le privilège, & le privilège avec le titre de possession; toutes choses qui n'ont rien de commun. Non rien, Monsieur. Eh détruisez toutes les communautés; rendez à tous les citoyens la liberté d'appliquer leurs facultés selon leur goût & leur intérêt; abolissez tous les privilèges, ceux même de librairie, j'y consens. Tout sera bien tant que les lois sur les contrats de vente et d'acquisition subsisteront.]

Diderot thus demonstrated the futility of the very institutions that he had been commissioned to defend tooth and nail.

History of Typography and Regulation of the Book Trade

In support of his argument, he rehearses the history of printing in France, for "things must be looked at from a distance" ["il faudra prendre les choses de loin"] (p. 481). The underlying thread of his narrative is the constant expansion of exclusive privileges, which were first established in the sixteenth century to protect enterprising publishers from counterfeits by dishonest competitors:

In fact, men like Estienne, Morel, and other skillful printers had no sooner published a work, in an edition prepared at great expense and whose success was ensured by careful workmanship and wise selection, than the same work was reprinted by drudges with none of their talents, who, having spent nothing, could sell at lower prices and who benefited from their preparation and care without having incurred any of their risks. What was the result of this? What must inevitably result, and what will result in any age. The competition ruined even the finest businesses. (pp. 486–87)

[En effet, les Estienne, les Morels & autres habiles imprimeurs n'avaient pas plus tôt publié un ouvrage dont ils avaient préparé à grands frais une édition, & dont l'exécution & le bon choix leur assuraient le succès que le même ouvrage était réimprimé par des incapables qui n'avaient aucun de leurs talents, qui n'ayant fait aucune dépense, pouvaient vendre à plus bas prix, & qui jouissaient de leurs avances & de leurs veilles, sans avoir couru aucun de leurs hasards. Qu'en arrivait-il? Ce qui devait arriver & ce qui en arrivera dans tous les temps. La concurrence rendit la plus belle entreprise ruineuse.]

To remedy this problem, which led audacious printers to ruin and discouraged ambitious projects, the king decided to grant them exclusive privileges. At first these were issued for a limited period of time, but later they were extended so as to protect the sales of editions that had not sold out their entire print run by the time the original *privilège* expired: "Thus, little by little, one moved toward perpetual and immutable *privilèges*" ["C'est ainsi qu'on s'avançait peu à peu à la perpétuité et à l'immutabilité du privilège"] (pp. 492–93). Furthermore, *privilèges* that had initially protected "old works and early manuscripts, that is, properties which, not having been acquired by anyone in particular, remained in the public domain" ["les anciens ouvrages & les premiers manuscrits, c'est-à-dire des effets qui n'appartenant proprement à aucun acquéreur étaient de droit commun"], were subsequently extended to works by contemporary authors (p. 494). As a result, if printing of the manuscript was allowed, the bookseller was granted a title that still bore the name of *privilège*, which authorized him to publish the work he had acquired and, by prescribing penalties for infringement, guaranteed his tranquil enjoyment of a property conveyed to him in perpetuity by a private contract between the author and himself. (p. 497)

[si l'impression du manuscrit était permise, on délivrait au libraire un titre qui retînt toujours le nom de privilège, qui l'autorisait à publier l'ouvrage qu'il avait acquis & qui lui garantissait, sous des peines spécifiées contre le perturbateur, la jouissance tranquille d'un bien dont l'acte sous seing privé signé de l'auteur & de lui lui transmettait la possession perpétuelle.]

Thus an equivalence was established between the perpetual property of the bookseller acquired through the contract with the author and the perpetuity of the *privilège*, made possible by successive renewals. Rewriting the history of royal *privilèges* in his own manner by making royal favor subject to the regime of contract,[7] Diderot suggests that the case he is attempting to make to the Director of the Book Trade is the natural culmination of a historical process: "So it was that the grant of *privilèges* became fixed, with the owners of manuscripts acquired from authors obtaining a permission to publish whose continuation they could solicit as often as it suited their interest to do so and transmitting their rights to others by sale, bequest, or abandonment" ["Voilà donc l'état des privilège devenu constant, & les possesseur de manuscrits acquis des auteurs, obtenant une permission de publier dont ils sollicitent la continuation autant de fois qu'il convient à leur intérêt, & transmettant leurs droits à d'autres à titre de vente, d'hérédité ou d'abandon"] (p. 503).

Turning from history to administration, Diderot argued that maintaining such permanent *privilèges* was indispensable to the printing and bookselling trades. To prove this, he listed the disastrous effects that would follow if "general competition" ["concurrence générale"] were to be allowed in publishing, that is, if *privilèges* were turned into mere permissions without any exclusivity clause. Apart from the fact that such a drastic change would be "to treat the bookseller's *privilège* as a favor to be granted or denied at will and to forget that it is simply the guarantee of a true title of ownership that cannot be infringed without injustice" ["traiter le privilège du libraire comme une grâce qu'on est libre de lui accorder ou de lui refuser, & oublier que ce n'est que la garantie d'une vraie propriété à laquelle on ne saurait toucher sans injustice"] (p. 526), it would have the most catastrophic consequences.

Booksellers would see a sharp decline in their profits, because several editions of the same title would compete for a share of the market. What had been "a profitable work for the exclusive owner would then become absolutely worthless to him and others" ["un ouvrage profitable au propriétaire exclusif, tombe absolument en non-valeur & pour lui & pour les autres"] (p. 516), and no bookseller would want to publish important works too costly to be remunerative in the slow market resulting from competing editions. Only works of high circulation would survive, and the drive to publish them at the lowest possible cost would ruin all the bookmaking arts, because these works would become "very common" and "as wretched with respect to typesetting, paper, and proofreading as the *Bibliothèque bleue*" ["très communs, tout aussi misérables de caractères, de papier & de correction que la Bibliothèque bleue"] (p. 516). Businesses related to bookmaking (font foundries, paper mills) would collapse, and, "what is worse, as these arts wither [in France], they will flourish abroad, and foreigners will be quick to supply us with the only good editions that will exist of our authors" ["ce qu'il y a de pis, c'est qu'à mesure que ces arts dépériront parmi nous, ils s'élèveront chez l'étranger, & qu'il ne tardera pas à nous fournir les seules bonnes éditions qui se feront de nos auteurs"] (p. 517).

In strict mercantilist logic, the state itself would ultimately become the victim of such a process, which would discourage French booksellers from engaging in publishing ventures and encourage them to deal instead in editions printed abroad:

A little more persecution and disorder and booksellers will seek suppliers abroad commensurate with their rate of sales. Because this would eliminate the risk of losing sums advanced to cover manufacturing costs, what could be more prudent? But the state will become poorer owing to the loss of workers and the disappearance of materials produced at home, and you will be sending out of the country the gold and silver that your own territory fails to yield. (p. 542).

[Encore un moment de persécution & de désordre, & chaque libraire se pourvoira au loin selon son débit. Ne s'exposant plus à perdre les avances de sa manufacture, que peut-il faire de plus prudent? Mais l'État s'appauvrira par la perte des ouvriers & la chute des matières que votre sol produit, & vous enverrez hors de vos contrées l'or et l'argent que votre sol ne produit pas.]

To avoid such foreseeable disasters, Diderot concludes with a proposal couched in the form of a legislative text:

That *privilèges* be regarded as pure and simple safeguards; that works acquired be considered irrevocable properties, and that the right to print and reprint same be granted exclusively to the acquirers thereof, unless the work itself contains a derogation clause. (p. 545)

[que les privilèges soient regardés comme de pures & simples sauvegardes, les ouvrages acquis comme des propriétés inattaquables, & leurs impressions et réimpressions continuées exclusivement à ceux qui les ont acquises, à moins qu'il n'y ait dans l'ouvrage même une clause dérogatoire.]

The Status of Men of Letters

Having thus examined the abominable effects that abolition of the *privilège* would have on the printing and bookselling trades, Diderot comes to the subject closest to his heart: the effects of the *privilège* on "literature," and, to begin with, on "the condition of the literary man" ["la condition des littérateurs & par contrecoup sur celle des lettres"] (p. 529). Writers are necessarily tied to booksellers, for it is entirely illusory for an author to think of publishing his own works. Diderot speaks from experience:

I have come close to practicing both professions, publisher as well as author; I have written, and I have on several occasions printed works on my own account; and I can assure you in passing that nothing accords less well with the active life of the businessman than the sedentary life of the man of letters. Incapable as we are of an endless round of petty chores, out of a hundred authors who would like to retail their own works, ninety-nine would suffer and be disgusted by it. (p. 513)

[J'ai à peu près exercé la double profession d'auteur & de libraire. J'ai écrit & j'ai plusieurs fois imprimé pour mon compte. Et je puis vous assurer, chemin faisant, que rien ne s'accorde plus mal que la vie active du commerçant & la vie sédentaire de l'homme de lettres. Incapables que nous sommes d'une infinité de petits soins, sur cent auteurs qui voudront débiter eux-mêmes leurs ouvrages, il y en quatre-vingt-dix-neuf qui s'en trouveront mal et s'en dégoûteront.]

The author who wished to publish himself would in fact have to contract with booksellers to sell books printed at his own expense. Such arrangements were not without risk and worry:

Provincial agents rob us with impunity; the merchant in the capital does not stand to profit from our work enough to push it. If he is granted a large discount, the author's profit evaporates. And then, keeping books of receipts and expenditures, answering, exchanging, receiving, sending—what occupations are these for a disciple of Homer or Plato! (p. 513)

[Les correspondants de province nous pillent impunément. Le commerçant de la capitale n'est pas assez intéressé au débit de notre ouvrage, pour le pousser. Si la remise qu'on lui accorde est forte, le profit de l'auteurs 'évanouit. Et puis tenir des livres de recette & de dépense, répondre, échanger, recevoir, envoyer, quelles occupations pour un disciple d'Homere ou de Platon!]

Booksellers are therefore inevitable, as Diderot had learned at some cost to himself. Authors, obliged to sell their manuscripts to people who would publish them, had only one hope: that their contracts would be as little disadvantageous as possible. As Diderot saw it, only full recognition of the writer's property rights in his "product" and full assurance of the bookseller's security through grant of perpetual *privilège* could guarantee that a just price would be paid for the work sold by the former and acquired by the latter.

To be sure, for authors unable to live on the income from their property or the emoluments of their position, literary activity could ideally be divorced from remuneration of any kind through the generosity of the sovereign, in the form of pensions, subsidies, or places. But such compensations were necessarily limited ("however kind and munificent a prince friendly to letters may be, his generosity can hardly be extended beyond known talents" ["Mais quelles que soient la bonté & la munificence d'un prince ami des lettres, elles ne peuvent guère s'étendre qu'aux talents connus"] (p. 530), and they were not always intelligently distributed:

There are few countries in Europe where letters are more honored or better compensated than in France. The number of places reserved for men of letters here is quite large: how delightful if all of them went to deserving individuals! Were I not afraid of being satirical, however, I might say that there are some for which the primary requirement is not a good book but a velvet habit. (p. 532)

[Il y a peu de contrées en Europe où les lettres soient plus honorées, plus récompensées qu'en France. Le nombre de places destinées aux gens de lettres y est très grand. Heureux si c'était toujours le mérite qui y conduisit. Mais si ne craignais d'être satirique, je dirais qu'il y en a où l'on exige plus scrupuleusement un habit de velours qu'un bon livre.]

For those who embark on a literary career, there is only one recourse: to draw their subsistence from the value of their writing when they sign their contract with a bookseller. The debut of the unknown writer is often difficult, "for it is success that instructs the merchant and the man of letters" ["c'est le succès qui instruit le commerçant et le littérateur"]. If the first book sells well, however, the author will be treated better:

At that moment the price of his talent changes, and I cannot deny that the increase in the commercial value of his second venture is unrelated to the decrease in the risk. It seems that the bookseller, anxious to keep his man, begins to calculate on a different basis. With the third success, the game is over: the author may still sign a bad contract, but he can have it more or less as he wishes. (p. 531)

[De ce moment, son talent change de prix; et je ne saurais le dissimuler, l'accroissement en valeur commerçante de sa seconde production n'a nul rapport avec la diminution du hasard. Il semble que le libraire, jaloux de conserver l'homme, calcule d'après d'autres éléments. Au troisième succès, tout est fini; l'auteur fait peut-être encore un mauvais traité, mais il le fait a peu près tel qu'il veut.]

Though no doubt idealized for the needs of the argument, the shift in the balance of power from publisher to author suggests a new image of the man of letters: the writer who tries as best he can to live by his pen.[8] In discussing equitable payment for manuscripts, Diderot sketches the mediocre but acceptable existence in store for the literary man without wealth, office, or patron. With a decent remuneration,

one might not get rich but would be able to live comfortably if the sums were not spread out over many years, did not slowly evaporate, and were not long gone by the time age arrived, needs increased, the eyes gave out, and the spirit was exhausted. Nevertheless, [payment] is an encouragement, and what sovereign is wealthy enough to meet the need with his liberalities? (p. 531)

[on ne s'enrichirait pas, mais on acquerrait de l'aisance si ces sommes n'étaient pas répandues sur un grand nombre d'années, ne s'évanouissaient pas à mesure qu'on les perçoit & n'étaient pas dissipées, lorsque les années sont venues, les besoins accrus, les yeux éteints, & l'esprit usé. Cependant c'est un encouragement! Et quel est le souverain assez riche pour y suppléer par ses libéralités?]

Thus the old representation of the prince as the protector of letters— and of men of letters—was not incompatible with the new insistence on just retribution for the writer.

But if just retribution was to be paid, the bookseller had to be assured of "tranquil and permanent possession of the works he acquires" ["possession tranquille & permanente des ouvrages qu'il acquiert"] (p. 532). That is why Diderot agreed to accept the commission from the Paris booksellers. He grasped the fact that the organization of the book trade in the old corporatist society meant that the independence (at least in a relative sense) of the writer depended on the existence of renewable and irrevocable *privilèges*:

Abolish these laws, force the insecure acquirer to give up ownership, and the consequences of this poorly conceived policy will be borne in part by the author. What benefit will I derive from my work, especially if my reputation is not yet secure, if, as

I suppose, the bookseller is afraid that a competitor—who has risked nothing to try out my talent, advanced nothing for a first edition, and paid me no honorarium—will instantly reap the benefits of acquiring it at the end of six years, or sooner if he dares? (p. 532)

[Abolissez ces lois. Rendez la propriété de l'acquéreur incertaine; & cette police mal entendue retombera en partie sur l'auteur. Quel parti tirerai-je de mon ouvrage, surtout si ma réputation n'est pas faite, comme je le suppose, lorsque le libraire craindra qu'un concurrent, sans courir le hasard de l'essai de mon talent, sans risquer les avances d'une première édition, sans m'accorder aucun honoraire, ne jouisse incessamment, au bout de six ans, plus tôt s'il l'ose, de son acquisition?]

Diderot is here taking six years as the average term of a *privilège* without renewal.

The booksellers who commissioned Diderot's brief were not very happy with it. They submitted it to Sartine in March 1764 only after revising it substantially and giving it a new title: *Représentations et observations en forme de mémoire sur l'état ancien et actuel de la librairie et particuliérement sur la propriété des privilèges* (Representations and Observations in the Form of a Brief on the Former and Present State of the Book Trade, and Particularly on the Ownership of *Privilèges*).[9] This new title is indicative of the gap between Diderot's most basic intentions—to plead for freedom of the press and establish the property rights of authors in their work—and the sole preoccupation of the booksellers, namely, to maintain the regime of *privilèges* and obtain recognition of the perpetuity, irrevocability, and transmissibility of their property. For their purposes, the form of Diderot's brief—a highly rhetorical dialogue—was pointless, as were the passages devoted to the possible abolition of communities, the discussion of social inequalities, and (on the pretext of discussing tacit permissions) the freedom of the press. Drastically revised by its publishers (as some articles of the *Encyclopédie* had been), Diderot's "Letter" would not be published in its original form until 1861.[10]

Condorcet: The Public Interest Versus the Privilege

Thirteen years after Diderot composed his brief, in 1776, Condorcet, probably writing in support of Turgot's decision in February of that year to abolish all *communautés des arts et métiers* (guilds in the arts and crafts),[11] drafted a pamphlet entitled *Fragments sur la liberté de la presse* (Fragments Concerning the Freedom of the Press).[12] Although the title has something in common with the one that Diderot ultimately gave to his "piece," the text undermines one after another of the principles on which Diderot based his 1763 brief. To begin with, Condorcet does not exempt *privilèges de librairie* from his blanket condemnation of privileges and exclusive rights of any kind:

Privilèges have the disadvantage in this as in other domains of reducing activity, concentrating it in a few hands, burdening it with a substantial tax, and making the manufactured goods of this country inferior to those of other countries. Hence they are neither necessary nor useful, and we have already seen that they are unjust.

[Les privilèges ont en ce genre, comme en tout autre, les inconvénients de diminuer l'activité, de la concentrer dans un petit nombre de mains, de la charger d'un impôt considérable, de rendre les manufactures du pays inférieures aux manufactures étrangères. Ils ne sont donc ni nécessaires, ni même utiles et nous avons vu qu'ils étaient injustes.]

Diderot's strategy, which was to maintain *privilèges de librairie* but only as a guarantee of contracts freely negotiated between authors and booksellers, was no longer acceptable in Condorcet's liberal perspective. But that is not all.

Whereas Diderot based his argument on the idea that literary property is identical to other forms of real property, Condorcet radically rejected this notion: "One feels that there can be no relation between the ownership of a work and that of a field which a man can cultivate, or a piece of furniture that can be used by only one person, the exclusive ownership of which is consequently based on the nature of the thing" ["on sent qu'il ne peut y avoir aucun rapport entre la propriété d'un ouvrage et celle d'un champ, qui ne peut être cultivé que par un homme; d'un meuble qui ne peut servir qu'à un homme, et dont, par conséquent, la propriété exclusive est fondée sur la nature des choses"]. Literary property is of a different order: "It is not a right but a privilege" ["ce n'est pas un véritable droit, c'est un privilège"] and, like all privileges, harmful to the "public interest" ["l'intérêt public"] because it is "a constraint imposed on freedom, a restriction of the rights of other citizens" ["une gêne imposée à la liberté, une restriction mise aux droits des auteurs citoyens"]. Just as a literary work cannot be protected by an exclusive privilege, neither can it be considered a form of personal property. Enlightenment must progress, and for that to happen everyone must be free to compose, improve, reproduce, and diffuse generally useful truths. Such truths can in no way be subject to appropriation by an individual.

For Diderot, every work is the legitimate property of its author because a work of literature is the irreducibly singular expression of that author's thoughts and feelings. As he put it in his brief,

What property can a man own if a work of the mind—the unique fruit of his up-bringing, his studies, his evenings, his age, his researches, his observations; if his finest hours, the most beautiful moments of his life; if his own thoughts, the feelings of his heart, the most precious part of himself, that which does not perish, which makes him immortal—does not belong to him? (pp. 509–10)

[Quel est le bien qui puisse appartenir à un homme, si un ouvrage d'esprit, le fruit unique de son éducation, de ses études, de ses veilles, de son temps, de ses recherches, de ses observations; si les plus belles heures, les plus beaux moments de sa vie; si ses propres pensées, les sentiments de son cœur; la portion de lui-même la plus précieuse, celle qui ne périt point; celle qui l'immortalise, ne lui appartient pas?]

For Condorcet, in stark contrast, that which forms the illegitimate basis of property and privilege—namely, "expressions," "sentences," "words," "pleasant turns of phrase" ["expressions . . . phrases . . . tournures agréables"]—is without importance compared to ideas and principles that belong to the realm of universal truths: "Let us assume that a book is useful. If it is useful, it is because of the universal truths it contains" ["Supposons un livre utile; c'est par les vérités qu'on y trouve qu'il est utile"].

Condorcet is well aware of the danger that such a position involves for anyone whose existence depends on income derived from the sale of his work: "A man of genius does not write books for money, but if he is not wealthy, and his books bring him no income, he will be obliged to find an occupation in order to live, and the public will lose thereby" ["Un homme de génie ne fait pas de livres pour de l'argent; mais s'il n'est pas riche et que ses livres ne lui rapportent rien, il sera obligé d'avoir une occupation pour vivre, et le public y perdra"].

The response to this objection comes in the form of two arguments. First, freedom of the press, by lowering the price of books, will ensure the greatest possible sale of the original edition, "prepared under the eyes of the author" ["faite sous les yeux de l'auteur"] and discourage others from publishing competing editions of the same text. Authors will therefore receive a just price for their works, the profits on which will no longer be threatened by counterfeits, "which are common only because of the exorbitant price charged for original editions, this price itself being a consequence of the [system of] *privilèges*" ["qui ne sont communes que par le prix exorbitant des éditions originales, prix qui lui-même est l'ouvrage des privilèges"]

Second, the writer's status may even improve if generalization of the subscription system allows the bookseller to amass the capital needed for a future edition and makes it possible for authors to be paid even before their works are published.[13]

The differences between Diderot's brief and Condorcet's pamphlet are substantial. They are due in part to the different contexts and different reasons for which they were written. Diderot defends, or at any rate accepts, existing institutions (guilds, *privilèges de librairie*, tacit permissions) even though he dislikes them, not only because he is writing on assignment but also because he believes that they can be invested with new content: the *privilège de librairie* is transformed into literary property and tacit permissions into freedom of the press. At a time when liberalism reigned triumphant, Condorcet refused such precautions and compromises: all privileges must be abolished because the progress of enlightenment demanded that truths be freely exposed and universally shared.

As for the property rights of authors in their works, the consequences of these differences are radical. For Diderot, the author's ownership of his work is a legitimate and inalienable right—inalienable, that is, except by the author himself. For Condorcet, it is a claim contrary to the general interest. Not only does this difference reflect two incompatible definitions of a "literary work"—for Diderot, the expression of a singular genius; for Condorcet, a vehicle of universal truths—it also reflects the two men's very different relations with the world of publishing. The writer who lived by his pen had little in common with the marquis who lived on his *rentes*. Nevertheless, revolutionary legislation would attempt to reconcile their incompatible theses, by recognizing both the ownership rights of the author (and his heirs) and the national interest in imposing strict temporal limits on authors' rights (restricted to five years by the decree of 13 January 1791 and ten years by the law of July 1793).[14]

Immaterial Objects

Ending this book with a commentary on Diderot's brief affords me an opportunity to return to the questions with which I began. Indeed, the brief can be seen as part of a process of abstraction of the text, which stands as a counterpoint or corollary to our interest in the various material embodiments of the written word. The early authors whose work we have examined along the way were acutely aware of those material embodiments and frequently transformed them into subjects of literature. Wax tablets, *librillos de memoria*, handwritten newsletters, philosophical and poetic manuscripts, printed works, writing as, literally or metaphorically, "woven words"—one or another of these material forms figured in the work of Baudri de Bourgueil, Cervantes,

Ben Jonson, Cyrano de Bergerac, and Goldoni, whose aesthetic inventiveness transformed them into literary motifs intended to delight, amuse, or divert the reader. Thus literary fiction continually reminds us of its dependence on practices and objects that enable us as readers to grasp not only the material embodiment of the text but also a part of what constitutes its soul.

Diderot, the reader of Richardson and defender of *privilèges de la librairie*, tells us that in every work, in each of its incarnations, there is also the presence of the work as an "immaterial object."[15] Before him, the lawsuits that developed in England following adopting of the Queen Anne Statute in 1710 led to the original formulation of this paradoxical category. The defense of the traditional rights of London booksellers and printers,[16] which had been undermined by legislation limiting the duration of the copyright to fourteen years, assumed that ownership of the manuscript implied a perpetual patrimonial right once the publisher acquired it from the author, and hence that the author possessed an inalienable but transmissible right to his compositions. The object of this primary right was not any particular manuscript, not even the autograph manuscript, but the work in its immaterial existence, "invisible and intangible" in the words of William Enfield.[17]

With its fundamental and perpetual identity so defined, the work transcended any possible material realization. According to Blackstone, another advocate of the cause of the London booksellers,

The identity of a literary composition consists intirely in the *sentiment* and the *language*; the same conceptions, cloathed in the same words, must necessarily be the same composition: and whatever method be taken of conveying that composition to the ear or the eye of another, by recital, by writing, or by printing, in any number of copies or at any period of time, it is always the identical work of the author which is so conveyed; and no other man can have a right to convey or transfer it without his consent, either tacitly or expressly given.[18]

After Diderot, Fichte, in the course of a debate about the reprinting of books in Germany, where the practice was especially widespread owing to the fragmentation of the Empire in many small states whose privileges were confined to the narrow territory of their sovereignty, restated this apparent paradox in a new way. To the classic dichotomy between the book's two natures, corporeal and spiritual, setting the object apart from the text, he added a second, between the ideas expressed by a book and the form given those ideas by the writing. Ideas are universal by nature, purpose, and use, hence no personal appropriation of ideas can be justified. Appropriation is legitimate only because

Each individual has his own thought processes, his own way of forming concepts and connecting them . . . Now, since pure ideas without sensible images cannot be thought, even less they capable of presentation to others. Hence, each writer must give his thoughts a certain form, and he can give them no other form than his own because he has no other. Hence "no one can *appropriate* his thoughts without thereby *altering their form*. This latter remains forever his exclusive property."

The textual form is the sole but powerful justification for individual appropriation of the common ideas conveyed to others by printed objects.[19] Property of this kind has one very special characteristic: since it is inalienable, it remains unavailable, intransmissible, and anyone such as a bookseller who acquires it is entitled only to be its beneficiary or representative, whose actions are constrained by a series of restrictions: for example, authorization to print only a limited number of copies per edition, with the right to reprint subject to additional compensation. The conceptual distinctions that Fichte introduced were thus intended to protect publishers against counterfeits without in any way limiting the author's sovereign and permanent ownership of his works.

Paradoxically, in order for texts to be subjected to the laws of property governing material objects, it was necessary to divorce them conceptually from any particular material embodiment. But composition, copying, and printing require a stylus or a pen, wax or paper, a hand or a press. And works reach their readers or listeners only by way of objects and practices that make them available to be read or listened to. Some early writers were more willing or adept than others when it came to referring to the practices, techniques, and places that gave literary productions and indeed all forms of writing material existence.

In their own way, they were the first to ask questions that have haunted writers in the modern era: What is a book? What is literature? Their answers varied widely. The readings proposed in this book were inspired above all by an answer given by one of the moderns:

A book is more than a verbal structure, or a series of verbal structures; a book is the dialogue with the reader, and the peculiar accent he gives to its voice, and the changing and durable images it leaves in his memory. That dialogue is infinite. Now the words *amica silentia lunae* mean "the intimate, silent, and shining moon" and then they meant the interlunar period, the darkness that permitted the Greeks to enter the citadel of Troy. Literature is not exhaustible, for the sufficient and simple reason that a single book is not. A book is not an isolated entity: it is a relationship, an axis of innumerable relationships.[20]

Notes

Introduction

1. D. F. McKenzie, *Bibliography and the Sociology of Texts*, Panizzi Lectures 1985 (London: British Library, 1986), p. 4.

2. Armando Petrucci, *La Scrittura: Ideologia e rapprezentazione* (Turin: Einaudi, 1986), pp. xviii–xxv. English translation: *Public Lettering: Script, Power, and Culture*, trans. Linda Lappin (Chicago: University of Chicago Press, 1993).

3. B. W. Ife, *Reading and Fiction in Golden-Age Spain: A Platonist Critique and Some Picaresque Replies* (Cambridge: Cambridge University Press, 1985).

4. Mark Rose, *Authors and Owners: The Invention of Copyright* (Cambridge, Mass.: Harvard University Press, 1993), and Joseph Lowenstein, *The Author's Due: Printing and the Prehistory of Copyright* (Chicago: University of Chicago Press, 2002).

5. Martha Woodmansee, *The Author, Art, and the Market: Rereading the History of Aesthetics* (New York: Columbia University Press, 1994).

6. Walter Greg, *Collected Papers*, ed. J. C. Maxwell (Oxford: Clarendon Press, 1966); R. B. McKerrow, *An Introduction to Bibliography for Literary Students* (Oxford: Clarendon Press, 1927); Fredson Bowers, *Principles of Bibliographical Description* (Princeton, N.J.: Princeton University Press, 1949), *Bibliography and Textual Criticism* (Oxford: Clarendon Press, 1964), and *Essays in Bibliography, Text, and Editing* (Charlottesville: University Press of Virginia, 1975).

7. Jacques Derrida, *De la Grammatologie* (Paris: Éditions de Minuit, 1967), esp. pp. 75–95 for the concept of "archi-writing" [English translation: *Of Grammatology*, trans. Gayatri Chakravorty Spivak (Baltimore: Johns Hopkins University Press, 1976)], and *Limited Inc.* (Paris: Galilée, 1990), esp. pp. 17–51 for the notion of "iterability" [English translation: *Limited Inc.* (Evanston, Ill.: Northwestern University Press, 1988)].

8. Stephen Greenblatt, *Shakespearean Negotiations: The Circulation of Social Energy in Renaissance England* (Berkeley: University of California Press, 1988), pp. 1–20.

9. David Scott Kastan, *Shakespeare and the Book* (Cambridge: Cambridge University Press, 2001), pp. 117–18.

10. See, for example, the edition of *Don Quixote* by Francisco Rico: Miguel de Cervantes, *Don Quijote de la Mancha*, edición del Instituto Cervantes, dirigida por Francisco Rico (Barcelona: Institututo Cervantes/Critica, 1998).

11. See, in regard to the two *King Lears* of 1608 and 1623, *The Division of the Kingdoms: Shakespeare's Two Versions of "King Lear"*, ed. Gary Taylor and Michael Warren (Oxford: Oxford University Press, 1983), and in regard to the three *Hamlet*s

of 1603, 1604, and 1623, Leah Marcus, "Bad Taste and Bad *Hamlet*," in her *Unediting the Renaissance: Shakespeare, Marlowe, Milton* (London: Routledge, 1996), pp. 132–76.

12. Jorge Luis Borges, "El libro," in *Borges oral* (Madrid: Alianza Editorial, 1998), pp. 9–23. Spanish text: "Yo he pensado, alguna vez, escribir una historia del libro. No desde el punto de vista físico. No me interesan los libros físicamente (sobre todo los libros de los bibliófilos, que suelen ser desmesurados), sino las diversas valoraciones que el libro ha recibido" (p. 10).

13. Jorge Luis Borges with Norman Thomas di Giovanni, *Autobiografía, 1899–1970* (Buenos Aires: El Ateneo, 1999), p. 26. Spanish text: "Todavía recuerdo aquellos volúmenes rojos con letras estampadas en oro de la edición Garnier. En algún momento la biblioteca de mi padre se fragmentó, y cuando leí *El Quijote* en otra edición tuve la sensación de que no era el verdadero. Más tarde hice que un amigo me consiguiera la edición de Garnier, con los mismos grabados en acero, las mismas notas a pie de página y también las mismas erratas. Para mí todas esas cosas forman parte del libro; considero que ése es el verdadero *Quijote*." English translation: *The Aleph and Other Stories, 1933–1969, Together with Commentaries and an Autobiographical Essay*, trans. Norman Thomas di Giovanni (New York: E.P. Dutton, 1970).

14. Margreta de Grazia and Peter Stallybrass, "The Materiality of the Shakespearean Text," *Shakespeare Quarterly* 44, 3 (1993: 255–83).

15. A comparable perspective can be found in Aurora Egido, *La voz de las letras en el Siglo de Oro* (Madrid: Abada Editores, 2003), esp. pp. 51–81, 83–93.

16. Erich Auerbach, *Mimesis: Dargestelle Wirklichkeit in der abendländischen Literatur* (Bern: C.A. Francke AG Verlag, 1946). English translation: *Mimesis: The Representation of Reality in Western Literature*, trans. Willard Trask (Garden City: N.Y.: Doubleday, 1953).

17. For very different perspectives, see Elizabeth L. Eisenstein, *The Printing Press as an Agent of Change: Communications and Cultural Transformations in Early Modern Europe* (Cambridge: Cambridge University Press, 1979), abridged in Elizabeth L. Eisenstein, *The Printing Revolution in Early Modern Europe* (Cambridge: Cambridge University Press, 1983); and Adrian Johns, *The Nature of the Book: Print and Knowledge in the Making* (Chicago: University of Chicago Press, 1998). See also Elizabeth L. Eisenstein, "An Unacknowledged Revolution Revisited," and Adrian Johns, "How to Acknowledge a Revolution," in "AHR Forum: How Revolutionary Was the Print Revolution?" *American Historical Review* 107, 1 (February 2002): 84–128.

18. Harold Love, *Scribal Publication in Seventeenth-Century England* (Oxford: Oxford University Press, 1993), and Fernando Bouza, *Corre manuscrito: Una historia cultural del Siglo de Oro* (Madrid: Marcial Pons, 2001).

19. François Moureau, ed., *De bonne main: La communication manuscrite au XVIIIe siècle* (Paris: Universitas; Oxford: Voltaire Foundation, 1993).

20. Peter Stallybrass, Roger Chartier, J. Franklin Mowery, and Heather Wolfe, "Hamlet's Tables and the Technologies of Writing in Renaissance England," *Shakespeare Quarterly* 55, 4 (2004): 1–41.

21. Sigmund Freud, "Notiz über den 'Wunderblock," *Internationale Zeitschrift für (ärztliche) Psychoanalyse* 11, 1 (1925): 1–5 [English translation: "A Note upon the 'Mystic Writing Pad," in Freud, *The Standard Edition of the Complete Psychological Works*, ed. James Strachey (London: Hogarth Press, 1961), vol. 19, pp. 227–32. Cf.

Jacques Derrida, "Freud et la scène de l'écriture," in Jacques Derrida, *L'écriture et la différence* (Paris: Éditions du Seuil, 1967), pp. 293–340 English translation: *Writing and Difference*, trans. Alan Bass (Chicago: University of Chicago Press, 1978).

22. Ann Rosalind Jones and Peter Stallybrass, *Renaissance Clothing and the Materials of Memory* (Cambridge: Cambridge University Press, 2000).

23. Michael Fried, *Absorption and Theatricality: Painting and Beholder in the Age of Diderot* (Berkeley: University of California Press, 1980).

24. Michel Foucault, *L'ordre du discours: Leçon inaugurale au Collège de France prononcée le 2 décembre 1970* (Paris: Gallimard, 1971), p. 11. English translation: "The Discourse on Language," in *The Archeology of Knowledge*, trans. A. M. Sheridan Smith (New York: Harper & Row, 1972), pp. 215–37.

25. Jorge Luis Borges, "William Shakespeare: Macbeth," *Prólogos con un prólogo de prólogos* (Madrid: Alianza Editorial, 1998), pp. 217–25: "*Art happens* (El arte ocurre), declaró Whistler, pero la conciencia de que no acabaremos nunca de descifrar el misterio estético no se opone al examen de los hechos que lo hicieron posible" (p. 218).

Chapter 1. Wax and Parchment

1. Miguel de Cervantes, *Don Quijote de la Mancha*, Edición del Instituto Cervantes, dirigida por Francisco Rico (Barcelona: Instituto Cervantes/Critica, 1998), p. 282. Spanish text: Y sería bueno, ya que no hay papel, que la escribiésemos, como hacían los antiguos, en hojas de árboles o en unas tablitas de cera, aunque tan dificultuoso será hallarse eso ahora como el papel." English translation: *Don Quixote*, trans. Samuel Putnam (New York: Modern Library, 1949), p. 204.

2. Pedro Mexia, *Silva de varia lección* [1540], edición de Antonio Castro (Madrid: Ediciones Cátedra, 1989), 2: 17–23.

3. Baudri de Bourgueil, *Poèmes*, ed. Jean-Yves Tilliette, 2 vols. (Paris: Les Belles Lettres, 1999, 2002). In citing Baudri's poems, I shall use the numbering of this edtion and give the Latin text and reference in the notes. An earlier edition of Baudri's poems was published by Phyllis Abrahams, *Les Œuvres poétiques de Baudri de Bourgueil (1046–1130): Étude critique publiée d'après le manuscrit du Vatican* (Paris, 1926). On the life of the poet-abbot, see the old biography by Abbé H. Pasquier, *Baudri de Bourgueil archévêque de Dol 1046–1130, d'après des documents inédits* (Paris, 1878).

4. Ernst Robert Curtius, *La littérature européenne et le Moyen Age latin* (1947; Paris: Presses Universitaires de France, 1956), pp. 493–94. English translation: *European Literature and the Latin Middle Ages* (London: Routledge & Kegan Paul, 1953).

5. Richard H. Rouse and Mary A. Rouse, "The Vocabulary of Wax Tablets," in *Vocabulaire du livre et de l'écriture au Moyen Age: Actes de la table ronde Paris 24–26 septembre 1987*, ed. Olga Weijers (Turnhout: Brepols, 1989), pp. 220–30.

6. Latin text: "Sed ueter mecum ludus perduret in aeuum, / A tabulis nunquam scilicet amouear. / Viuam uobiscum; uos autem, uiuite mecum; / Tandem nos unus suscipiat tumulus. Amen" (vol. 1, p. 37).

7. Latin text: "In latum, uersus uix octo pagina uestra, /In longum uero, uix capit exametrum; /Attamen in uobis pariter sunt octo tabelle, /Quae dant bis geminas paginulasque decem— /Cera nanque carent altrinsecus exteriores: /Sic faciunt

octo, quatuor atque decem. / Sic bis sex capiunt, capiunt et carmina centum: /Id quoque multiplices paginulae faciunt" (vol. 1, p. 37).

8. Elisabeth Lalou, "Les tablettes de cire médiévale," *Bibliothèque de l'École des Chartes* 147 (1989): 123–40 (list of tablets, nos. 11 and 13, pp. 138–39).

9. Armando Petrucci, *Le Tavolette cerate fiorentine di casa Majorfi* (Rome, 1965).

10. A less amiable example of the "genre" can be found in Ovid, *The Love Books*, Book 1, 12, lines 7–10, 27–30: "Away with you, ye ill-omened tablets, away, thou sullen wood, and as for thee, thou wax that bringest her refusal, thou wast sucked from the flower of the towering hemlock; surely thou art the dregs of the vile honey of some Corsican bee. . . . O lying tablets, little wonder that men call ye double; faith, 'twas a number of evil augury. What is the worst fate my wrath can wish you? May time devour you and rot you, and may the wax which covers you grow damp and foul with mildew!" Ovid, *The Love Books*, trans. J. Lewis May (New York: Rarity Press, 1930). Latin text: "Ite hinc, difficiles, funebria ligna, tabellae, / Tuque, negaturis cera referta notis, / Quam, puto, de longae collectam flores circulae / Melle sub infami Corsica misit apis . . . / Ergo uos rebus duplices pro nomine sensi; / Auspicii numerus non erat ipse boni. Quid precer iratus, nisi uos cariosa senectus / Rodat et immundo cera sit alba situ?" In Ovid, *Les Amours/Amores*, ed. Henri Bornecque, rev. Pierre Néraudeau (Paris: Les Belles Lettres, 2002), pp. 44–46. The word *duplices* designated both a diptych constituted by two tablets and duplicity.

11. Latin text: "Nescio quis uel quid iuncturam corrigiarum / Discidit: at spero quod senium nocuit. / Huic uestro morbo nostra pietate medebor, / Nostro restituam munere corrigiam. / Cera quidem uetus est, palearum fusca fauilla, / Et turpat uestram cera uetus speciem. / Idcirco minor est scribenti gratia uestra, / Cum uelut offensum reicitis grafium. / Ergo pro nigra uiridantem preparo ceram, / Quo placeat scribe gratia uestra" (vol. 2, p. 122).

12. Latin text: "Qui michi uos misit—hoc est abbast magis Sagiensis— / Sollers ploranti misit auem puero" (vol. 1, p. 37).

13. Latin text: "Quas tibi promisi tabulas, quas ipsa requiris, / Reddam cum potero, nam modo non habeo" (vol. 2, p. 48).

14. Latin text: "Pulchras misissem tabulas tibi si uoluisses; / Mittere quas nolo, comminus ipse dabo" (vol. 2, p. 138).

15. M. T. Clanchy, *From Memory to Written Record: England, 1066–1307*, 2nd ed. (Oxford: Blackwell, 1993), pp. 118–19: "It seems to have been common practice for monastic authors to write on wax and then have a fair copy made on parchment." For a similar distinction between wax and papyrus in the Roman world, see Guglielmo Cavallo, "Testo, libro, lettura," in *Lo spazio letterario di Roma antica*, ed. Cavallo et al., vol. 2, *La circolazione del testo* (Rome: Salerno Editrice, 1989), pp. 307–41, esp. 313–14.

16. Latin text: "Carmina carminibus nostris superapposuissem, / Si superapposita susciperent tabulae. / Impleui nostras, dum tu pigritare, tabellas, / Dum scriptum in cera lentus es excipere. / ut uero ceram uacues, opus excipe nostrum; / ut probus a solita te excute pigricia" (vol. 1, p. 34).

17. On the meaning of the verbs *dictare* and *dicitare* when referring to the composition of texts, regardless of the modality, see Clanchy, *From Memory to Written Record*, p. 271.

18. Latin text: "Talia dictabat noctibus aut euitans" (vol. 1, p. 3).

19. Rouse and Rouse, "The Vocabulary," p. 220.

20. Latin text: "Praecepi fieri capitales aere figuras, / Vt quod non sensus, res tribuat precium— / Ad nos miserunt Arabes huc forsitam aurum, / Materiarum quo signa priora micant. / Introitus alios minio uiridiue colore, / Vt mirabilius omne nitescat opus. / Vt quos allicere sententia plena nequibit, / Hos saltem species codicis alliciat." (vol. 1, pp. 3–4).

21. Latin text: "Sumptibus ipse meis uolo te nunc ducere Romam, / Vt leuies nostrum per mutua uerba laborem. / Tunc tibi nonanceps signum redolebit amoris / Cum iocundabor uerborum melle tuorum" et "Ipse tuum nomen in saecula perpetuabo, / Si ualeant aliquem mea carmina perpetuare" (vol. 1, p. 80).

22. Natalie Zemon Davis, *The Gift in Sixteenth-Century France* (Madison: University of Wisconsin Press, 2000).

23. Latin text: "Perlege sola meos uersus indagine cauta, / Perlege: quicquid id est, scripsit amica manus; / Scripsit amica manus et idem dictauit amicus , / Idem qui scripsit carmina composuit" (vol. 2, p. 125).

24. Latin text: "Ecce meae manui, mi stile, subtraheris ! / Quo perarabo meas tam digno pectine ceras / Tamque meis tabulis qui stilus aptus erit?" (vol 1, p. 90).

25. Latin text: "Et michi sufficerent et stilus et tabulae" (vol. 1, p. 133).

26. Mary Carruthers, *The Book of Memory: A Study of Memory in Medieval Culture* (Cambridge: Cambridge University Press, 1990).

27. Peter Stallybrass, Roger Chartier, J. Franklin Mowery, and Heather Wolfe, "Hamlet's Tables and the Technologies of Writing in Renaissance England," *Shakespeare Quarterly* 55, 4 (2004): 379–419.

28. Carruthers, *The Book of Memory*, pp. 285–87, 296–97.

29. Latin text: "In te praeterea uiget excellentia quaedam, / Cunctis qui recitant qua supermineas. / Quicquid enim recitas, recitas ita uoce sonora / Vt, quicquid dicas, omnibus id placeat; / Nam sic uerba sonis uerbisque sonos moderaris / Quatenus a neutro dissideat neutrum" (vol. 1, p. 105).

30. Latin text: "Denique quod dictas, sed et illud quod semel audis, / Viuaci semper ore referre potes" (vol. 1, p. 105).

31. Latin text: "Quod legis aut audis memori sic mente retractas / Vt recitantem te nil queat effugere" (vol. 1, p. 120).

32. Latin text: "Huc ades ergo, puer, ut iocundemur in orto / Iocundoque situ recreentur pectora nostra. / Vel tua cantabis uel ego mea carmina cantem / Et fidibus lentis aptabimus organa nostra" (vol. 1, p. 138).

33. See Albert Bates Lord, *The Singers of Tales* (Cambridge, Mass.: Harvard University Press, 1960).

34. Latin text: "Nam dictare acuit ebetatum mentis acumen; / Dictando siquidem sepe reuoluo libros" (vol. 1, p. 109).

35. "Ipse locum noui qui floridus ocia gignit, / Libros et carta et cuncta studentibus apta." And "Littera quam queris uastum dispersa per orbem / Optat te, nostri complens armaria claustri" (vol. 1, p. 75).

36. Latin text: "O utinam uerum iurauerit, ut michi reddat / Quem male decepto sustulit Ouidium !" (vol. 1, p. 117).

37. Cf. Jean-Yves Tilliette, "Introduction," in Baudri de Bourgeuil, *Poèmes*, pp. xix–xxii.

38. Latin text: "Ille mihi puer est, puero iocundior omni, / Qui proprium tabulis applicat ingenium. / Si cupis ergo mihi, cupiasque, Geraude, placere, / Libros et tabulas sedulus insequere. / Volue, reuolue libros, que nescis quere, require, / Fac aliquid dignum quod recites sociis" (vol. 2, p. 124).

39. Latin text: "Sed tibi nunc totum nostrum commendo libellum / Vt studiosa legas, sollicite uideas . . . Ore Sibillino respondeat Emma roganti, / Perlegat, extollat, corrigat, adiciat" (vol. 2, pp. 59–60).

40. Latin text: "Perlegi uestram studiosa indagine cartam / Et tetigi nuda carmina uestra manu. / Explicui gaudens bis terque quaterque uolumen / Nec poteram refici singula discutiens. / Ille liber mihi gratus erat, gratissima dicta; / Ergo, consumpsi sepe legendo diem" (vol. 2, p. 130).

41. Dolbeau, "Noms de livres," in *Vocabulaire du livre et de l'écriture au Moyen Age*, pp. 79–99.

42. Latin text: "Composui gremio posuique sub ubere laeuo / Scedam, quod cordi iunctius esse ferunt. / Si possem cordi mandare uolumina uestra, / Cordi mandarem singula, non gremio. / Tandem fessa dedi nocturno membra sopori, / Sed nescit noctem sollicitatus amor. / Quid non sperabam? Quid non sperare licebat? / Spem liber ediderat, ocia nox dederat. / In somnis insomnis eram, quia pagina uestra / Scilicet in gremio uiscera torruerat" (vol. 2, pp. 130–31).

43. On the Latin vocabulary of reading, which Baudri borrowed, see Emmanuelle Valette-Cagnac, *La lecture à Rome: Rites et pratiques* (Paris: Belin, 1997), pp. 19–28.

44. Guglielmo Cavallo, "Testo, libro, lettura," in *Lo spazio letterario di Roma antica*, pp. 329–41.

45. Armando Petrucci, "Lire au Moyen Age," *Mélanges de l'École française de Rome* 96 (1984): 603–16.

46. Franco Alessio, "Conservazione e modelli di sapere nel Medioevo," in *La memoria del sapere: Forme di conservazione e strutture organizzative dall'Antichità a oggi*, ed. Pietro Rossi (Rome-Bari: Laterza, 1988), pp. 99–133.

47. Paul Saenger, *Spaces Between Words: The Origins of Silent Reading* (Stanford, Calif.: Stanford University Press, 1997).

48. Petrucci, "Lire au Moyen Age," p. 604. For a similar analysis of the relations between styles of reading and speech situations in the Roman world, see Valette-Cagnac, *La lecture à Rome*, pp. 29–71.

49. Latin text: "Nec michi librorum nec desit copia carte / Excerpamque legens carta quod excipiat" (vol. 1, p. 134).

50. Armando Petrucci, *Le scritture ultime: Ideologia della morte e strategie dello scrivere nella tradizione occidentale* (Turin: Einaudi, 1995), pp. 67–69, and the reproduction of the mortuary scroll for Abbé Vital of the monastery of Savigny, early twelfth century. English translation: *Writing the Dead: Death and Writing Strategies in the Western Tradition* (Stanford, Calif.: Stanford University Press, 1998).

51. Latin text: "In rotulo multi, cum sollicitudine quadam, / Dicendi seriem semper moetantur ab Adam. [. . .] Nos pro Natali carmen faceremus anheli, / Si multum carmen posset prodesse fideli; / Sed quia non prosunt odarum garrulitates, / Odarum, queso, seponamus leuitates. / Intenti precibus, breuiter loca subtitulate, / Ne calamus uehemens pariat dispendia cartae" (vol. 1, p. 39).

52. Latin text: "Colligit ultra fas rotuiaris epistola multa, / Quae, quasi parcentes nugis, transimus inulta. / Et fuit exiguae condignum parcere cartae" (vol. 1, p. 40).

53. Sebastián de Covarrubias Orozco, *Tesoro de la Lengua Castellana o Española*, (1611), Edición de Felipe C. R. Maldonado, revisada por Manuel Camarero (Madrid: Editorial Castalia, 1995), p. 301. Spanish text: "Cera. Antes que se hubiese hallado el papel y la tinta, escribían en tablas enceradas, y con unos punteros abrían en la cera las letras."

54. Lalou, "Les tablettes de cire médiévales," pp. 133, 129.

55. Latin text: "Inter amicos sunt commertia mutua magni, / Quas res communis iungit amicitias " (vol. 2, p. 151).

56. Latin text: "Ergo alternus amor me scribere pauca coegit / Vt sic te cogam scribere multa michi" (vol. 1, p. 108).

57. Latin text: "O utinam ueniat ! ueniat, rogo, terminus ille, / Lucrer ut alterius commoda colloquii ! / Ipsa dares animum respondens plura roganti / Et responderem plura rogatus ego. / Interea nobis nos mutua carmina mandent, / Duxque comesque suus sit taciturna fides" (vol. 2, p. 46).

58. "Ergo salutat te praesentis epistola cartae / Et monet ut redeas: Stephane, tolle moras, / Fac, precor, ut redeas, ut mutuo nos uideamus / Nosque reconcilient altera colloquia. / O michi quam laetam reddet fortuna dietam / Te tempestiuum si michi reddiderit. / Sola dies sine te mecum decernitur annus, / Mille dies tecum parua breuisque dies" (vol. 1, p. 87).

59. Latin text: "Noster Auite,/ Huc uenias ad me, uenias mecumque moreris / Nos ut nostrorum dulcedine colloquiorum / Condelectemur, laetum quoque tempus agamus " (vol. 1, p. 138).

60. On the Roman model of literary friendships and sociability, see Catherine Salles, *Lire à Rome* (Paris: Les Belles Lettres, 1992), pp. 111–35.

61. See Michel Jeanneret, *Des mets et des mots: Banquets et propos de table à la Renaissance* (Paris: Librairie J. Corti, 1987), on "metaphors of bibliophagy," pp. 123–29, and on the banquets of "gourmand grammarians," pp. 151–60. English translation: *A Feast of Words: Banquets and Table Talk in the Renaissance* (Chicago: University of Chicago Press, 1991).

62. Latin text: "His onerabuntur mensae sapientis amici: / Nos inuitat ad has, his cupio refici./ Inuenies uarios libros relegendo sapores / Qui superent illud manna saporiferum. [. . .] Promptus ad hanc mensam properet quicumque uocatur, / Quo prebet mammas philosophia suas. / Hanc inuitatus ab amico promptus adibo / Postpositis aliis rebus et officiis; / Maturando pedes actus celerabo seniles, / Ne quas innectam dissimulando moras. / Nolo tristentur quos debeo laetificare / Aduentu propero colloquioque meo" (vol. 2, p. 142).

Chapter 2. Writing and Memory: Cardeno's Librillo

1. Miguel de Cervantes, *Don Quijote de la Mancha*, Edición del Instituto Cervantes, p. 251. Spanish text: "un cojín y una maleta asida a él, medio podridos, o podridos del todo, y deshechos." Putnam translation, p. 180.

2. *Don Quijote de la Mancha*, pp. 251–52. Spanish text: "cuatro camisas de

delgada holanda y otras cosas de lienzo no menos curiosas que limpias, y en un pañizuelo halló un buen montoncillo de escudos de oro, y así como los vio dijo: — ¡Bendito sea todo el cielo, que nos ha deparado una aventura que sea de provecho! — Y, buscando más, halló un librillo de memoria ricamente guarnecido." Putnam translation, p. 180.

3. Miguel de Cervantes, *L'Ingénieux hidalgo don Quichotte de la Manche* [1837], trans. Louis Viardot (Paris: Garnier-Flammarion, 1969), p. 215.

4. Miguel de Cervantes, *L'Ingénieux hidalgo don Quichotte de la Manche*, trans. Aline Schulman (Paris: Éditions du Seuil, 1997), p. 215.

5. Miguel de Cervantes, *L'Ingénieux Hidalgo Don Quichotte de la Manche*, in *Don Quichotte suivi de La Galatée, Œuvres romanesques*, vol. 1, trans. Jean Canavaggio, Claude Allaigre, and Michel Moner (Paris: Gallimard, 2001), p. 576.

6. Miguel de Cervantes, *Le Valeureux Don Quixote de la Manche*, trans. César Oudin (Paris, 1639), vol. 1, p. 215.

7. Miguel de Cervantes, *Histoire de l'Admirable Don Quichotte de la Manche*, trans. Filleau de Saint-Martin (Paris, 1798), p. 251.

8. For example, Miguel de Cervantes, *Don Quixote*, A New Translation by Edith Grossman (New York: Ecco, HarperCollins, 2003), translates *librillo de memoria* as "small diary," p. 175, and "notebook," pp. 177, 199, 201, 209.

9. Miguel de Cervantes, *The History of the Valorous and Witty Knight-Errant Don Quixote of the Mancha*, trans. Thomas Shelton (London, 1652), p. 48; *The Life and Exploits of the Ingenious Gentleman Don Quixote de la Mancha*, trans. Charles Jarvis (London, 1747), p. 44; *The History of the Renowned Don Quixote de la Mancha*, trans. Charles Henry Wilmot (London, 1774), vol. 1, p. 179. Thanks to Peter Stallybrass for these references.

10. *Don Quijote de la Mancha*, p. 252. Spanish text: "y lo primero que halló en él, escrito como en borrador, aunque de muy buena letra, fue un soneto, que, leyéndole alto porque Sancho también lo oyese, vio que decía desta manera." Putnam translation, p. 180.

11. *Don Quijote de la Mancha*, p. 253. Spanish text: "Volvió la hoja don Quijote y dijo: 'Esto es prosa y parece carta." Putnam translation, p. 181.

12. *Don Quijote de la Mancha*, p. 254. Spanish text: "Y hojeando casi todo el librillo, halló otros versos y cartas, que algunos pudo leer y otros no; pero lo que todo contenían eran quejas, lamentos, desconfianzas, sabores y sinsabores, favores y desdenes, solenizados los unos y llorados los otros." Putnam translation, p. 182.

13. *Don Quijote de la Mancha*, p. 262. Spanish text: "querría pasar brevemente por el cuento de mis desgracias, que el traerlas a la memoria no me sirve de otra cosa que añadir otras de nuevo." Putnam translation, p. 189.

14. *Don Quijote de la Mancha*, p. 263. Spanish text: "¡Ay, cielos, y cuántos billetes le escribí! ¡Cuán regaladas y honestas respuestas tuve! ¡Cuántas canciones compuse y cuántos enamorados versos, donde el alma declaraba y trasladaba sus sentimientos, pintaba sus encendidos deseos, entretenía sus memorias y recreaba sus voluntad!" Putnam translation, p. 190.

15. *Don Quijote de la Mancha*, pp. 275, 276. Spanish text: "haciendo aquí del desesperado, del sandio y del furioso," and "locura de lloros y sentimientos." Putnam translation, p. 199.

16. *Don Quijote de la Mancha*, p. 282. Spanish text: "Pero ¿qué haremos para escribir la carta? —Y la libranza pollinesca también—añadió Sancho." Putnam translation, p. 203.

17. *Don Quijote de la Mancha*, p. 1234. Spanish text: "Don Quijote, que vio el llanto y supo la causa, consoló a Sancho con las mejores razones que pudo y le rogó que tuviese paciencia prometiéndole de darle una cédula de cambio para que le diesen tres [asnos] en su casa, de cinco que había dejado en ella." My translation.

18. *Don Quijote de la Mancha*, p. 282. Spanish text: "y sería bueno, ya que no hay papel, que la escribiésemos, como lo hacían los antiguos, en hojas de árboles o en unas tablitas de cera, aunque tan dificultuoso será hallarse eso ahora como el papel." Putnam translation, p. 204.

19. Pedro Mexía, *Silva de varia lección* [1540], ed. Antonio Castro (Madrid: Ediciones Cátedra, 1989), vol. 2, part 3, chap. 2, "En qué escrivían los antiguos, antes que huviesse papel, y de qué manera," pp. 17–23: "También escrivieron los antiguos en tablicas enceradas muy lisas, en las quales hazían las letras con unos puçoncicos delgados que llamavan estilos; y de aquí quedó que el que bien escrive dizen que tiene buen estilo, tomando el nombre del instrumento."

20. *Don Quijote de la Mancha*, p. 282. Spanish text: "Mas ya me ha venido a la memoria dónde será bien, y aun más que bien, escribilla, que es en el librillo de memoria que fue de Cardenio, y tú tendrás cuidado de hacerla trasladar en papel, de buena letra, en el primer lugar que hallares donde haya maestro de escuela de muchachos, o, si no cualquiera sacristán te la trasladará; y no se la des a trasladar a ningún escribano, que hacen letra procesada, que no la entenderá Satanás." Putnam translation, p. 204.

21. William Shakespeare, *Henry VI, Part 2*, ed. Stanley Wells and Gary Taylor, in William Shakespeare, *The Complete Works* (Oxford: Oxford University Press, 1988) Act IV, Scene 2, p. 79.

22. *Don Quijote de la Mancha*, p. 282. Spanish text: "—Pues ¿qué se ha de hacer con la firma? —dijo Sancho.

—Nunca las cartas de Amadís se firman—respondió don Quijote.

—Está bien —respondió Sancho—, pero la libranza forzosamente se ha de firmar, y esa, si se traslada, dirán que la firma es falsa y quedaréme sin pollinos.

—La libranza irá en el mesmo librillo firmada, que en viéndola mi sobrina no pondrá dificultad en cumplilla. Y en lo que toca a la carta de amores, pondrás por firma "Vuestro hasta la muerte, el Caballero de la Triste Figura." Y hará poco al caso que vaya de mano ajena, porque, a lo que yo me sé acordar, Dulcinea no sabe escribir ni leer y en toda su vida ha visto letra mía ni carta mía." Putnam translation, p. 204.

23. Béatrice Fraenkel, *La signature: Genèse d'un signe* (Paris: Gallimard, 1992).

24. Armando Petrucci, "Scrivere per gli altri," *Scrittura e Civiltà* 13 (1989): 475–87.

25. *Don Quijote de la Mancha*, p. 286. Spanish text: "Llamó a Sancho y le dijo que se la quería leer porque la tomáse de memoria, si acaso se le perdiese por el camino, porque de su desdicha todo se podía temer. A lo cual respondió Sancho:

—Escríbala vuestra merced dos o tres veces ahí en el libro, y démele, que yo le llevaré bien guardado; porque pensar que yo la he de tomar en la memoria es disparate, que la tengo tan mala, que muchas veces se me olvida cómo me llamo." Putnam translation, pp. 206–7.

26. Pedro Mexía, *Silva de varia lección*, II.3.7, "Quán excelente cosa es la memoria," p. 49 ["Aristótiles dize que comúnmente los agudos de ingenio son [. . .] muy prestos en el tomar y flacos en el retener; y los rudos, por el contrario: con dificultad lo reciben y aprenden, pero sosténlo más."]

27. *Don Quijote de la Mancha*, p. 287. Spanish text: "—Buena está —dijo Sancho- fírmela vuestra merced.—No es de menester firmarla —dijo don Quijote—, sino solamente poner mi rúbrica, que es lo mesmo que firma, y para tres asnos y aun para trecientos, fuera bastante." Putnam translation, p. 208.

28. Miguel de Cervantes, *The History of the Most Renowned Don Quixote of Mancha*, trans. J. Philips (London, 1687), p. 117. Thanks to Peter Stallybrass for this reference.

29. On stenographic methods and practices, see Adele Davidson, "'Some by Stenography'? Stationers, Shorthand, and the Early Shakespearean Quartos," *Papers of the Bibliographical Society of America* 90, 4 (1996): 417–49 and "*King Lear* in an Age of Stenographical Publication," *Papers of the Bibliographical Society of America* 92 (1998): 297–324; and Michael Mendle, "News and the Pamphlet Culture of Mid-Seventeenth-Century England," in *The Politics of Information in Early Modern Europe*, ed. Brendan Dooley and Sabrina A. Baron (London: Routledge, 2001), pp. 56–79, esp. pp. 63–67.

30. Roger Chartier, *Publishing Drama in Early Moden Europe*, Panizzi Lectures 1998 (London: British Library. 1999), and "'*Coppied onely by the eare*': Le texte de théâtre entre la scène et la page au XVIIe siècle," in *Du Spectateur au lecteur: Imprimer la scène aux XVIe et XVIIe siècles*, ed. Larry F. Norman, Philippe Desan, and Richard Strier (Fasano: Schena Editore; Paris, Presses de l'Université de Paris-Sorbonne, 2002), pp. 31–53.

31. *Don Quijote de la Mancha*, p. 292. Spanish text: "Y, así, se entretenía paseándose por el pradecillo, escribiendo y grabando por las cortezas de los árboles y por la menuda arena muchos versos, todos acomodados a su tristeza, y algunos en alabanza de Dulcinea." Putnam translation, p. 211.

32. William Shakespeare, *As You Like It*, Act III, Scene 2, p. 639.

33. William Shakespeare, *The Most Lamentable Roman Tragedy of Titus Andronicus*, Act IV, Scene 1, p. 141.

34. *Don Quijote de la Mancha*, p. 293. Spanish text: "no se pudieron sacar en limpio ni enteros más destas tres coplas."

35. *Don Quijote de la Mancha*, p. 295. Spanish text: "Metió la mano en el seno Sancho Panza, buscando el librillo, pero no le halló, ni le podía hallar si le buscara hasta agora, porque se había quedado don Qujote con él y no se le había dado, nia él se le acordó de pedírsele." Putnam translation, p. 214.

36. *Don Quijote de la Mancha*, p. 296. Spanish text: "Consolóle el cura, y díjole que en hallando a su señor él le haría revalidar la manda y que tornase a hacer la libranza en papel, como era uso y costumbre, porque las que se hacían en libros de memoria jamás se acetaban ni cumplían." Putnam translation, p. 214.

37. *Don Quijote de la Mancha*, p. 296. Spanish text: "—Por Dios, señor licenciado, que los diablos lleven la cosa que de la carta se me acuerda, aunque en el principio decía: 'Alta y sobajada señora.'"

—No diría —dijo el barbero— *sobajada,* sino *sobrehumana* o *soberana señora.*

—Así es —dijo Sancho—. Luego, si mal no me acuerdo, proseguía, si mal no me acuerdo: 'el llego y falto de sueño, y el ferido besa a vuestra merced ias manos, ingrata y muy desconocida hermosa,' y no sé qué decia de salud y de de enfermedad que le enviaba, y por aquí iba escurriendo hasta que acababa en 'Vuestro hasta la muerte, el Caballero de la Triste Figura.'" Putnam translation, p. 215.

38. Cf. Mary Carruthers, *The Book of Memory: A Study of Memory in Medieval Culture* (Cambridge: Cambridge University Press, 1990), and Fernando Bouza, *Comunicación, conocimiento y memoria en la España de los siglos XVI y XVII* (Salamanca: Publicaciones del Seminario de Estudios Medievales y Renacentistas, 1999). English translation: *Communication, Knowledge, and Memory in Early Modern Spain* (Philadelphia: University of Pennsylvania Press, 1999).

39. *Don Quijote de la Mancha,* p. 213. Spanish text: "Si desa manera cuentas tu cuento, Sancho —dijo don Quijote—, repitiendo dos veces lo que vas diciendo, no acabarás en dos días: dilo seguidamente y cuéntalo como hombre de entendimiento y si no, no digas nada.

—De la misma manera que yo lo cuento, —respondió Sancho— se cuentan en mi tierra todas las consejas, y yo no sé contarlo de otra, ni es bien que vuestra merced me pida que haga usos nuevos.

—Di como quisieres —respondió don Quijote—, que pues la suerte quiere que no pueda dejar de escucharte, prosigue." Putnam translation, p. 149.

40. *Diccionario de la lengua castellana* [. . .] *Compuesto por la Real Academia Española,* vol. 4 (Madrid, 1734), p. 400. Spanish text: "Libro de memoria. El librito que se suele traher en la faltriquera, cuyas hojas están embetunadas y en blanco, y en él se incluye una pluma de metal, en cuya punta se inxiere un pedazo agudo de piedra lápiz, con la qual se annóta en el librito todo aquello que no se quiere fiar a la fragilidad de la memoria: y se borra despues para que vuelvan a servir las hojas, que tambien se suelen hacer de marfil."

41. Sebastián de Covarrubias Orozco, *Tesoro de la Lengua Castellana o Española,* (1611), ed. Felipe C. R. Maldonado rev. Manuel Camarero (Madrid: Editorial Castalia, 1995), p. 167, "Barniz. Es una especie de goma [. . .] Y della y del aceite de linaza o de olivo, se hace el compuesto que vulgarmente llamamos barniz, con que se da lustre a toda pintura y se barniza el hierro al fuego, las tablas en blanco para escribir, *latine tabelle gypsata seu dealbata, graece palimpsestos.*"

42. This is the hypothesis favored by Alicia Marchant Rivera, *Literatura e historia de la cultura escrita: Prácticas bibliófilas y escriturarias en el Quijote de Cervantes* (Malaga: Universidad de Málaga, 2003), pp. 59–61. See also Antonio Castillo Gómez, "La escritura representada: Imágenes de lo escrito en la obra de Cervantes," in *Volver a Cervantes, Actas del IV Congreso Internacional de la Asociación de Cervantistas, Lepanto 1/8 de octubre de 2000,* ed. Antonio Bernat Vistarini (Palma, Universitat de les Illes Balears, 2001), pp. 311–25.

43. William Shakespeare, *The Tragical History of Hamlet Prince of Denmark.* The text is that of the 1604 Quarto, Act I, Scene 5, lines 98–104, p. 662.

44. Ibid., lines 107–11.

45. Peter Stallybrass, Roger Chartier, J. Franklin Mowery, and Heather Wolfe,

"Hamlet's Tables and the Technologies of Writing in Renaissance England," *Shakespeare Quarterly* 55, 4 (2004): 379–419.

46. Robert Triplet, *Writing Tables with a Kalendar for XXIII Years* (London, 1604).

47. *Hamlet*, Act I, Scene 5. Cf. Francis Goyet, *Le sublime du "lieu commun": L'invention rhétorique à la Renaissance* (Paris: Honoré Champion, 1996), pp. 568–69.

48. Thanks to Peter Blayney for this information.

49. John Florio, *Queen's Anna New World of Words* (London, 1611): "Cartella, a kind of sleeked pasteboard to write upon and may be blotted out againe. Also leaves of writing tables." Cf. Jessie Ann Owens, *Composers at Work: The Craft of Musical Composition 1450–1600* (Oxford: Oxford University Press, 1997), pp. 74–107.

50. Randle Cotgrave, *A Dictionarie of the French and English Tongues* (London, 1611).

51. Fernando Bouza devotes several pages to *libros de memoria* in his book *Palabra e imagen en la corte: Cultura oral y visual de la nobleza en el Siglo de Oro* (Madrid: Abada Editores, 2003), pp. 48–58.

52. Thanks to Pedro Rueda for this information, taken from a document in the Archivo General de Indias in Seville (Contratación, 221, no. 2).

53. Bouza, *Palabra e imagen en la corte*, pp. 53–56.

54. Spanish text: "no es bronce la memoria / sino tabla con barniz, /que se borra fácilmente / y encima se sobre escrive."

55. Spanish text: "Dixo una vez un letrado, / que era el amor de muger / como tabla de barniz / en cuyo blanco matiz, memoria suelen poner. / Que borrando con saliva / lo primero que se escrive / aquello que después vive / hazen que encima se escriva. / Como blanca tabla están / las almas de las mujeres. / Si oy el escrito eres, / mañana te borrarán. / Con sólo faltar un día / como es de barniz su amor, / pondrán don Pedro, señor, / adonde don Iuan dezía."

56. Princeton University Library, Rare Books, Manuscript Collection, CO938 (n°8). Thanks to Don Skemer, the curator of this collection, for showing us this *librillo de memoria*, which is written in Spanish, was used in Venezuela in the seventeenth century, and is probably not very different from Cardenio's.

57. Another example of Cervantes' reference to the erasability of the "libros de memoria" is the one owned by Monipodio in the *Novela of Rinconete y Cortadillo*; cf. Miguel de Cervantes, Saavedra, *Novelas ejemplares*, ed. Harry Sieber (Madrid: Cátedra, 1997), pp. 235–36. English translation: *Exemplary Stories*, trans. Lesley Lipson (Oxford, New York: Oxford University Press, 1998.

58. *Don Quijote de la Mancha*, p. 356. Spanish text: "Señor —respondió Sancho—, si va a decir la verdad, la carta no me la trasladó nadie, porque yo no llevé carta alguna." Putnam translation, p. 265.

59. *Don Quijote de la Mancha*, p. 357. Spanish text: "Así fuera —respondió Sancho—, si no la hubiera yo tomado en la memoria cuando vuestra merced me la leyó, de manera que se la dije a un sacristán, que me la trasladó del entendimiento tan punto por punto, que dijo que en todos los días de su vida, aunque había leído muchas cartas de descomunión, no había visto ni leído tan linda carta como aquella." Putnam translation, p. 265.

60. *Don Quijote de la Mancha*, p. 357. Spanish text: "No señor —respondió

Sancho—, porque después que la di, como vi que no había de ser de más provecho, di en olvidalla." Putnam translation, p. 265.

    61. *Don Quijote de la Mancha*, p. 104: "Pero está el daño de todo esto que en este punto y término deja pendiente el autor desta historia esta batalla, disculpándose que no halló más escrito destas hazañas de don Quijote, de las que deja referidas" ("What is annoying about all this is that at this very point in the story, the author leaves this battle in suspense, with the excuse that he has found no writings about the exploits of Don Quixote other than those related here").

    62. *Don Quijote de la Mancha*, p. 904. Spanish text: "Ahora que estamos solos y que aquí no nos oye nadie, querría yo que el señor gobernador me asolviese ciertas dudas que tengo, nacidas de la historia que del gran don Quijote anda ya impresa. Una de las cuales dudas es que pues el buen Sancho nunca vio a Dulcinea, digo, a la señora Dulcinea del Toboso, ni le llevó la carta del señor don Quijote, porque se quedó en el libro de memoria en Sierra Morena, cómo se atrevió a fingir la respuesta." Putnam translation, pp. 728–29.

    63. *Don Quijote de la Mancha*, pp. 647–48. Spanish text: "y a mí se me trasluce que no ha de haber nación ni lengua donde no se traduzga."

Chapter 3. The Press and Fonts: Don Quixote in the Print Shop

    1. *Don Quijote de la Mancha*, p. 1142. Spanish text: "y, así, él y Sancho, con otros dos criados que don Antonio le dio, salieron a pasearse." Putnam translation, p. 922.

    2. *Don Quijote de la Mancha*, p. 1142. Spanish text: "Sucedió, pues, que yendo por una calle alzó los ojos don Quijote y vio escrito sobre una puerta, con letras muy grandes: 'Aquí se imprimen libros,' de lo que se contentó mucho, porque hasta entonces no había visto emprenta alguna y deseaba saber cómo fuese." Putnam translation, p. 922.

    3. William Baldwin, *A Marvelous Hystory intituled Beware the Cat* (London, 1570). For a modern edition, see *Beware the Cat: The First English Novel*, by William Baldwin, Introduction and Text by William A. Ringler and Michael Flachmann (San Marino, Calif.: Huntington Library, 1988). Thanks to Joshua Phillips for calling this text to my attention.

    4. Jorge Luis Borges, "Magias parciales del *Quijote*," in Jorge Luis Borges, *Otras inquisiciones* (1952; Madrid: Alianza Editorial, Biblioteca Borges, 1997), pp. 74–79. Spanish text, p. 76: "Cervantes se complace en confundir lo objetivo y lo subjetivo, el mundo del lector y el mundo del libro." English translation: "Partial Enchantments of the *Quixote*," in *Other Inquisitions, 1937–1952*, trans. Ruth L. C. Simms (Austin: University of Texas Press, 1964), p. 44.

    5. *Don Quijote de la Mancha*, pp. 1142–43. Spanish text: "y vio tirar en una parte, corregir en otra, componer en esta, enmendar en aquella, y, finalmente, toda aquella máquina que en las emprentas grandes se muestra." Putnam translation, p. 922.

    6. Hieronymus Hornschuch, *Orthotypographia, Hoc est Instructio operas typographicas correcturis, et Admonitio scripta sua in lucem edituris utilis et necessaria)*

(1608). English translation: *Hornschuch's Orthotypographia*, ed. and trans. Philip Gaskell and Patricia Bradford (Cambridge: University Library, 1972).

7. Alonso Víctor de Paredes, *Institución y origen del arte de la imprenta y reglas generales para los componedores*, ed. Jaime Moll (Madrid: El Crotalón, 1984); reprinted with a "Nueva noticia editorial" by Víctor Infantes (Madrid: Calambur, Biblioteca Litterae, 2002).

8. Ibid., fol. 42r–45r.

9. Joseph Moxon, *Mechanick Exercises on the Whole Art of Printing (1683–4)*, ed. Herbert Davis and Harry Carter (London: Oxford University Press, 1958), pp. 311–12.

10. Ibid., p. 247.

11. Melchor de Cabrera Nuñez de Guzman, *Discurso legal, histórico y político en prueba del origen, progressos, utilidad, nobleza y excelencias del Arte de la Imprenta; y de que se le deben (y a sus Artífices) todas las Honras, Exempciones, Inmunidades, Franquezas y Privilegios de Arte Liberal, por ser, como es, Arte de las Artes* (Madrid, 1675), fol. 117v. Spanish text: "porque es en ella (la imprenta) muy superior la parte intelectual, y especulativa, a la operacion manual." Thanks to Fernando Bouza for pointing out the existence of this text, of which there exists a facsimile published by Amalia Sarría Rueda (Madrid: Singular, 1993). On Melchor de Cabrera's writings from 1636 on in defense of fiscal exemptions for printers, see Miguel María Rodríguez San Vincente, "Argumentos historico-jurídicos para la defensa de la inmunidad fiscal del libro español en el siglo XVII," *Cuadernos bibliográficos* 44 (1982): 5–31.

12. Ibid., fol. 15, recto et verso. Spanish text: "El componedor percibe el concepto, y discurso [. . .] Contar bien qualquiera original; porque los Libros no se componen consecutivo, sino alternando el original. [. . .] Hazer interrogacion, admiracion, y parentesis; porque muchas vezes la mente de los Escritores se confunde, por falta de estos requisitos, necessarios, è importantes para el entendimiento, y comprehension de lo que se escrive, ò imprime; porque qualquiera que falte, muda, truëca, y varia el sentido."

13. Ibid. fol. 15, verso. Spanish text: "El Corrector ha de saber, por lo menos Gramatica (ay, y ha avido graduados en diversas Ciencias) Ortografia, Etimologia, Puntuacion, colocacion de acentos; Ha de tener noticia de las Ciencias, y buenas letras, de los caracteros Griëgos, y Hebreos; de reglas de Musica, para sus Libros; Ha de ser dotado de locucion, Arte, y elegancia para conocer, y enmendar barbarismos, solecismos, y los demàs defectos que se hallan en el Latin, Romance, y otras Lenguas." A similar definition of tasks and skills can be found in a 1619 memoir by the proofreader Gonzalo de Ayala and the lawyer Juan de Valdes, who differentiated printers from booksellers on the grounds that printing was a liberal art, but not bookselling. See Víctor Infantes, "La apologia de la imprenta de Gonzalo de Ayala: un texto desconocido en un pleito de impresores del Siglo de Oro," *Cuadernos bibliográficos* 44 (1982): 33–47.

14. Cf. Jeffrey Masten, "Pressing Subjects or, the Secret Lives of Shakespeare's Compositors," in *Language Machines: Technologies of Literary and Cultural Production*, ed. Jeffrey Masten, Peter Stallybrass, and Nancy Vickers (New York and London: Routledge, 1997), pp. 75–107.

15. Cf. Ernst Robert Curtius, *Europaïsche Literatur und lateinisches Mittelalter*

(1947), trans. Jean Bréjoux, *La Littérature européenne et le Moyen Age latin* (Paris: Presses Universitaires de France, 1957), pp. 522–26. English translation: *European Literature and the Latin Middle Ages*, trans. Willard Trask (London: Routledge, 1953).

16. Paredes, *Institución y Origen del Arte de la Imprenta*, fol. 44v. Spanish text: "Assimilo yo un libro à la fabrica de un hombre, el qual consta de anima racional, con que la criò Nuestro Señor con tantas excelencias como su Divina Magestad quiso darle; y con la misma omnipotencia formò al cuerpo galan, hermoso, y apacible."

17. Ibid., fol. 3v–6r, citation fol. 4v. Spanish text: "Puso Dios en la prensa su Imagen, y Sello, para que la copia saliesse cõforme à la que avia de tomar [. . .] y quiso juntamente alegrarse con tantas, y tan varias copias de su mysterioso Original."

18. Paredes, *Institución y Origen del Arte de la Imprenta*, fol. 44v. Spanish text: "un libro perfectamente acabado, el cual constando de buena doctrina, y acertada disposicion del Impresor, y Corrector, que equiparo al alma del libro; y impresso bien en la prensa, con limpieza, y asseo, le puedo comparar al cuerpo airoso y galan."

19. On the rejection of the contrast between "substantive essence" and "accidentals" and an example of the effect of different typographic forms (including format, composition, and punctuation) on meaning, see the pioneering study by D. F. McKenzie, "Typography and Meaning: The Case of William Congreve," in *Buch und Buchhandel in Europa im achtzehnten Jahrhundert*, ed. Giles Barber and Bernhard Fabian (Hamburg: Hauswedell, 1981), pp. 81–125, reprinted in D. F. McKenzie, *Making Meaning: "Printers of the Mind" and Other Essays*, ed. Peter McDonald and Michael F. Suarez, S.J. (Amherst: University of Massachusetts Press, 2002), pp. 198–236.

20. *Don Quijote de la Mancha*, pp. 280, 339, 499. Spanish text: chapter 25, "Bien haya quien nos quitó ahora del trabajo de desenalbardar al rucio"; chapter 29, "Luego subió don Quijote sobre Rocinante, y el barbero se acomodó en su cabalgadura, quedándose Sancho a pie, donde de nuevo se le renovó la pérdida del rucio, con la falta que entonces le hacía"; chapter 42, "Sólo Sancho Panza se desesperaba con la tardanza del recogimiento, y sólo él se acomodó mejor que todos, echándose sobre los aparejos de su jumento." Putnam translation, pp. 202, 252, 386.

21. *Don Quijote de la Mancha*, pp. 1233–35.

22. *Don Quijote de la Mancha*, p. 270. Spanish text: "Despidióse del cabrero don Quijote y, subiendo otra vez sobre Rocinante, mandó a Sancho que le siguiese, el cual lo hizo, con su jumento, de muy mala gana." Putnam translation, p. 195.

23. Francisco Rico, "Historia del texto" and "La presente edición," in *Don Quijote de la Mancha*, pp. CXCII–CCXLII and CCLXXIII–CCLXXXVI.

24. For a magisterial example, see Jean Bollack, *L'Œdipe roi de Sophocle: Le texte et ses interprétations* (Lille: Presses Universitaires de Lille, 1990), vol. 1, *Introduction, Texte, Traduction*, pp. XI–XXI, 1–178.

25. See, for example, Margreta De Grazia and Peter Stallybrass, "The Materiality of the Shakespearean Text," *Shakespeare Quarterly* 44, 3 (1993): 255–83; Leah S. Marcus, *Unediting the Renaissance: Shakespeare, Marlowe, Milton* (London: Routledge, 1996), and Stephen Orgel, "What Is a Text," in *Staging the Renaissance: Reinterpretations of Elizabethan and Jacobean Drama*, ed. David Scott Kastan and Peter Stallybrass (New York: Routledge, 1991), pp. 83–87.

26. D. F. McKenzie, *Bibliography and the Sociology of Texts*, Panizzi Lectures 1985 (London: British Library, 1986), pp. 29–30.

27. Stephen Greenblatt, "Textual Note," in *The Norton Shakespeare Based on the Oxford Edition*, ed. Stephen Greenblatt (New York: W.W. Norton, 1997), pp. 738–40.

28. Francisco Rico, "Prólogo," in Miguel de Cervantes Saavedra, *Don Quijote de la Mancha*, ed. Silvia Iriso y Gonzalo Pontón (Barcelona: Galaxia Gutenberg / Círculo de Lectores, 1998), pp. 22, 20. Spanish text: "Cervantes revoluciona la ficción concibiéndola no en el estilo artificial de la literatura, sino en la prosa doméstica de la vida" and "El *Quijote* no está tanto *escrito* como *dicho*, redactado sin someterse a las constricciones de la escritura: ni las de entonces, con las mañas barrocas requeridas por los estilos en boga, ni, naturalmente, las nuestras."

29. For other examples of this treatment of writing, especially in Milton, see D. F. McKenzie, "Speech-Manuscript-Print," in *New Directions in Textual Studies*, ed. Dave Oliphant and Robin Bradford (Austin: Harry Ransom Humanities Research Center, 1990), pp. 86–109, reprinted in *Making Meaning*, pp. 237–58.

30. *Don Quijote de la Mancha*, p. 1143. Spanish text: "yo sé algún tanto del toscano y me precio de cantar algunas estancias del Ariosto." Putnam translation, p. 922. Cf. Maxime Chevalier, *L'Arioste en Espagne (1530–1650): Recherches sur l'influence du "Roland furieux"* (Bordeaux: Institut d'Études Ibériques et Ibéro-Américaines de l'Université de Bordeaux, 1966).

31. *Don Quijote de la Mancha*, pp. 1143–44. Spanish text: "Yo apostaré una buena apuesta que adonde diga en el toscano *piache*, dise vuesa merced en el castellano 'place', y adonde diga *più* dice 'más', y el *su* declara con 'arriba' y el *giù* con 'abajo'." Putnam translation, p. 923.

32. *Don Quijote de la Mancha*, p. 1144. Spanish text: "me parece que el traducir de una lengua en otra, como no sea de las reinas de las lenguas, griega y latina, es como quien mira los tapices flamencos por el revés, que aunque se veen las figuras, son llenas de hilos que las escurecen y no se veen con la lisura y tez de la haz." Putnam translation, p. 923.

33. *Don Quijote de la Mancha*, p. 1144. Spanish text: "Pero dígame vuestra merced: este libro ¿imprímese por su cuenta o tiene ya vendido el privilegio a algún librero? —Por mi cuenta lo imprimo —respondió el autor— y pienso ganar mil ducados, por lo menos, con esta primera impresión, que ha de ser de dos mil cuerpos, y se han de despachar a seis reales cada uno en daca las pajas." Putnam translation, p. 923.

34. Fernando Bouza, "'Aun en lo material del papel y inpresión'. Sobre la cultura escrita en el Siglo de Gracián," in *Libros libres de Baltasar Gracián*, Exposición bibliográfica, siendo comisario Angel San Vincente Pino (Saragossa: Gobierno de Aragón, 2001), pp. 11–50.

35. Paredes, *Institución y Origen del Arte de la Imprenta*, fol. 43v.

36. Francisco Rico, "Historia del texto," in *Don Quijote de la Mancha*, p. CXCIV.

37. Ian Michael, "How *Don Quixote* came to Oxford: The Two Bodleian Copies of *Don Quixote*, Part I (Madrid: Juan de la Cuesta, 1605)," in *Culture and Society in Habsburg Spain: Studies Presented to R. W. Truman by His Pupils and Colleagues on the Occasion of His Retirement*, ed. Nigel Griffin, Clive Griffin, Eric Southworth, and Colin Thompson (London: Tamesis, 2001), pp. 95–120.

38. *Don Quijote de la Mancha*, p. 1145. Spanish text: "Yo no imprimo mis libros

para alcanzar fama en el mundo, que ya en él soy conocido por mis obras: provecho quiero, que sin él no vale un cuatrín la buena fama." Putnam translation, p. 924.

39. See, for example, the contracts that Parisian booksellers signed with the translator Nicolas de Herberay for his translations of *Amadis de Gaule* in 1540 and 1542, and Palmerin in 1543, published in Annie Parent, *Les métiers du livre à Paris au XVIe siècle (1535–1560)* (Geneva: Droz, 1974), pp. 300–304.

40. Sebastián de Covarrubias Orozco, *Tesoro de la lengua castellana o Española*, (1611), ed. Felipe C. R. Maldonado, rev. Manuel Camarero (Madrid: Editorial Castalia, 1995): "Trasladar: Vale algunas veces interpretar alguna escritura de una lengua en otra; y también vale copiar," p. 933.

41. *Don Quijote de la Mancha*, p. 619. Spanish text: "una de las mayores [tentaciones del demonio] es ponerle a un hombre en el entendimiento que puede componer y imprimir un libro con que gane tanta fama como dineros y tantos dineros cuanta fama." Putnam translation, p. 506.

42. *Don Quijote de la Mancha*, p. 1145. Spanish text: "¡Bien está vuesa merced en la cuenta ! —respondió don Quijote—. Bien parece que no sabe las entradas y salidas de los impresores y las correspondencias que hay de unos a otros. Yo le prometo que cuando se vea cargado de dos mil cuerpos de libros vea tan molido su cuerpo, que se espante, y más si el libro es un poco avieso y nonada picante." Putnam trnaslation, p. 923.

43. Deception by printers to conceal the true number of copies printed when books were published for the author's account was denounced in the first manual for confessors concerning the typographic art. This was written in Latin by Juan Caramuel Lobkowitz, abbot of the monastery of Emmaüs in Prague and later bishop of Satriano and Campagna. It can be found in the *Theologia moralis fundamentalis*, vol. 4, *Theologia praeterintentionalis* (Lyon, 1664), pp. 185–200. For a recent edition of this text, which cites Cervantes in support of its condemnation, see Juan Caramuel, *Syntagma de Arte Typographica*, ed. Andrés Escapa (Salamanca: Instituto de Historia del Libro y de la Lectura, 2004), pp. 134–43.

44. Miguel de Cervantes, "Novela del licenciado vidriera," in *Novelas ejemplares*, Edición, prólogo y notas de Jorge García López (Barcelona: Crítica, 2001), pp. 265–301. English translation: *Three Exemplary Novels*, trans. Samuel Putnam (Westport, Conn.: Greenwood Press, 1982). Spanish text, p. 285: "Arrimóse un día con grandísimo tiento, porque no se quebrase, a las tiendas de un librero, y díjole: —Este oficio me contentara mucho, si no fuera por una falta que tiene. Preguntóle el librero se la dijese. Respondióle: —Los melindres que hacen cuando compran un privilegio de un libro y de la burla que hacen a su autor si acaso le imprime a su costa, pues en lugar de mil y quinientos, imprimen tres mil libros, y cuando el autor piensa que se venden los suyos, se despachan los ajenos."

45. See Fernando Bouza, "Para qué imprimir: De autores, públicos, impresores y manuscritos en el Siglo de Oro," *Cuadernos de Historia Moderna* 18 (1997): 31–50.

46. *Don Quijote de la Mancha*, p. 1145. Spanish text: "Dios le dé a vuesa merced buena manderecha —respondió don Quijote." Putnam translation, p. 924.

47. Here I am following the brilliant argument of Francisco Rico, *Visita de imprentas: Páginas y noticias de Cervantes viejo*, dissertation defense, University of Valladolid, 1996.

48. *Don Quijote de la Mancha*, p. 1145. Spanish text: "Estos tales libros, aunque hay muchos deste género, son los que se deben imprimir, porque son muchos los pecadores que se usan y son menester infinitas luces para tantos desalumbrados." Putnam translation, p. 924.

49. *Don Quijote de la Mancha*, pp. 1145–46. Spanish text: "Pasó adelante y vio que asimesmo estaban corrigiendo otro libro, y, preguntando su título, le respondieron que se llamaba la *Segunda parte del ingenioso hidalgo don Quijote de la Mancha*, compuesta por un tal, vecino de Tordesillas. —Ya yo tengo noticias deste libro —dijo don Quijote." Putnam translation, p. 924.

50. Alonso Fernández de Avellaneda, *El Ingenioso hidalgo Don Quijote de la Mancha*, ed. Fernando García Salinero (Madrid: Clásicos Castalia, 1971). Cf. Edward C. Riley, "Three Versions of *Don Quijote*," *Modern Language Review* 68 (1973): 807–19.

51. *Don Quijote de la Mancha*, p. 591. Spanish text: "el autor desta historia, puesto que con curiosidad y diligencia ha buscado los hechos que don Quijote hizo en su tercera salida, no ha podido hallar noticia de ellas, a lo menos por escrituras auténticas: solo la fama ha guardado, en las memorias de la Mancha, que don Quijote la tercera vez que salió de su casa fue a Zaragoza, donde se halló en una famosas justas que en aquella ciudad se hicieron." Putnam translation, p. 459.

52. Pedro Malo, cf. Lluís C. Viada i Llluch, "L'estampa barcelonina d'En Pere i d'En Pau Malo davant de la rectoria del Pi: una conjectura cervàntica," *Bulletí de la Biblioteca de Catalunya* 4 (1925): 225–37. Thanks to Manuel Peña for pointing out this article.

53. This hypothesis is endorsed by Rico in *Visitas de imprentas*, pp. 48–49. Rico notes that in the same year, 1614, that the continuation of Avellaneda appeared, Sebastián de Cormellas also printed a new edition of the *Obras de Ludovico Blesio*.

54. Cf. Ian Michael, "How *Don Quixote* Came to Oxford," p. 97.

55. Cf. Luis Gómez Canseco, "Introduccón," in Fernández de Avellaneda, *El Ingenioso hidalgo Don Quijote de la Mancha*, pp. 29–59, "Pesquisa en torno a Avellaneda."

56. *Don Quijote de la Mancha*, pp. 1110–11. Spanish text: "Por vida de vuestra merced, señor don Jerónimo, que en tanto que traen la cena leamos otro capítulo de la segunda parte de *Don Quijote de la Mancha*. —¿Para qué quiere vuestra merced, señor don Juan, que leamos estos disparates, si el que hubiere leído la primera parte de la historia de don Quijote de la Mancha no es posible que pueda tener gusto en leer este segunda?" Putnam translation, p. 895.

57. *Don Quijote de la Mancha*, pp. 646–56.

58. The figure is entirely plausible, given the fact that between 1605 and 1615 the book went through three editions in Madrid (two in 1605, one in 1608), two editions in Lisbon in 1605, one edition in Valencia, two in Brussels (1607 and 1611), and one in Milan (1610). Cf. Michael, "How *Don Quixote* Came to Oxford," pp. 116–17.

59. *Don Quijote de la Mancha*, p. 655. Spanish text: "algunos han puesto falta y dolo en la memoria del autor, pues se le olvida de contar quien fue el ladrón que hurtó el rucio a Sancho, que allí no se declara, y solo se infiere de lo escrito que se le hurtaron, y de allí a poco lo vemos a caballo sobre el mesmo jumento, sin haber parecido." Putnam translation, p. 532.

60. *Don Quijote de la Mancha*, p. 657. Spanish text: "el yerro [está] en que antes de haber parecido el jumento dice el autor que iba a caballo Sancho en el mesmo rucio —A eso —dijo Sancho— no sé que responder, sino que el historiador se engañó, o ya sería descuido del impresor. " Putnam translation, p. 534.

61. Jorge Luis Borges, "Magias parciales del *Quijote*," [1952], in Borges, *Otras inquisiciones*, p. 79: "¿Por qué nos inquieta que Don Quijote sea lector del *Quijote* y Hamlet espectador de *Hamlet*? Creo haber dado con la causa: tales inversiones sugieren que si los caracteres de una ficción pueden ser lectores o espectadores, nosotros, sus lectores o espectadores, podemos ser ficticios." English translation: "Partial Enchantments of the *Quixote*," in *Other Inquisitions, 1937–1952*, p. 46.

62. *Don Quijote de la Mancha*, p. 1115. Spanish text: "no pondré los pies en Zaragoza y así sacaré a la plaza del mundo la mentira dese historiador moderno, y echarán de ver las gentes como yo no soy el don Quijote que él dice." Putnam translation, p. 898.

63. *Don Quijote de la Mancha*, p. 1112. Spanish text: "la tercera, que más le confirma por ignorante, es que yerra y se desvía de la verdad en lo más principal de la historia, porque aquí dice que la mujer de Sancho Panza mi escudero se llama Mari Gutiérrez, y no llama tal, sino Teresa Panza: y quien en esta parte tan principal yerra, bien se podrá temer que yerra en todas las demás de la historia." Putnam translation, p. 896.

64. Cf. Edward C. Riley, "Who's Who in *Don Quijote*? Or, Approach to the Problem of Identity," *Modern Language Notes* 81 (1966): 113–30.

65. *Don Quijote de la Mancha*, p. 1131. Spanish text: "Bien sea venido el valeroso don Quijote de la Mancha: no el falso, no el ficticio, no el apócrifo que en falsas historias estos días nos han mostrado, sino el verdadero, el legal y el fiel que nos describió Cide Hamete Benengeli, flor de los historiadores. [. . .] —Estos bien nos han conocido: yo apostaré que han leído nuestra historia, y aun la del aragonés recién impresa." Putnam translation, p. 912.

66. *Don Quijote de la Mancha*, p. 1146. Spanish text: "en verdad y en mi conciencia que pensé que ya estaba quemado y hecho polvos por impertinente." Putnam translation, p. 912.

67. *Don Quijote de la Mancha*, p. 1195. Spanish text: "'Mirad qué libro es ese.' Y el diablo le respondió: 'Esta es la *Segunda parte de la historia de don Quijote de la Mancha*, no compuesta por Cide Hamete Benengeli, su primer autor, sino por un aragonés, que él dice ser natural de Tordesillas'. 'Quitádmele de ahí —respondió el otro diablo— y metedle en los abismos del infierno, no lo vean más mis ojos.' '¿Tan malo es? —respondió el otro.' 'Tan malo —replicó el primero—, que si de propósito yo mismo me pusiera a hacerle peor, no acertara'." Putnam translation, pp. 965–66.

68. *Don Quijote de la Mancha*, p. 1208. Spanish text: "no conocía a don Quijote de la Mancha, que asimismo estaba allí presente, y que no era aquel que andaba impreso en una historia intitulada *Segunda parte de don Quijote de la Mancha*, compuesta por un tal de Avellaneda, natural de Tordesillas." Putnam translation, p. 976.

69. Mateo Alemán, *Guzmán de Alfarache*, Edición, introducción y notas de Francisco Rico (Barcelona: Planeta, 1983), p. 708. Spanish text: "Se mareó Sayavedra;

dióle una calentura, saltóle a modorra y perdió el juicio. Dice que él es Guzmán de Alfarache y con la locura se arrojó a la mar, quedando ahogado en ella." English translation: *The Rogue, or the Life of Guzman de Alfarache*, trans. James Mabbe (New York: Knopf, 1924).

70. Jorge Luis Borges, "Magias parciales del *Quijote*" [1952], in Borges, *Otras inquisiciones*, pp. 76–75. Spanish text: "A las vastas y vagas geografías del Amadís opone los polvorientos caminos y los sórdidos mesones de Castilla." English translation: "Partial Enchantments of the *Quixote*," in *Other Inquisitions, 1937–1952*, p. 43.

71. *Don Quijote de la Mancha*, pp. 1220–21. Spanish text: "Iten, suplico a los dichos señores mis albaceas que si la buena suerte les trujere a conocer el autor que dicen que compuso una historia que anda por ahí con el título de *Segunda parte de las hazañas de don Quijote de la Mancha*, de mi parte le pidan, cuan encarecidamente ser pueda, perdone la ocasión que sin yo pensarlo le di de haber escrito tantos y tan grandes disparates como en ella escribe, porque parto desta vida con escrúpulo de haberle dado motivo para escribirlos." Putnam translation, p. 987.

72. *Don Quijote de la Mancha*, p. 1217. Spanish text: "Yo tengo juicio ya libre y claro, sin las sombras caliginosas de la ignorancia que sobre él me pusieron mi amarga y continua leyenda de los detestables libros de las caballerías." Putnam translation, p. 984.

73. *Don Quijote de la Mancha*, p. 1217. Spanish text: "Dadme albricias, buenos señores, de que ya no soy don Quijote de la Mancha, sino Alonso Quijano, a quien mis costumbres me dieron renombre de 'bueno'." Putnam translation, p. 984.

74. Francisco Rico, "Quexana," *Euphrosyne: Revista de Filología Clásica* 22 (1994): 431–39.

75. *Don Quijote de la Mancha*, p. 42. Spanish text: "se vino a llamar 'don Quijote.'"

76. *Don Quijote de la Mancha*, p. 1220. Spanish text: "Yo fui loco y ya soy cuerdo; fui don Quijote de la Mancha y soy agora, como he dicho, Alonso Quijano el Bueno. Pueda con vuestras mercedes mi arrepentimiento y mi verdad volverme a la estimación que de mí se tenía." Putnam translation, p. 986.

77. *Don Quijote de la Mancha*, p. 35. Spanish text: "un hidalgo de los de lanza en astillero, adarga antigua, rocín flaco y galgo corredor." Putnam translation, p. 25. On the historic identity indicated by this description, see the splendid essay by Pierre Vilar, "Le temps du 'Quichotte'," *Europe* (January-February 1956): 3–16, reprinted in Vilar, *Une histoire en construction: Approche marxiste et problématiques conjoncturelles* (Paris: Gallimard, 1982), pp. 233–246.

78. *Don Quijote de la Mancha*, p. 40. Spanish text: "fue que le pareció convenible y necesario, así para el aumento de su honra como para el servicio de su república, hacerse caballero andante y irse por todo el mundo con sus armas y caballo a buscar las aventuras y a ejercitarse en todo aquello que él había leído que los caballeros andantes se ejercitaban." Putnam translation, p. 27.

79. *Don Quijote de la Mancha*, pp. 36–37. Spanish text: "Quieren decir que tenía el sobrenombre de 'Quijada' o 'Quesada', que en esto hay alguna diferencia en los autores que deste caso escriben, aunque por conjeturas verisímiles se deja entender que se llamaba 'Quijana'." Putnam translation, pp. 25–26.

80. Francisco Rico, "La *princeps* del Lazarillo: Título, capitulación y epígrafes

de un texto apócrifo," in Rico, *Problemas del Lazarillo* (Madrid: Cátedra, 1988), pp. 113–151.

81. Peter Stallybrass, "Shakespeare, the Individual, and the Text," in *Cultural Studies*, ed. Lawrence Grossberg, Cary Nelson, and Paula A. Treichler (New York: Routledge, 1992), pp. 593–612; Random Cloud, "'The Very Names of the Persons': Editing and the Inventions of Dramatic Character," in *Staging the Renaissance*, pp. 88–96.

82. This was the case with novels of chivalry in the second half of the sixteenth century, when new works in a genre abandoned by the presses circulated as manuscript copies. José Manuel Lucía Megías, *De los libros de caballerías manuscritos al Quijote* (Madrid: SIAL Ediciones, Colección Trivium, 2004).

83. Nuñez de Guzman, *Discurso legal, histórico y polític*, fol. 23r. Spanish text: "gustô que la escriviessen su nombre en la palma de la mano; y sacaba las letras de los caxonzillos, donde la dezían estaban, y las ponía en el componedor".

84. Ibid., fol. 23r. Spanish text: "Su Magestad entrò en la Oficina, mandô à los Artifices, no se mudassen de sus puestos, y asientos, sino que continûassen su exercicio en la forma que se hallaban; y quando llegaba à las Caxas, el rato que se detenia en ver componer, descansaba la mano en el ombro izquierdo del Componedor."

85. *Don Quijote de la Mancha*, p. 1143. Spanish text: "Llegábase don Quijote a un cajón y preguntaba qué era aquello que allí se hacía; dábanle cuenta los oficiales; admirábase y pasaba adelante." Putnam translation, p. 922.

Chapter 4. Handwritten Newsletters, Printed Gazettes: Cymbal and Butter

1. Ben Jonson, *The Staple of Newes*, in Ben Jonson, *Complete Works*, ed. C. H. Herford Percy and Evelyn Simpson, vol. 6 (Oxford: Clarendon Press, 1938), pp. 273–381 (English quotations are from this edition). Other editions: Ben Jonson, *The Staple of News*, ed. De Winter (New York: Henry Holt, 1905); Ben Jonson, *The Staple of News*, ed. Devra Rowland Kifer (Lincoln: University of Nebraska Press, 1975); and Ben Jonson, *The Staple of News*, ed. Anthony Parr (Manchester: Manchester University Press, 1988).

2. On the Folio of 1616, see Jennifer Brady and W. H. Herendeen, eds., *Ben Jonson's 1616 Folio* (Newark: University of Delaware Press, 1991), and Joseph Loewenstein, *Ben Jonson and Posssessive Authorship* (Cambridge: Cambridge University Press, 2002). For a comparison with Shakespeare's Folio of 1623, see Margreta de Grazia, *Shakespeare Verbatim: The Reproduction of Authenticity and the 1790 Apparatus* (Oxford: Clarendon Press, 1991), pp. 29–41.

3. Ben Jonson, *Newes from the New World Discover'd in the Moone*, in *Complete Works*, vol. 7 (1941) , pp. 511–25, quotation pp. 514–15.

4. Ibid., p. 515.

5. This, at any rate, is the hypothesis put forward by De Winter in Jonson, *The Staple of News*, pp. XXV–XXXI.

6. *The Staple of Newes*, pp. 285–89.

7. Ibid., p. 286. Pennyboy Junior: "What is't, an *Office*, Thom?" Thomas: "Newly erected / Here in the house, almost on the same floore, / Where all the newes

of all sorts shall be brought, / And there be examin'd, and then registred, / And so be issu'd under the Seal of the *Office*, / As *Staple Newes*; no other newes be currant."

8. See the description in Francis Osborne, *Traditionall memoyres of the raigne of King James*, 1658: "It was fashion of those times, and did so continue 'till these for the principall Gentry, Lords, Courtiers and men of all professions not meerely Mechanick, to meet in *Pauls Church* by eleven, and walk in the middle Ile till twelve, and after dinner from three to six; during which time some discoursed commerce, others of Newes." Quoted in Harold Love, *Scribal Publication in Seventeenth-Century England* (Oxford: Oxford University Press, 1993), p. 193.

9. *The Staple of Newes*, p. 288.

10. Ibid., p. 293.

11. Ibid., p. 295.

12. Francis Goyet, *Le sublime du "lieu commun": L'invention rhétorique à la Renaissance* (Paris: H. Champion, 1996).

13. See Folke Dahl, *Dutch Corantos 1618–1650: A Bibliography Illustrated with 334 Facsimile Reproductions of Corantos Printed 1618–1625 and an Introductory Essay on Seventeenth Century Stop Press News* (Göteborg, 1945), and Otto Lankhorst, "Newspapers in the Netherlands in the Seventeenth Century," in *The Politics of Information in Early Modern Europe*, ed. Brendan Dooley and Sabrina A. Baron (London: Routledge, 2001), pp. 150–59.

14. For a compilation of the earliest English periodicals, see Folke Dahl, *A Bibliography of English Corantos and Periodical Newsbooks 1620–1642* (London: Bibliographical Society, 1952). Cf. C. John Sommerville, *The News Revolution in England: Cultural Dynamics of Daily Information* (New York: Oxford University Press, 1996), and Joad Raymond, *The Invention of the Newspaper: English Newsbooks 1641–1649* (Oxford: Clarendon Press, 1996).

15. Quoted in Dahl, *Bibliography of English Corantos*, p. 19.

16. Cf. Appendix B. The Staple and the News Syndicate, in *The Staple of News*, ed. Anthony Parr, pp. 258–59. The six partners were Archer, Bourne, Butter, Downes, Newbery, and Sheffard.

17. Mark H. Curtis, "The Alienated Intellectuals of Early Stuart England," *Past and Present* 23 (1962): 25–43, and Roger Chartier, "Espace social et imaginaire social: Les intellectuels frustrés au XVIIe siècle," *Annales E.S.C.* (1982): 389–400. English translation: "Time to Understand: The 'Frustrated Intellectuals,'" in Chartier, *Cultural History: Between Practices and Representations*, trans. Lydia Cochrance (Ithaca, N.Y.: Cornell University Press, 1988), pp. 127–50.

18. *The Staple of News*, p. 293.

19. Ibid., p. 295.

20. Jonson, *Newes from the New World*, p. 515.

21. William Shakespeare, *The Winter's Tale*, in William Shakespeare, *The Complete Works*, ed. Stanley Wells and Gary Taylor (Oxford: Oxford University Press, 1988), p. 1120.

22. *The Staple of Newes*, p. 295.

23. Ibid. The text reads: "Why, me thinkes Sir, if the honest common people / Will be abus'd, why should not they ha' their pleasure, / In the believing Lyes, are made for them; / As you i'th' *Office*, making them your selves?"

24. Ibid.

25. Cf. Steven Shapin, *A Social History of Truth. Civility and Science in Seventeenth-Century England* (Chicago: University of Chicago Press, 1994), and Adrian Johns, *The Nature of the Book: Print and Knowledge in the Making* (Chicago: University of Chicago Press, 1998).

26. *Newes from the New World*, p. 515.

27. *The Staple of Newes*, p. 295.

28. Ibid., p. 296.

29. Ibid., p. 296.

30. Quote from Somerville, *The News Revolution*, p. 28.

31. Ibid.

32. Ibid., pp. 31–32.

33. Quoted in Dahl, *Bibliography of English Corantes*, p. 23.

34. Ibid., p. 22. Of 349 printed gazettes published between 1620 and 1642, only 508 individual copies have survived, whereas the total number of issues published can be estimated as at least 1,000 and the total number of copies published at 400,000 (assuming a print run of 400 copies per issue).

35. *The Staple of Newes*, p. 328.

36. Ibid., p. 325.

37. Ibid.

38. See the analysis of Stuart Sherman, "Eyes and Ears, News and Plays: The Argument of Ben Jonson's *Staple*," in *The Politics of Information*, pp. 23–40, esp. pp. 34–38.

39. *The Staple of Newes*, p. 329. Fitton says: "Witnesse the Engine, that they have presented him, / To winde himselfe with, up, into the *Moone*: / And thence make all his discoveries."

40. Ibid., p. 328.

41. See Paul R. Sellin, "The Politics of Ben Jonson's *Newes from the New World Discover'd in the Moone*," *Viator: Medieval and Renaissance Studies* 17 (1986): 321–37.

42. *The Staple of Newes*, p. 337. Customer 4: "All the countrey /Expected from the city most brave speeches, / Now, at the Coronation."

43. Ibid., p. 331. Register: "'Tis the house of *fame*, Sir, / Where both the curious, and the negligent; / The scrupulous, and carelesse; wilde, and stay'd; / The idle, and laborious; all doe meet,/ To tast the *Cornu copiae* of her rumors, / Which she, the mother of sport, pleaseth to scatter / Among the vulgar."

44. Ibid., p. 334. "There is the *Legacy* left to the *Kings Players*, / Both for their various shifting of their *Scene*, / And dext'rous change o' their persons to all shapes, / And all disguises: by the right reverend. / *Archbishop of Spalato*."

45. Thomas Middleton, *A Game at Chess*, ed. T. H. Howard-Hill (Manchester: Mancheser University Press, 1993), and Thomas Middleton, *The Bridgewater Manuscript of Thomas Middleton's A Game at Chess (1624)*, ed. T. H. Howard-Hill (Lewiston, N.Y.: Edwin Mellen, 1995). See also F. J. Levy, "Staging the News," in *Print, Manuscript, Performance: The Changing Relations of the Media in Early Modern England*, ed. Arthur F. Marotti and Michael D. Bristol (Columbus: Ohio State University Press, 2000), pp. 252–78.

46. *The Staple of Newes*, p. 334. Lickfinger: "What newes of *Gundomar*?"

Thomas: "A second *Fistula*, / Or an *excoriation* (at the least) / For putting the poore *English-play*, was writ of him, / To such a sordid use, as (is said) he did. / Of cleansing his *posterior's.*"

47. Ibid., p. 366.

48. The emphasis on Jonson's paradoxical relation to print can be found in the interpretations of Sommerville, *The News Revolution*, p. 31 ("It wounded him to think that print was adding its authority to something so insubstantial as the news, and that attention that might have been devoted to the great themes of the English stage should be squandered on gossip"), and Julie Sanders, *Ben Jonson's Theatrical Republics* (London: Macmillan, 1998), p. 135 ("A crucial paradox of print is that although it was the medium expected [certainly by Jonson] to bring new depths of consideration and greater durability to already-circulating manuscripts, it was itself highly dependent upon surface appearance, and matters of immediacy, fashion, and the visual").

49. Cf. Raymond, *The Invention of the Newspaper*, p. 92 ("The anxieties which Jonson expressed in the 1620s over the power of the journalist to supplant the poet as counselor to princes were not fully realized by the corantos of the 1620s and 1630s; but they were by the 1640's newsbooks "), and Sellin, "The Politics of Ben Jonson's *Newes*," pp. 330–31, who argues that Jonson supported the king's position that "mysteries of church and state were not for the common mind, and to air them publicly came near to infringing upon the royal prerogative."

50. D. F. McKenzie, "The *Staple of News* and the Late Plays," in *A Celebration of Ben Jonson*, ed. Wiklliam Blissett (Toronto: University of Toronto Press, 1973), pp. 83–128, reprinted in D. F. McKenzie, *Making Meaning: "Printers of the Mind" and Other Essays*, ed. Peter McDonald and Muchael Suarez, S.J. (Amherst: University of Massachusetts Press, 2002), pp. 169–97, esp. "*The Staple of News* marks the end of theatre as the only secular mass medium, the end of the play-house as the principal forum of public debate, the end of actor's popular function as the abstracts and brief chronicles of the time. The dramatic poet, as rhetor in the truest sense, has lost his vocation to the journalist."

51. *Newes of the New World*, p. 514.

52. Love, *Scribal Publication*, pp. 9–12. By way of comparison, for France, see François Moureau, "Préface," in Moureau, *Répertoire des nouvelles à la main: Dictionnaire de la presse manuscrite clandestine XVIe-XVIIIe siècle* (Oxford: Voltaire Foundation, 1999), pp. VII–XXXVII, and François Moureau, "Les nouvelles à la main dans le système d'information de l'Ancien Régime," in *De bonne main: La communication manuscrite au XVIIIe siècle*, ed. François Moureau (Paris, Universitas; Oxford, Voltaire Foundation, 1993), pp. 117–34; and for Spain, Fernando Bouza, *Corre manuscrito: Una historia cultural del Siglo de Oro* (Madrid: Marcial Pons, 2001), pp. 136–77.

53. The letter from Henry Ball to Sir Joseph Williamson is quoted in Love, *Scribal Publication*, pp. 130–31.

54. This hypothesis is due to Sabrina A. Baron, "The Guises of Dissemination in Early Seventeenth-Century England: News in Manuscript and Print," in *The Politics of Information*, ed. Dooley and Baron, pp. 41–56.

55. See the data in Love, *Scribal Publication*, pp. 11–12, and Baron, "The Guises of Dissemination.

56. On John Pory, cf. William S. Powell, *John Pory, 1572–1636: The Life and*

Letters of a Man of Many Parts (Chapel Hill: University of North Carolina Press, 1977); Love, *Scribal Publication*, p. 14; and Baron, "The Guises of Dissemination," pp. 45–46.

57. D. F. McKenzie insists on the close relationship between copyists and printers and between handwritten newsletters and printed gazettes in "The London Book Trade in the Later Seventeenth Century," Cambridge, Sandars Lectures, 1976, typescript, p. 5. I wish to thank Mark Bland for providing me with a copy of these lectures by McKenzie, which have never been published.

58. As Winter explicitly recognizes in his edition of the play, when he says (Introduction, p. xliv) that "I believe it [the staple-office] to be a composite of various features of the newsmongering of the time."

59. *The Staple of Newes*, p. 332.

60. Tessa Watt, *Cheap Print and Popular Piety 1550–1640* (Cambridge: Cambridge University Press, 1991), pp. 11–12.

61. Raymond, *The Invention of the Newspaper*, p. 230.

62. Love, *Scribal Publication*, p. 131.

63. Baron, "The Guises of Dissemination," p. 48.

64. To borrow an expression from Sherman, "Eyes and Ears," p. 30.

65. *Newes of the New World*, p. 519. The first herald is speaking.

Chapter 5. Talking Books and Clandestine Manuscripts: The Travels of Dyrcona

1. Cyrano de Bergerac, *L'Autre monde ou les états et empires de la Lune*, in *Œuvres complètes*, vol. 1, ed. Madeleine Alcover (Paris: H. Champion, 2000), pp. 1–161, quote pp. 136–37. As the notes will make clear, this essay is greatly indebted to the philological and critical work of Madeleine Alcover. The English translations are taken from Cyrano de Bergerac, *Voyages to the Moon and the Sun*, trans. Richard Aldington (New York: Orion, 1962).

2. Josef Balogh, "Voces paginarum. Beiträge zur Geschichte des lauten Lesens und Schreibens," *Philologus* 82 (1926–27): 84–109, 202–40, and Bernard M. W. Knox, "Silent Reading in Antiquity," *Greek, Roman, and Byzantine Studies* 9 (1968): 421–35.

3. Spanish text: "Cuando he de escribir una comedia, / Encierro los preceptos con seis llaves; / Saco a Terencio y Plauto de mi estudio, / Para que no den voces, porque suele / Dar gritos la verdad en libros mudos," in Lope de Vegas, *Arte nuevo de hacer comedias en este tiempo* (1609), in *Lope de Vega esencial*, ed. Felipe Pedraza (Madrid: Taurus, 1990), pp. 124–34.

4. Cyrano de Bergerac, *Œuvres complètes*, vol. 1, p. 137. French text: "Sachant lire aussitôt que parler, ils ne sont jamais sans lecture; dans la chambre, à la promenade, en ville, en voyage, à pied, à cheval, ils peuvent avoir dans la poche, ou pendus à l'arçon de leurs selles, une trentaine de ces livres dont ils n'ont qu'à bander un ressort pour en ouïr un chapitre seulement, ou bien plusieurs, s'ils sont en humeur d'écouter un livre. Ainsi vous avez éternellement autour de vous les grands hommes et morts et vivants qui vous entretiennent de vive voix."

5. Henri-Jean Martin, *Livre, pouvoirs et société à Paris au XVIIe siècle (1598–1701)* (Geneva: Droz, 1969), vol. 2, pp. 597–98 and Plate III, 2, p. 1064.

6. Cyrano de Bergerac, *Œuvres complètes*, vol. 1, p. 66; English translation, p. 81. French text: "C'est une invention toute ensemble bien utile et bien agréable; car quand ils sont las de parler, ou quand ils dédaignent de prostituer leur gorge à cet usage, ils prennent tantôt un luth, tantôt un autre instrument, dont ils se servent aussi bien que de la voix à se communiquer leurs pensées; de sorte que quelquefois ils se rencontreront jusqu'à quinze ou vingt de compagnie, qui agiteront un point de théologie ou les difficultés d'un procès, par un concert le plus harmonieux dont on puisse chatouiller l'oreille."

7. Francis Godwin, *L'Homme dans la lune ou le voyage chimérique fait au Monde de la Lune, nouvellement découvert par Dominique Gonzales, Adventurier Espagnol, autrement dit le Courrier Volant* (Paris: Piat et Guignard, 1648).

8. See M. B. Parkes, *Pause and Effect: An Introduction to the History of Punctuation in the West* (Berkeley: University of California Press, 1993), and Roger Chartier, "The Text Between the Voice and the Book," in *Text, Hypertext: Emerging Practrices in Textual Studies*, ed. Raimonda Modiano, Leroy F. Searle, and Peter Dhillingsburg (Seattle: University of Washington Press, 2004), pp. 54–71.

9. See Ronsard, "Au Lecteur," *Les Quatre premiers livres de la Franciade* (1572), in *Œuvres complètes*, ed. Gustave Cohen (Paris: N.R.F., Bibliothèque de la Pléiade, 1950), vol. 2, pp. 1009–13, and Georges Forestier, "Lire Racine," in Racine, *Œuvres complètes*, vol. 1, *Théâtre-Poésie*, ed. Georges Forestier (Paris: Gallimard, Bibliothèque de La Pléiade, 1999), pp. LVIX–LXVIII.

10. See Joseph Moxon, *Mechanick Exercises on the Whole Art of Printing (1683–4)*, ed. Herbert Davis and Harry Carter (Oxford: Oxford University Press, 1958), pp. 216–17, and Louis Van Delft, "Principes d'édition," in La Bruyère, *Les Caractères*, ed. Louis Van Delft (Paris, Imprimerie Nationale, 1988), pp. 45–57.

11. Francis Yates, *The French Academies of the Sixteenth Century* (London: Warburg Institute, 1947).

12. Cyrano de Bergerac, *Œuvres complètes*, vol. 1, pp. 66–67; translation, p. 82. French text: "L'agitation, par exemple, d'un doigt, d'une main, d'une oreille, d'une lèvre, d'un bras, d'une joue, feront chacun en particulier une oraison ou une période avec tous ses membres. D'autres ne servent qu'à désigner des mots, comme un pli sur le front, les divers frissonnements des muscles, les renversements des mains, les battements de pied, les contorsions de bras de façon qu'alors qu'ils parlent, avec la coutume qu'ils ont prise d'aller tout nus, leurs membres, accoutumés à gesticuler leurs conceptions, se remuent si dru, qu'il ne semble pas d'un homme qui parle, mais d'un corps qui tremble."

13. Cyrano de Bergerac, *Histoire comique par Monsieur Cyrano de Bergerac Contenant les Estats et Empires de la Lune* (Paris: Charles de Sercy, 1657).

14. Jacques Prévot, *Cyrano de Bergerac romancier* (Paris: Belin, 1977), p. 15. See also his introductory "Notice" to *L'Autre monde*, in *Libertins du XVIIe siècle*, vol. 1, ed. Jacques Prévot (Paris: Gallimard, Bibliothèque de la Pléiade, 1988), pp. 1543–57.

15. René Pintard, *Le Libertinage érudit dans la première moitié du XVIIe siècle*, (1943; Geneva: Slatkine, 1983), pp. 329–330.

16. This is Madeleine Alcover's position in *La pensée philosophique et scientifique de Cyrano de Bergerac* (Geneva: Droz, 1970).

17. This is the position taken by Jacques Prévot in *Cyrano de Bergerac romancier*.

18. Madeleine Alcover, "Analyse," in Cyrano de Bergerac, *Œuvres complètes*, vol. 1, pp. CLXXXVII–CLXXXVIII.

19. Cyrano de Bergerac, *Œuvres complètes*, vol. 1, p. 7–8; translation, p. 46. French text: "J'étais de retour à mon logis et, pour me délasser de la promenade, j'étais à peine entré dans ma chambre quand, sur ma table, je trouvai un livre ouvert que je n'y avais point mis. . . . C'étaient les oeuvres de Cardan."

20. Jerôme Cardan (Hieronymus Cardanus, Girolamo Cardano), *Les Livres de Hiéronime Cardanus médecin milanais, intitulez de la subtilité et subtiles inventions, ensemble les causes occultes et raisons d'icelles* (Paris: Cavellat, 1578).

21. Cyrano de Bergerac, *Œuvres complètes*, vol 1, p. 8. French text: "Je pris toute cette enchaînure d'incidents pour une inspiration de Dieu qui me poussait à faire connaître que la lune est un monde."

22. See Anthony Grafton, *Cardano's Cosmos: The World and Works of a Renaissance Astrologer* (Cambridge, Mass.: Harvard University Press, 1999).

23. Cyrano de Bergerac, *Œuvres complètes*, vol. 1, p. 55; translation, p. 77. French text: "Un jour, entre autres, j'apparus à Cardan comme il étudiait; je l'instruisis de quantité de choses, et en récompense il me promit qu'il témoignerait à la postérité de qui il tenait les miracles qu'il s'attendait d'écrire."

24. Ibid., p. 61; translation, p. 78. French text: "Je suis né dans le soleil. Mais parce que quelquefois notre monde se trouve trop peuplé, à cause de la longue vie de ses habitants, et qu'il est presque exempt de guerres et de maladies, de temps en temps nos magistrats envoient des colonies dans les mondes d'autour."

25. Ibid., p. 135; translation, p. 135. French text: ". . . prouve que toutes les choses sont vraies, et déclare la façon d'unir physiquement les vérités de chaque contradictoire, comme par exemple que le blanc est noir et que le noir est blanc; qu'on peut être et n'être pas en même temps; qu'il peut y avoir une montagne sans vallée; que le néant est quelque chose et que toutes les choses qui sont ne sont point." On these various interpretations, see Madeleine Alcover's note on lines 2745–55.

26. *Nouvelles oeuvres de Monsieur Cyrano de Bergerac contenant l'Histoire comique des Estats et Empires du Soleil, plusieurs lettres et autres pièces divertissantes* (Paris: Charles de Sercy, 1662). In Cyrano de Bergerac, *Œuvres complètes*, vol. 1, pp. 163–343.

27. On the difficult problem of the date of composition of Cyrano's two works, which preceded their appearance in print by ten years, see the overview in Alcover, "Analyse," pp. CLIII–CLVII; for the reference to Davity's work, see pp. CLXVI–CLXIX; and for the titles, see Madeleine Alcover, "Essai de titrologie: les récits de Cyrano de Bergerac," in *Libertinage et Philosophie au XVIIe siècle*, workshop organized by Anthony McKenna and Pierre-François Moureau (Saint-Etienne: Publications de l'Université de Saint-Etienne, 1996), pp. 75–94.

28. On narratives of publishing in the seventeenth century, see Christian Jouhaud, ed., *De la publication entre Renaissance et Lumières* (Paris et Alain Viala: Fayard, 2002).

29. Cyrano de Bergerac, *Œuvres complètes*, vol. 1, pp. 167–68; translation, p. 157. French text: "A mesure que j'achevais un cahier, impatient de ma gloire, qui lui démangeait plus que la sienne, il allait à Toulouse le prôner dans les plus belles assemblées. Comme on l'avait en réputation d'un des plus forts génies de son siècle, mes louanges, dont il semblait l'infatigable écho, me firent connaître de tout le monde."

30. Ibid., p. 167. French text: "Déjà les graveurs sans m'avoir vu, avaient buriné mon image; et la ville retentissait, dans chaque carrefour, du gosier enroué des colporteurs qui criaient à tue-tête: 'Voilà le portrait de l'auteur des *États et Empires de la Lune.*'"

31. On the various engraved portraits of Cyrano, see Madeleine Alcover, *Cyrano relu et corrigé* (Geneva: Droz, 1990), pp. 68–74.

32. Harold Love, *Scribal Publication in Seventeenth-Century England* (Oxford: Clarendon Press, 1993), reprinted as *The Culture and Commerce of Texts: Scribal Publication in Seventeenth-Century England* (Amherst: University of Massachussetts Press, 1998).

33. Cyrano de Bergerac, *Œuvres complètes*, vol 1, p. 168. French text: "un potpourri de contes ridicules, un amas de lambeaux décousus, un répertoire de Peaud'Ane à bercer les enfants."

34. Ibid., p. 168. French text: "Ce contraste d'opinions entre les habiles et les idiots augmenta son crédit. Peu aprés, les copies en manuscrit se vendirent sous le manteau; tout le monde, et ce qui est hors du monde, c'est-à-dire depuis le gentilhomme jusqu'au moine, acheta cette pièce; les femmes mêmes prirent parti. Chaque famille se divisa, et les intérêts de cette querelle allèrent si loin, que la ville fut partagée en deux factions, la lunaire et l'antilunaire."

35. Ibid., p. 170. French text: "Vous n'avez seulement qu'à nous le mettre entre les mains; et pour l'amour de vous, nous engageons notre honneur à le faire brûler sans scandale."

36. On this trial, see Prévot's remarks in *Libertins du XVIIe siècle*, pp. XXXI–XXXIII, and the documents published by Didier Foucault, "Documents toulousains sur le supplice de Vanini," *La Lettre clandestine* 5 (1996): 15–31.

37. See Robert Mandrou, *Magistrats et sorciers en France au XVIIe siècle: Une analyse de psychologie historique* (Paris: Plon, 1968), on the new jurisprudence of the Parlement of Paris, which ceased to "recognize sorcerers" after around 1640, pp. 341–63, and on doubts in the provincial parlements (among which the Parlement of Toulouse was not the most reluctant), pp. 383–404.

38. Cyrano de Bergerac, *Œuvres complètes*, vol. 1, pp. 180–83; translation, p. 168. French text: "Quand ils aperçurent tous les cercles par lesquels ce philosophe a distingué le mouvement de chaque planète, tous d'une voix hurlèrent que c'étaient les cernes que je traçais pour appeler Belzébuth. Celui qui le tenait le laissa choir d'appréhension, et par malheur en tombant il s'ouvrit dans une page où sont expliquées les vertus de l'aimant; je dis par malheur, pour ce qu'à l'endroit dont je parle il y a une figure de cette pierre métallique, où les petits corps qui se déprennent de sa masse pour accrocher le fer sont représentés comme des bras. À peine un de ces marauds l'aperçut, que je l'entendis s'égosiller que c'était là le crapaud qu'on avait trouvé dans l'auge de l'écurie de son cousin Fiacre, quand ses chevaux moururent."

39. Cyrano de Bergerac, *Œuvres complètes*, vol 1, p. 184. French text: "criait à gorge déployée, qu'on se gardât de toucher à rien, que tous ces livres-là étaient de francs grimoires, et le mulet un Satan."

40. For other examples of the magical powers attributed to books by peasant

communities, see Daniel Fabre, "Le livre et sa magie," in *Pratiques de la lecture*, ed. Roger Chartier (Paris: Payot, 1993), pp. 231–63.

41. Cyrano de Bergerac, *Œuvres complètes*, vol. 1, p. 178; translation, p. 166. French text: une longue robe tissue des feuillets d'un livre de plain-chant, le couvrait jusqu'aux ongles, et son visage était caché d'une carte où l'on avait écrit *l'In principio*" [i.e., les premiers mots de l'*Évangile* de Jean].

42. Ibid., pp. 171–72; translation, p. 160. French text: "Les plaisirs innocents dont le corps est capable ne faisaient que la moindre partie. De tous ceux que l'esprit peut trouver dans l'étude et la conversation, aucun ne nous manquait; et nos bibliothèques unies comme nos esprits, appelaient tous les doctes dans notre société. Nous mêlions la lecture à l'entretien; l'entretien à la bonne chère; celle-là à la pêche ou à la chasse, aux promenades; et en un mot, nous jouissions pour ainsi dire et de nous-mêmes, et de tout ce que la nature a produit de plus doux pour notre usage, et ne [mettions] que la raison pour borne à nos désirs."

43. Ibid., p. 57; translation, p. 77. French text: "Je connus aussi Campanella; ce fut moi qui l'avisai, pendant qu'il était à l'Inquisition à Rome, de styler son visage et son corps aux grimaces et postures ordinaires de ceux dont il avait besoin de connaître l'intérieur, afin d'exciter chez soi par une même assiette les pensées que cette même situation avait appelées dans ses adversaires, parce qu'ainsi il ménagerait mieux leur âme quand il la connaîtrait. . . . Il commença, à nos prières, un livre que nous intitulâmes *De sensu rerum*."

44. Ibid., p. 301. French text: "conformant tout à fait mon corps au vôtre, et devenant pour ainsi dire vôtre gémeau, il est impossible qu'un même branle de matière ne nous cause à tous deux un même branle d'esprit.

45. Tommaso Campanella, *De sensu rerum et magia liber quatuor, pars mirabilis occulta philosophiae* (Frankfurt, 1620), and *La Cité du Soleil*, Latin text of the Paris edition, 1637, ed. and trans. Roland Crahay (Brussels: Académie Royale de Belgique, 1993). On the radical difference between Cyrano's two voyages (and on the libertine attitude and utopian genre more generally), see Prévot, "Introduction," in *Libertins du XVIIe siècle*, p. LXVIII.

46. Cyrano de Bergerac, *Œuvres complètes*, vol. 1, p. 59. French text: "J'y ai connu aussi quantité d'autres gens, que votre siècle traite de divins, mais je n'ai rien trouvé en eux que beaucoup de babil et beaucoup d'orgueil."

47. Madeleine Alcover, "Un gay trio: Cyrano, Chapelle, Dassoucy," in *L'Autre au XVIIe siècle: Actes du 4e colloque du Centre International de Rencontres sur le XVIIe siècle, University of Miami, 23–25 Avril 1998*, ed. Ralph Heyndals and Barbara Woshinsky (Tübingen: Narr, 1999), pp. 265–75, and "Biographie" and "Analyse," pp. XXXIV, CCII–CCVIII.

48. Edmond Rostand, *Cyrano de Bergerac*, intro. Jacques Truchet (Paris: Imprimerie Nationale, 1983).

49. The idea of giving Cyrano a long nose, already present in Théophile Gautier, comes from the passage in *States and Empires of the Moon* in which the moon people explain why they castrate children with short noses by saying that "thirty centuries of observation have taught us that, among us, a big nose is a sign that says, 'Herein resides a man who is clever, cautious, courteous, affable, generous, and liberal,' while a small one is a stopper holding the opposite vices in. That is why we

turn the snub-nosed into eunuchs, because the republic would rather not have their children than have children who resemble them." Cyrano de Bergerac, *Œuvres complètes*, vol. 1, pp. 141–42. French text: "Sachez que nous le faisons après avoir observé depuis trente siècles qu'un grand nez est à la porte de chez nous une enseigne qui dit: 'Céans loge un homme spirituel, prudent, courtois, affable, généreux et libéral' et qu'un petit est le bouchon des vices opposés. C'est pourquoi des camus on bâtit les eunuques parce que la république aime mieux n'avoir point d'enfants d'eux, que d'en avoir de semblable à eux." See Rostand, *Cyrano de Bergerac*, ed. Pierre Citti (Paris: Livre de Poche classique, 1990), p. 13 and note pp. 50–51.

50. The most recent and trustworthy biographical information can be found in Alcover, "Biographie."

51. "Préface," in Cyrano de Bergerac, *Œuvres complètes*, vol. 1, pp. 483–84, 488. French text: "Cet âge, où la nature se corrompt plus aisément, et la grande liberté qu'il avait de ne faire que ce que bon lui semblait, le portèrent sur un dangereux penchant, où j'ose dire que je l'arrêtai, parce qu'ayant achevé mes études, et mon père voulant que je servisse dans les Gardes, je l'obligeai d'entrer avec moi dans la compagnie de M. de Carbon Castel-Jaloux" (pp. 483–84) and "Il accompagnait ces deux qualités d'une si grande retenue envers le beau sexe, qu'on peut dire qu'il n'est jamais sorti du respect que le nôtre lui doit."

52. Cyrano de Bergerac, *Œuvres complètes*, vol. 1, pp. 51–52, pp. 75–77; translation, pp. 51, 89. French text: "à cause qu'ils habillent, par hasard, en ce pays-là, les singes à l'espagnole, et que, l'ayant à son arrivée trouvé vêtu de cette façon, elle n'avait point douté qu'il ne fût de l'espèce. [. . .] Le roi commanda aux gardeurs des singes de nous ramener, avec ordre exprès de nous faire coucher ensemble, l'Espagnol et moi, pour faire en son royaume multiplier notre espèce. On exécuta de point en point la volonté du prince, de quoi je fus très aise pour le plaisir que je recevais d'avoir quelqu'un qui m'entretint pendant la solitude de ma brutification."

53. Carlos García, *Antipatía de los franceses y españoles, obra apacible y curiosa [. . .] Antipathie des français et des espagnols, oeuvre curieuse et agréable*, 1617. See also the commentary by Jean-Frédéric Schaub, *La France espagnole: Les racines hispaniques de l'absolutisme français* (Paris: Éditions du Seuil, 2003), pp. 160–66.

54. Cyrano de Bergerac, *Œuvres complètes*, vol. 1, p. 283. French text: "On n'avait pas sitôt mangé des pommes de l'un, qu'on devenait éperdument passionné pour quiconque avait mangé du fruit de l'autre."

55. Ibid., pp. 284–85. French text: "car chacun de ces braves au combat, pour garantir son amant, ou pour mériter d'en être aimé, hasardait des efforts si incroyables, que l'Antiquité n'a rien vu de pareil."

56. On this incident, see Alcover, "Biographie," pp. LXII–LXIV.

57. The Sydney manuscript, which is preserved in the Fisher Library at the University of Sydney, was published by Margaret Sankey, *Édition diplomatique d'un manuscrit inédit: Cyrano de Bergerac, L'Autre Monde ou Les Empires et Estats de la Lune* (Paris: Lettres Modernes, 1995). The manuscript at the Bibliothèque Nationale in Paris is the reference text for Madeleine Alcover's edition in the first volume of Cyrano's *Œuvres complètes*, published by Honoré Champion, as well as Jacques Prévot's edition: Cyrano de Bergerac, *Les États et Empires de la Lune*, in *Libertins du XVIIe siècle*, vol. 1, pp. 901–90. The manuscript in the Bayerische Staatsbibliothek in

Munich served as the reference text for Leo Jordan's edition, which was published in Dresden in 1910.

58. Cf. Joan DeJean, *Libertine Strategies. Freedom and the Novel in Seventeenth-Century* (Columbus: Ohio State University Press, 1981), p. 106.

59. Sankey, *Édition diplomatique*, pp. XXXV, XXVI.

60. Alcover, "Critique textuelle," p. CXVIII.

61. See the catalog published by Miguel Benitez, *La Face cachée des Lumières: Recherches sur les manuscrits philosophiques clandestins à l'âge classique* (Paris; Universitas; Oxford: Voltaire Foundation, 1996), pp. 1–61. On the *Colloquium heptaplomeres de abditis sublimium rerum arcanis*, see Prévot, "Introduction," pp. LXV–LXVI.

62. Cf. Love, *Scribal Publication*; H. R. Woudhuysen, *Sir Philip Sydney and the Circulation of Manuscripts 1558–1640* (Oxford: Clarendon Press, 1996); and Arthur Marrotti, *Manuscript, Print, and the English Renaissance Lyric* (Ithaca, N.Y.: Cornell University Press, 1995).

63. Fernando Bouza, *Corre manuscrito: Una historia cultural del Siglo de Oro* (Madrid: Marcial Pons, 2001).

64. See *De bonne main. La communication manuscrite au XVIIIe siècle*, ed. François Moureau (Paris: Universitas; Oxford; Voltaire Foundation, 1993), and Roger Chartier, "Le manuscrit à l'âge de l'imprimé (XVe-XVIIIe siècles). Lectures et réflexions," *La Lettre clandestine* 7 (1998): 175–93.

65. Cyrano de Bergerac, *Œuvres complètes*, vol. 1, p. 77.

66. *L'École des filles*, in *Libertins du XVIIe siècle*, pp. 1099–1202; cf. Joan DeJean, *The Reinvention of Obscenity: Sex, Life, and Tabloids in Early Modern France* (Chicago: University of Chicago Press, 2002), pp. 56–83.

67. See Joan DeJean's comments in her edition of the uncensored version of the play, in Molière, *Le Festin de Pierre (Dom Juan): Édition critique du texte d'Amsterdam (1683)*, ed. Joan DeJean (Geneva: Droz, 1999), pp. 7–46.

68. Alcover, "Critique textuelle," CXL–CXLI.

69. Cyrano de Bergerac, *Œuvres complètes*, vol. 1, pp. 44–45; translation, p. 69. French text: En effet, j'ai remarqué que comme ce serpent essaie toujours de s'échapper du corps de l'homme, on lui voit la tête et le cou sortir au bas de nos ventres. Mais aussi Dieu n'a pas permis que l'homme seul en fût tourmenté; il a voulu qu'il se bandât contre la femme pour lui jeter son venin, et que l'enflure durât neuf mois après l'avoir piquée. Et pour vous montrer que je parle suivant la parole du Seigneur, c'est qu'il dit au serpent, pour le maudire, qu'il aurait beau faire trébucher la femme en se raidissant contre elle, qu'elle lui ferait enfin baisser la tête."

70. For a comparison of the two endings, see Cyrano de Bergerac, *Œuvres complètes*, vol. 1, pp. 153–61 (Paris manuscript) and pp. 451–53 (printed edition of 1657).

71. "Preface," ibid., p. 491. French text: "de sorte qu'enfin le libertinage, dont les jeunes gens sont pour la plupart soupçonnés, lui parut un monstre, pour lequel je puis témoigner qu'il eut depuis cela toute l'aversion qu'en doivent avoir ceux qui veulent vivre chrétiennement."

72. Alcover, "Critique textuelle," p. CXLIII.

73. Cyrano de Bergerac, *Œuvres complètes*, vol. 1, p. 453.

74. See Philip Gaskell, *A New Introduction to Bibliography* (Oxford: Clarendon

Press, 1972), and Jeanne Veyrin-Forrer, "Fabriquer un livre au XVIe siècle," in *Histoire de l'Édition française*, vol. 2, *Le Livre triomphant: Du Moyen Age au milieu du XVIIe siècle*, ed. Roger Chartier and Henri-Jean Martin (Paris: Fayard/Cercle de la Librairie, 1989), pp. 336–69.

75. Alcover, *Cyrano relu et corrigé*, pp. 48–68.

76. Alcover, *Cyrano relu et corrigé*, pp. 1–23, and "Biographie," pp. LX–LXI (for identifications of possible censors, see p. LXXX).

77. Cyrano de Bergerac, *Œuvres complètes*, vol. 1, pp. 477–91 and Alcover, "Critique textuelle," pp. CXIX–CXXII.

78. Cyrano de Bergerac, *Le Pédant joué*, in *Œuvres complètes*, vol. 3, *Théâtre*, critical edition, ed. André Blanc (Paris: H. Champion, 2001), pp. 11–222 (esp. pp. 41–44).

79. Cyrano de Bergerac, *Œuvres complètes*, vol. 1, pp. 72–74. French text: "Je lui demandai si c'était une obligation pour la valeur de l'écot. Il me répartit que non, qu'il ne lui devait plus rien et que c'étaient des vers."

80. Ibid., p. 73. French text: "Là les versificateurs officiers mettent les pièces à l'épreuve, et si elles sont jugées de bon aloi, on les taxe, non pas selon leur poids, mais selon leur pointe."

81. Ibid. French text: "Je ne craignais pas de demeurer court; car quand nous ferions ripaille pendant huit jours, nous ne saurions dépenser un sonnet, et j'en ai quatre sur moi, avec neuf épigrammes,deux odes et une églogue."

82. Ibid. French text: "Ha! vraiment, dis-je en moi-même, voilà justement la monnaie dont Sorel fait servir Hortensius dans *Francion*, je m'en souviens. C'est là sans doute qu'il l'a dérobé. Mais de qui diable peut-il l'avoir appris ? Il faut que ce soit de sa mère, car j'ai ouï dire qu'elle était lunatique."

83. Charles Sorel, *Histoire comique de Francion*, in *Romanciers du XVIIe siècle*, ed. Antoine Adam (Paris: Gallimard, Bibliothèque de La Pléiade, 1958), pp. 59–527 (quote p. 450).

84. Cyrano de Bergerac, *Œuvres complètes*, vol. 1, p. 415. French text: "Et plût à Dieu, lui dis-je, que cela fût de même en notre monde! J'y connais beaucoup d'honnêtes poètes qui meurent de faim et qui feraient bonne chère si on payait les traiteurs en cette monnaie."

85. Ibid., p. 74. French text: "Ils écrivent dans un grand registre, qu'ils appellent *les comptes de Dieu*, à peu près ainsi: 'Item; la valeur de tant de vers, délivrés un tel jour, à un tel, que Dieu me doit rembourser aussitôt l'acquit reçu du premier fonds qui se trouvera.'"

86. Ibid., p. 415. French text: "Ils écrivent dans un grand registre, qu'ils appellent *les comptes du Grand Jour*, à peu près ainsi: '*Item*; la valeur de tant de vers, délivrés un tel jour, à un tel, qu'on m'y doit rembourser aussitôt l'acquit reçu du premier fonds qui se trouvera '."

87. Ibid., p. 74. French text: "Lorsqu'ils se sentent malades, en danger de mourir, ils font hacher ces registres en morceaux et les avalent, parce qu'ils croient que, s'ils n'étaient ainsi digérés, Dieu ne les pourrait pas lire."

88. Francis Goyet, *Le sublime du "lieu commun": L'invention rhétorique à la Renaissance* (Paris: H. Champion, 1996) emphasizes the presence of the words *digerere* and *digesta* in the "methods" of the commonplace books, pp. 505–6 (Cicero),

pp. 534–35 (Melanchton). See also Ann Moss, *Printed Commonplace-Books and the Structuring of Renaissance Thought* (Oxford: Clarendon Press, 1996).

89. Quoted from the King James Version. See Louis Marin, *La parole mangée et autres essais théologico-politiques* (Paris: Méridiens Klincksieck, 1986).

90. Cyrano de Bergerac, *Œuvres complètes*, vol. 1, p. 415. French text: "parce qu'ils croient que, s'ils n'étaient pas ainsi digérés, cela ne leur profiterait de rien."

91. Ibid., p. 66. French text: "n'est autre chose qu'une différence de tons non articulés, à peu près semblable à notre musique, quand on n'a pas ajouté les paroles."

92. Ibid., pp. 92, 127, 134, 138. In the Sydney manuscript edited by Margaret Sankey, the musical notations are found on pp. 53, 80, 85, 87.

93. Ibid., p. 217; translation pp. 193–94. French text: "Il me discourut pendant trois grosses heures en une langue que je sais bien n'avoir jamais ouïe, et qui n'a aucun rapport avec pas une de ce monde-ci, laquelle toutefois je compris plus vite et plus intelligiblement que celle de ma nourrice."

Chapter 6. Text and Fabric: Anzoletto and Philomela

1. Carlo Goldoni, *Mémoires pour servir à l'histoire de sa vie et à celle de son théâtre*, ed. Norbert Jonard (Paris: Aubier, 1992), p. 443. English translation: *Memoirs of Carlo Goldoni*, trans. John Black (New York: Knopf, 1926). [Since this text was unavailable to me, the translations given in the text are mine.—Trans.] French text: "Le nouveau genre l'emportait sur l'ancien, et les Italiens qui faisaient la base de ce Théâtre, n'étaient plus que les accessoires du Spectacle." On this text, see Franco Fido, *Nuova guida a Goldoni. Teatro e società nel Settecento* (Turin: Einaudi, 1977, 2000), esp. "I Mémoires e la letteratura autobiografica del Settecento," pp. 281–312.

2. Fido, *Nuova guida a Goldoni*, "Un veneziano a Parigi: esperienze e commedie del periodo francese," pp. 258–80.

3. On this comedy, see Luigi Squarzina, "Gli addii del Goldoni all' Italia e *Una delle ultime sere di carnovale*," in *Atti del colloquio "Goldoni in Francia"* (Rome: Accademia nazionale dei Lincei, 1971), pp. 121–31, and Franca Angelini, "Anzoletto in Moscovia," in *Istituzioni culturale e sceniche nell' età delle riforme*, a cura di Guido Nicastro (Milan: Franco Angeli, 1986), pp. 87–100.

4. Quotations from Carlo Goldoni, *Una delle ultime sere di carnovale*, ed. Gilberto Pizzamiglio, *Le Opere*, Edizione Nazionale (Venice: Marsilio, 1993).

5. Goldoni, *Una delle ultime sere di carnovale*, p. 41. Italian text: "In fondo di questa Commedia è un'allegoria, che ha bisogno di spiegazione. Essendo io in quell'anno chiamato in Francia, e avendo risolto di andarvi, per lo spazio almeno di due anni, immaginai di prender congedo dal Pubblico di Venezia col mezzo di una Commedia; e come non mi pareva ben fatto di parlare sfacciatamente ed alla scoperta di me, e delle cose mie, ho fatto de' Commedianti una società di Tessitori, o sia fabbricanti di stoffe, ed io mi sono coperto col titolo di Disegnatore. L'allegoria non è male adattata. I Comici esguiscono le opere degli Autori, ed i Tessitori lavorano sul modello de' loro Designatori."

6. Goldoni, *Mémoires*, p. 431. French text: "La Pièce eut beaucoup de succès; elle fit la clôture de l'année comique 1761, et la Soirée du Mardi gras fut la plus

brillante pour moi, car la Salle retentissait d'applaudissements, parmi lesquels on entendait distinctement crier: *Bon voyage*: *Revenez*: *N'y manquez pas.* J'avoue que j'en étais touché jusqu'aux larmes."

7. Ibid., p. 431. French text: "Une Brodeuse française, appelée Madame Gatteau, se trouve pour des affaires à Venise. Elle connaît Anzoletto; elle aime autant sa personne que ses desseins ; elle l'engage, et va l'emmener à Paris ; voilà une énigme qu'il n'était pas difficile à deviner."

8. Ibid., pp. 256–57. French text: "Le langage Vénitien est sans contredit le plus doux et le plus agréable de tous les autres dialectes de l'Italie. La prononciation en est claire, délicate, facile; les mots abondants, expressifs; les phrases harmonieuses, spirituelles; et comme le fond du caractère de la Nation Vénitienne est la gaieté, ainsi le fond du langage Vénitien est la plaisanterie. Cela n'empêche pas que cette langue ne soit susceptible de traiter en grand les matières les plus graves et les plus intéressantes; les Avocats plaident en Vénitien, les harangues des Sénateurs se prononcent dans le même idiome; mais sans dégrader la majesté du Trône, ou la dignité du Barreau, nos Orateurs ont l'heureuse facilité naturelle d'associer à l'éloquence la plus sublime, la tournure la plus agréable et la plus intéressante. . . . Les succès de mes premières Pièces Vénitiennes m'encouragèrent à en faire d'autres."

9. Goldoni, *Una delle ultime sere di carnovale*, Act I, Scene 5, p. 86.

10. Ibid., Act 2, Scene 6, p. 117.

11. Ibid., Act 3, Scene V, p. 130.

12. See the studies by Gianfranco Folena, *L'italiano in Europa: Esperieze linguistiche del Settecento* (Turin: Einaudi, 1981), esp. "Itinerario dialectale goldoniano," pp. 182–87 and "Il francese de Goldoni," pp. 374–78.

13. Cf. the remarks by Huguette Hatem in her French translation, Carlo Goldoni, *Une des dernières soirées de carnaval* (Paris: L'Arche, 1980), pp. 128–29, note 5, 137–42, "Postface: Sur le langage et la traduction."

14. John Scheid and Jesper Svenbro, *Le métier de Zeus: Mythe du tissage et du tissu dans le monde gréco-romain* (Paris: Editions La Découverte, 1994), pp. 149, 160–62. English translation: *The Craft of Zeus: Myths of Weaving and Fabric*, trans. Carol Volk (Cambridge, Mass.: Harvard University Press, 1996). See also the remarks of D. F. McKenzie, *Bibliography and the Sociology of Texts*, Panizzi Lectures 1985 (London: British Library, 1986), pp. 5–6.

15. Goldoni, *Una delle ultime sere di carnovale*, Act I, Scene 15, p. 87. Italian text: "Xe un pezzo che i dessegni de sto paese piase, e incontra per tutto. Sia merito dei dessegnadori, o sia merito dei testori, i nostri drapi ha chiapà concetto. Xe andà via dei laoranti, e i xe stai ben accolti. Se gh'ha mandà dei dessegni, i ha avù del compatimento; ma no basta gnancora. Se vol provar, se una man italiana, dessegnando sul fatto, sul gusto dei Moscoviti, possa formar un misto, capace de piàser ale do nazion."

16. Goldoni, *Mémoires*, p. 184. French text: "Allons, continuais-je dans mes réflexions; voici le moment peut-être d'essayer cette réforme que j'ai en vue depuis si longtemps. Oui, il faut traiter des sujets de caractère; c'est là la source de la bonne Comédie: c'est par là que le grand Molière a commencé sa carrière, et est parvenu à ce degré de perfection, que les anciens n'ont fait que nous indiquer, et que les modernes n'ont pas encore égalé."

17. Ibid., p. 453. French text: "La plupart des Comédiens Italiens ne me demandaient que des canevas; le Public s'y était accoutumé, la Cour les souffrait; pourquoi aurais-je refusé de m'y conformer? [. . .] Je réussis plus que je ne croyais: mais quel que fût le succès de mes Pièces, je n'allais guère les voir, j'aimais la bonne Comédie, et j'allais au Théâtre Français pour m'amuser et pour m'instruire."

18. Goldoni, *Il Teatro comico Memorie italiane*, ed. Guido Davico Bonino (Milan: Oscar Mondadori, 1983), p. 31.

19. Goldoni, *Mémoires*, p. 267. French text: "Une poétique mise en action."

20. Goldoni, *Il Teatro comico*, Act I, Scene 4, p. 39. English translation: *The Comic Theater*, trans. John W. Miller (Lincoln: University of Nebraska Press, 1969), pp. 11–12. Italian text: "Un povero commediante che ha fatto el so studio segondo l'arte, e che ha fatto l'uso de dir all'improviso ben o mal quel che vien, trovandose in necessià de studiar e de dover dir el premedità, se el gh'ha reputazione, bisogna che el ghe pensa, bisogna che el se sfadiga a studiar, e che el trema sempre, ogni volta che se fa una nova commedia, dubitando o de no saverla quanto basta, o de no sostegnir el carattere come xe necessario."

21. Goldoni, *Mémoires*, p. 449. French text: "je faisais part de mes idées à mes Comédiens. Les uns m'encourageaient à suivre mon plan, les autres ne me demandaient que des farces : les premiers étaient les Amoureux qui désiraient des Pièces écrites ; les derniers c'étaient les Acteurs comiques, qui, habitués à ne rien apprendre par cœur, avaient l'ambition de briller sans se donner la peine d'étudier."

22. Goldoni, *Mémoires*, p. 452. French text: "Je voyais de loin que les Acteurs qui avaient perdu l'habitude d'apprendre leurs rôles m'auraient sans malice et sans mauvaise volonté mal servi ; je me vis contraint à borner mes idées, et à me contenir dans la médiocrité du sujet pour ne pas hasarder un ouvrage qui demanderait plus d'exactitude dans l'exécution."

23. Goldoni, *Il Teatro comico*, Act II, Scene 10, pp. 66–67. Italian text: "Guai a noi, se facessimo una tal novità: non è ancor tempo di farla" et "anzi convien cercare di bene allogarle e di sostenerle con merito nel loro carattere ridicolo, anche a fronte del serio più lepido e più grazioso."

24. Ibid., Act III, Scene 3, pp. 80–81; translation, p. 67. Italian text: "Guardatevi sopra tutto dalla cantilena e dalla declamazione, ma recitate naturalmente, come se parlaste, mentre essendo la commedia una imitazione della natura, si deve fare tutto quello che è verisimile. Circa al gesto, anche questo deve essere naturale. Movete le mani secondo il senso della parola."

25. Ibid., Act III, Scene 10, p. 88.

26. Carlo Goldoni, *Le Baruffe Chiozzotte/Baroufe à Chioggia*, Italian comedy translated and presented in a bilingual edition by Felice Del Beccaro and Raymond Laubreaux (Paris: Aubier-Flammarion, 1968), pp. 38–39. Italian text: "I Teatri d'Italia sono frequentati da tutti gli ordini di persone; e la spesa è si mediocre, che il bottegaio, il servitore ed il povero pescatore possono partecipare di questo pubblico divertimento, alla differenza de' Teatri Francesi, ne' quali si paga dodici paoli in circa per un solo posto nell'ordine nobile, e due per istare in piedi in platea. Io aveva levato al popolo minuto la frequenza dell'Arlecchino; sentivano parlare della riforma delle Commedie, voleano gustarle; ma tutti i caratteri non erano adattati alla loro intelligenza: ed era bien giusto, che per piacere a quest'ordine di persone, che pagano

come i Nobili e come i Ricchi, facessi delle Commedie, nelle quali riconoscessero i loro costumi e i lori defetti e, mi sia permesso di dirlo, le loro virtù."

27. The first two of these comedies were presented in an unforgettable performance by Giorgio Strehler and the troupe of the Piccolo Teatro in Milan in the 1964/65 season (for *Le Baruffe chiozzotte*, which received a new production in 1992/93) and the 1974/75 season for *Il Campiello*.

28. Goldoni, *Una delle ultime sere di carnovale*, Act 2, Scene 4, p. 113. Italian text: "Co no se' vu assistente al teler, credéu che i testori possa redur i drappi segondo la vostra intenzion?"

29. Ibid., p. 114. Italian text: "Per maggior cautela, farò dessegni più sminuzzadi, con tutti quei chiari e scuri, e con tutti quel ombrizamenti che sarà necessari. Minierò le carte; ghe sarà su i colori. No la s'indubita; gh' ho tanta speranza che i aventori sarà contenti; e che 'l so servitore Anzoletto no ghe sarà desutile gnanca lontan."

30. Ibid., Act I, scene 2, p. 54. Italian text: "El xe mercante de sea, ch' el me dà tutto l' anno da laorar."

31. See Nicolà Mangini, *I teatri di Venezia* (Milan: Mursia, 1974).

32. Goldoni, *Mémoires*, pp. 316–17. French text: "Je passai du Théâtre Saint-Ange à celui de Saint-Luc: il n'y avait pas là de Directeur; les Comédiens partageaient la recette, et le propriétaire de la salle, qui jouissait du bénéfice des loges, leur faisait des pensions à proportion du mérite ou de l'ancienneté. C'était à ce Patricien que j'avais à faire; c'était à lui que je remettais mes Pièces, qui m'étaient payées sur le champ, et avant la lecture; mes émoluments étaient presque doublés: j'avais liberté entière de faire imprimer mes Ouvrages, et point d'obligation de suivre la Troupe en Terre-Ferme: ma condition était devenue beaucoup plus lucrative, et infiniment plus honorable."

33. Goldoni, *Una delle ultime sere di carnovale*, Act I, Scene 13, p. 79: Italian text: "Cossa serve? Nu altri marcanti gh'avemo bisogno de' testori; i testori ha bisgno del dessegnador."

34. Ibid., Act I, Scene 14, p. 83. Italian text: "Dasseno me despiase anca a mi; perché in materia de drapi, la sa che ogni ghe vol dele novità; e lu, per dir quel che xe, per la nostra bottega, l'ha sempre trovà qualcossa, che ha dà int'el genio all'universal."

35. Ibid., Act II, Scene 1, p. 92. Italian text: "Anzoletto: Caro sior Zamaria, vu parlé con tropa bontà. De cento e più dessegni che ho fatto qualchedun ghe n'è andà mal, e qualche volta avé butà via la seda, l'oro e l'arzento per causa mia. / Zamaria: Mi no digo cussì. So che i mii drapi laorai sui vostri dessegni, se no i ho smaltii a Venezia, i ho smaltii in terraferma; e se in qualcun ho descapità, m'ho reffatto sora la brocca con queli che xe andai ben."

36. Ibid., Act I, scene 11, p. 76. Italian text: "Ghe digo ben, che ho visto desuso in teler un drapo, che no ho visto el più belo. Un dessegno de sior Anzoletto, che xe una cossa d'incanto. Che no gh' ha invidia a uno dei più beli de Franza."

37. Ibid., Act I, Scene 11, p. 76: "Lazaro: Cossa diséu, sior Bastian, de quei drapi che st'anno xe vegnui fora dai mii teleri? \ Bastian: Stupendi: i me li ha magnai dale man. V'arecordéu quel raso con quei finti màrtori? Tutti lo credeva de Franza. I voleva fina scometter; ma per grazia del Cielo, roba forastiera inte la mia bottega no ghe ne vien."

38. Ibid., Act II, Scene 3, p. 102. Italian text: "Domenica: Sti maledetti danari

xe queli che lo fa andar via / Anzoletto: No solamente i danari, ma anca un pocheto de onor."

39. Ibid., Act II, Scene 7, p. 122. Italian text: "El va via, più per capricio che per interese. Bezzi no credo che 'l ghe ne voggia avanzar. Lo conosso, el xe un galantomo: vadagna poco, vadagna assae, in fin dell'anno sarà l' istesso. El dise che 'l va via per l' onor; cossa vorlo de più de quel che l'ha avudo qua? No s'ha visto fina quatro, o cinque teleri int'una volta laorar sui so dessegni? No xe piene le boteghe de roba dessegnada da lu? Vorlo statue? Vorlo trombe? Vorlo tamburi? Sarave forsi meggio per elo, e per mi, che 'l restasse qua: che se a diese ghe despiaseria che 'l restasse, ghe sarà cento che gh'averà da caro che 'l resta."

40. Goldoni, *Mémoires*, pp. 235–36. French text: "Voilà donc ma muse et ma plume engagées aux ordres d'un particulier. Un Auteur Français trouvera peut-être cet engagement singulier. Un homme de lettres, dira-t-on, doit être libre, doit mépriser la servitude et la gêne. Si cet Auteur est à son aise comme l'était Voltaire, ou cynique comme Rousseau, je n'ai rien à lui dire; mais si c'est un de ceux qui ne se refusent pas au partage de la recette et au profit de l'impression, je le prie en grâce de vouloir bien écouter ma justification. [. . .] les gratifications et le Cour, les pensions, les bienfaits du Roi. Rien de tout cela en Italie."

41. See Ivo Mattozzi, "Carlo Goldoni e la professione di scrittore," *Studi e Problemi di Critica Testuale* 1 (1972): 95–153.

42. Goldoni, *Mémoires*, p. 318. French text: "qu'il ne pouvait plus recevoir de moi mes originaux, qu'il les tenait de la main de Medebac, et que c'était pour le compte de ce Comédien qu'il allait continuer l'Édition."

43. Ibid., pp. 318–19. French text: "contre le Directeur qui me disputait la propriété de mes Pièces et contre le Libraire qui était en possession de la faculté de les publier [. . .] Imprimeur très accrédité et très honnête homme [. . .] des changements et des corrections."

44. Ibid., pp. 5–6. French text: "Voyant qu'après ma première édition de Florence, mon Théâtre était au pillage partout, et qu'on m'avait fait quinze éditions sans mon aveu, sans m'en faire part, et ce qui est encore pis, toutes très mal imprimées, je conçus le projet d'en donner une seconde à mes fais [. . .] Je conçus le projet [. . .] de placer dans chaque volume, au lieu de Préface, une partie de ma vie, imaginant qu'à la fin de l'Ouvrage l'histoire de ma Personne, et celle de mon Théâtre, auraient pu être complètes [. . .] qu'un Ouvrage qui devait être porté jusqu'à trente volumes, et devait être achevé dans l'espace de huit années, n'est encore, au bout de vingt ans, qu'au tome XVII, et je ne vivrai pas assez pour voir cette édition terminée."

45. Ibid., p. 7. French text: "jusqu'au commencement de ce qu'on appelle en Italie la réforme du Théâtre Italien." The seventeen autobiographical capsules can be found in Goldoni, *Il Teatro comico/Memorie italiane*, pp. 95–231. See Ginette Herry, "Goldoni de la *Préface Bettinelli* aux *Préfaces Pasquali* ou le destin des souvenirs," in *Il tempo vissuto*, Proceedings of Gargnano colloquium, 9–11 September 1985 (Rome: Cappelli, 1988), pp. 197–211.

46. Goldoni, *Mémoires*, pp. 477–78, 544–45.

47. On the themes of Gozzi's attack on Goldoni, see Gérard Luciani, *Carlo Gozzi (1720–1806): L'homme et l'oeuvre* (Lille: Atelier de reproduction des thèses;

Paris: H. Champion, 1977), reprinted in *Carlo Gozzi ou l'enchanteur désenchanté* (Grenoble: Presses Universitaires de Grenoble, 2001); Paolo Bosisio, *Carlo Gozzi e Goldoni. Una polemica letteraria con versi inediti e rari* (Florence: Olschski, 1979), and Ginette Herry, "Une poétique mise en action," in Goldoni, *Le Théâtre comique,* pp. 9–92.

48. Goldoni, *Una delle ultime sere di carnovale,* Act III, Scene 12, pp. 154–55. Italian text: "Momolo: E se vien fora critiche, voléu che ve le manda? / Anzoletto: Ve dirò; se le xe critiche, sior, sì; se le xe satire, sior, no. Ma al dì d'ancuo par che sia dificile e criticar senza satirizar; onde no ve incomodé de mandarmele. No le me piase, né per mi, né per altri. Se vegnirà fora dele cosse contra de mi, pazzenzia: za el responder no serve a gnente; perché se gh'avé torto, fé pezo parlar; e se gh'avé rason, o presto, o tardi, el mondo ve la farà."

49. Gilberto Pizzamiglio, "Introduzione," in Goldoni, *Una delle ultime sere di carnovale,* p. 9. Italian text: "commedia delgi adii e della nostalgia, metafora autobiografica di una sofferta partenza, nonché dubitoso bilancio della riforma."

50. On this essential aspect of the comedy, see Franca Angelini Frajese, *"Una delle ultime sere di carnovale:* Il mestiere, la festa, il teatro," *Problemi* 38 (1973): 409–13.

51. Scheid and Svenbro, *Le métier de Zeus,* pp. 119–38.

52. Jean-Pierre Vernant, *Mythe et pensée chez les Grecs: Etudes de psychologie historique* (Paris: François Maspéro, 1965), pp. 222–25. English translation: *Myth and Thought Among the Greeks* (London: Routledge, 1983).

53. Scheid and Svenbro, *Le métier de Zeus,* pp. 149–55.

54. William Shakespeare, *The Winter's Tale,* in William Shakespeare, *The Complete Works,* ed. Stanley Wells and Gary Taylor (Oxford: Oxford University Press, 1988), pp. 1101–30. The text is that of the 1623 Folio.

55. Margaret Spufford, *The Great Reclothing of Rural England: Petty Chapmen and Their Wares in the Seventeenth Century* (London: Hambledon Press, 1984).

56. *The Winter's Tale,* Act IV, Scene 4, p. 1119.

57. Ibid.

58. Ibid., p. 1120.

59. Ibid., p. 1123.

60. Ann Rosalind Jones and Peter Stallybrass, *Renaissance Clothing and the Materials of Memory* (Cambridge: Cambridge University Press, 2000), which mentions two examples, pp. 159, 162–63.

61. Ovid, *Metamorphoses,* trans. David Raeburn (London: Penguin, 2004).

62. On Velazquez's treatment of the myth in *Las Hilanderas,* painted between 1655 and 1660, see the note by Jonathan Brown in the catalogue of the exhibition *Velázquez, Rubens y Van Dick: Pintores cortesanos del siglo XVII* (Madrid: Museo del Prado and Ediciones El Viso, 1999), pp. 219–22, and the interpretation proposed by Jones and Stallybrass, *Renaissance Clothing and the Materials of Memory,* pp. 89–103.

63. Ovid, *Metamorphoses,* Book VI, lines 129–31: "Non illud Pallas, non illud carpere Liuor / Possit opus; doluit successu flaua uirago / Et rupit pictas, caelestia crimina, uestes."

64. Ibid., Book VI, lines 134–35: "Non tulit infelix laqueoque animosa ligauit / Guttura."

65. Ibid., Book VI, lines 144–45: "de quo tamen illa remittit / Stamen et antiquas exercet aranea telas."

66. Ibid., Book V, lines 294–678.

67. Ibid., Book V, lines 677–78: "Nunc quoque in alitibus facundia prisca remansit / Raucaque garrulitas studiumque immane loquendi."

68. Scheid and Svenbro, *Le métier de Zeus*, pp. 139–44.

69. Ovid, *Metamorphoses*, Book VI, lines 555–56: "Luctantemque loqui comprensam forcipe linguam: Abstulit ense fero."

70. Ibid., Book VI, lines 570–74: "Quid faciat Philomela? fugam custodia claudit, / Structa rigent solido stabulorum moenia saxo / Os mutum facti caret indice."

71. Ibid., Book VI, lines 574–80: "Grande doloris / Ingenium est miserisque uenit sollertia rebus. / Stamina barbarica suspendit callida tela / Purpureasque notas filis intexuit albis, / Indicium sceleris, perfectaque tradidit uni, / Vtque ferat dominae gestu rogat; illa rogata / Pertulit ad Prognem; nescit quid tradat in illis." Translated here by David A. Raeburn in Ovid, *Metamorphoses: A New Verse Translation* (London: Penguin, 2004), p. 238. In her book *L'homme-cerf et la femme-araignée: Figures grecques de la métamorphose* (Paris: Gallimard, 2003), p. 236, Françoise Frontisi-Ducroux follows certain Alexandrian mythographers in interpreting Philomela's weaving as a figurative representation of her suffering rather than as a text recounting it.

72. Ibid., Book VI, lines 645–46: "Pars inde cauis exsultat aenis, / Pars ueribus stridunt; manant penetralia tabo."

73. Ibid., Book VI, lines 650–51: "Ipse sedens solio Tereus sublimis auito / Vescitur inque suam sua uiscera congerit aluum."

74. Baudri de Bourgueil, *Poèmes*, éd. Jean-Yves Tilliette (Paris: Les Belles Lettres, 1998), Poem 126, vol. 1, p. 133, *De sufficientia uotorum suorum*: "Philomela spent the night within my walls recounting her ancient sorrows in a plaintive tone" [Latin text: "Sepibus in nostris pernox, Filomela maneret, / Antiquos fletus et querulos replicans"]; Poem 129, vol. 1, p. 138, *Ad Auitum ut ad eum ueniret:* "There, throughout the night, Philomela wailed her ancient lament, and once again her trills recalled her suffering of long ago" [Latin text: "Huc agit antiquam pernox Philomela querelam / Et replicat ueteres lubricata uoces dolores."]

75. William Shakespeare, *The Most Lamentable Roman Tragedy of Titus Andronicus*, in *The Complete Works*, pp. 125–52. The quoted text is from the Quarto of 1594.

76. Ibid., Act II, Scene 4, p. 137.

77. Ovid, *Metamorphoses*, lines 520–21: "Cum rex Pandione natam / In stabula alta trahit, siluis obscura uetustis."

78. Shakespeare, *Titus Andronicus*, Act IV, Scene 1, p. 141.

79. Ibid.

80. On this scene, see the commentary by Eve Rachele Sanders, *Gender and Literacy on Stage in Early Modern England* (Cambridge: Cambridge University Press, 1998), pp. 62–63, 174–75.

81. Seneca, *Thyestes*, trans. Caryl Churchill (London: Nick Hern Books, 1995).

82. Shakespeare, *Titus Andronicus*, Act V, Scene 2, p. 148.

83. Ibid., Act V, Scene 3, p. 150.

84. Aristotle, *Poetics*, 16, in *The Complete Works of Aristotle*, vol. 2, ed. Jonathan Barnes (Princeton, N.J.: Princeton University Press, 1985), p. 2328 (1454b36). Charles-Émile Ruelle, in his French translation of this chapter on various forms of recognition in the theater, preferred the expression "le langage de la toile" (the language of fabric) to render the allusion to the letters embroidered by Philomela; cf. Aristotle, *Poétique et Rhétorique*, trans. Ch-Emile Ruelle (Paris: Librairie Garnier frères, 1883).

85. Jones and Stallybrass, *Renaissance Clothing and the Materials of Memory*, pp. 158–59 and fig. 37, reproduction of an embroidered counterpane of wool and silk depicting Philomela embroidering and an old woman spinning (circa 1600).

86. Ibid., p. 141.

87. William Shakespeare, *A Midsummer Night's Dream*, in *The Complete Works*, ed. Stanley Wells and Gary Taylor (Oxford: Oxford University Press, 1988), Act III, Scene 2, lines 204–9, p. 323. The text is that of the 1600 Quarto edition.

88. For initial results of ongoing research, see Lilian Maria de Lacerda, "Letras bordadas sob livros: pelo imaginário tecido como a palavra," paper presented at the XXVI Congresso Intercom, Belo Horizonte, 2003.

89. Richard Shorleyker, *A Schole-house for the Needle* (London, 1624), reprinted by the Widow Shorleyker, London, 1632.

90. John Taylor, *The Needles Excellency: A new booke wherein are divers admirable workes wrought with the needle*, Printed for James Boler (London, 1631). The work was reprinted in 1634 (at which time it was described as the "tenth edition"), in 1636, and in 1640 ("twelfth edition").

91. Cesare Vecellio, *Corona delle nobili e virtuose Donnne: Libro primo Nel quale si dimostra in varii dissegni tutte le sorti di Mostre di punti tagliati [. . .] che con l'Aco si usano hoggi per tutta Europa*, Venise, 1591.

92. André Labarre, *Le livre dans la vie amiénoise du XVIe siècle. L'enseignement des inventaires après décès, 1503–1576* (Paris: Nauwelaerts, 1971), pp. 164–77.

93. *La fleur des patrons de lingerie a deux endroitz a point croise a point couche et a point picque, en fil dor fil dargent et fil de soye en quelque ouvrage que ce soit en comprenant lart de broderie et tissuterie* (Lyon: Pierre de Saincte Lucie dict le Prince, 1549) (which presents twenty-two patterns). In the 1520s, Claude Nourry published a book with a similar title, un *Livre nouveau dict patrons de lingerie*, which Pierre de Saincte-Lucie reprinted in 1549. He proposed forty-six patterns, and the title page included an image of the type of loom used in commercial workshops. Cf. Henri Baudrier, *Bibliographie lyonnaise* (Lyon, 1895–1915), vol. 12, p. 92 (for Claude Nourry) and pp. 187–89 (for Pierre de Sainte-Lucie).

94. Yvonne Verdier, *Façons de dire, façons de faire: La laveuse, la couturière, la cuisinière* (Paris: Gallimard, 1979), pp. 157–258, and the commentary by Daniel Fabre, "Passeuses aux gués du destin," *Critique* 402 (1990): 1075–99.

95. See Roger Chartier, "Culture écrite et littérature à l'âge moderne," and Marina Roggero, "L'alphabétisation en Italie: Une conquête féminine?" *Annales. Histoire, Sciences Sociales* (July-October 2001): 783–802, 903–25.

96. Goldoni, *La Locandiera*, in Goldoni, *Commedie*, ed. Guido Davico Bonino (Milan: Garzanti, 1976), vol. 1, pp. 335–421, Act I, Scene 15, p. 355. English translation: "Mine Hostess," trans. Clifford Bax, in Goldoni, *Three Comedies* (London: Oxford

University Press, 1961), pp. 20–21. Italian text: "Questa biancheria, l'ho fatta per personaggi di merito, per quelli che la sanno conoscere." On this comedy, see Mario Baratto, *Sur Goldoni* (Paris: L'Arche, 1971), pp. 87–106.

97. Ibid., Act II, Scene 15, p. 392; translation, pp. 65–66. Italian text: Fabrizio: "È vero, signore, che vuole il conto?" / Cavaliere: "Sì, l'avete portato?" / Fabrizio: "Adesso la padrona lo fa." / Cavaliere: "Ella fa i conti?"/ Fabrizio: "Oh, sempre ella. Anche cuando viveva suo padre. Scrive e sa far di conto meglio di qualche giovane di negozio."

98. Fido, *Nuova guida a Goldoni*, p. 128. Italian text: "C'era la donna coquette certo, ma anche amabile e intelligente, laboriosa e spiritosa, pienamente degna della nostra simpatia e ammirazione."

Chapter 7. Commerce in the Novel: Damilaville's Tears and the Impatient Reader

1. Quotes here are taken from the published version in Diderot, *Arts et lettres (1739–1766), Critique I*, ed. Jean Varloot (Paris: Hermann, 1980): *Éloge de Richardson*, pp. 181–208 (with an introduction by Jean Sgard). See also the recent version in the appendix to Diderot, *Contes et romans*, ed. Michel Delon, with the collaboration of Jean-Christophe Abramovici, Henri Lafon, and Stéphane Pujol (Paris: Gallimard, Bibliothèque de la Pléiade, 2004), pp. 895–911. [English translation: "In Praise of Richardson," in Denis Diderot, *Selected Writings on Art and Literature*, trans. Geoffrey Bremner (London: Penguin, 1994), pp. 82–97. The translations of quoted passages are not take from this volume, however, but are my own.—Trans.].

2. *Dictionnaire des journaux (1600–1789)*, ed. Jean Sgard (Paris: Universitas, 1991), n° 732, *Journal étranger* 1 (1754–1762): 731–32.

3. See the bibliography established by Henri Lafon in Diderot, *Contes et romans*, pp. 1264–66.

4. Roland Mortier, *Diderot en Allemagne (1750–1850)* (Paris: Presses Universitaires de France, 1954), pp. 325–28. On the German reception of Diderot, cf. Anne Saada, *Inventer Diderot: Les constructions d'un auteur dans l'Allemagne des Lumières* (Paris: CNRS, 2003).

5. Louis Marin, *Des pouvoirs de l'image: Gloses* (Paris: Seuil, 1993), "Le descripteur fantaisiste; Diderot, *Salon de 1765, Casanove, n° 94, 'Une marche d'armée',* description," pp. 72–101 (quote, pp. 72–73). French text: "Autrement dit, quels pouvoirs de langage convoquer et mobiliser pour qu'à la lecture—à voix haute, basse, ou voix silencieuse—une image apparaisse, flottante d'abord, errante comme une ombre élyséenne, puis insistante, obsessive, bientôt envoûtante, envahissant l'âme, occupant l'esprit, travaillant le sens et les sens, prête à franchir les frontières de l'intérieur et de l'extérieur, en voie de vision ou d'hallucination?"

6. Diderot, *Éloge de Richardson*, in *Œuvres esthétiques*, ed. Paul Vernière (Paris: Garnier, 1959), pp. 21–48 (quote p. 25). French text: "L'auteur laisse errer sa plume au gré de son imagination. Mais à travers le désordre et la négligence aimable d'un pinceau qui s'abandonne, on reconnaît aisément la main sûre et savante d'un grand peintre."

7. See Jean Sgard, *Prévost romancier* (Paris: Librairie José Corti, 1989), pp. 538–51, 610.

8. For modern editions of the three novels, see Samuel Richardson, *Pamela, or Virtue Rewarded*, ed. Thomas Keymer and Alice Wakely (Oxford: Oxford University Press, 2001); *Clarissa or, the History of a Young Lady*, ed. Angus Ross (Harmondsworth: Penguin, 1985), and *The History of Sir Charles Grandison*, ed. Jocelyn Harris (Oxford: Oxford University Press, 1972). For French translations, see Samuel Richardson, *Paméla ou la Vertu récompensée* (Bordeaux: Ducros, 1970) (which wrongly attributes the translation to Prévost), and *Lettres anglaises ou Histoire de Miss Clarisse Harlove* (Paris: Desjonquères, 1999) (which was in fact translated by Prévost).

9. Diderot, *Correspondance*, ed. Laurent Versini (Paris: Robert Laffont, Bouquins), p. 272. French text: "On disputa beaucoup de Clarisse. Ceux qui méprisaient cet ouvrage, le méprisaient souverainement. Ceux qui l'estimaient, aussi outrés dans leur estime que les premiers dans leur mépris, le regardaient comme un des tours de force de l'esprit humain."

10. Ibid., p. 348. French text: "Ce que vous me dites de l'enterrement et du testament de Clarisse, je l'avais éprouvé. C'est seulement une preuve de plus de la ressemblance de nos âmes."

11. See June S. Siegel, "Diderot and Richardson: Manuscripts, Missives, and Mysteries," in *Diderot Studies XVIII*, ed. Otis Fellows and Diana Guiragossian (Geneva: Droz, 1975), pp. 145–67, and the Introduction by Jean Sgard to *Éloge de Richardson* in Diderot, *Arts et lettres (1739–1766)*, pp. 181–84.

12. Diderot, *Correspondance*, p. 348. French text: "Seulement encore mes yeux se remplirent de larmes; je ne pouvais plus lire; je me levai et me mis à me désoler, à apostropher le frère, la sœur, le père, la mère et les oncles, et à parler tout haut, au grand étonnement de Damilaville qui n'entendait rien ni à mon transport ni à mes discours, et qui me demandait à qui j'en avais."

13. Leah Price, *The Anthology and the Rise of the Novel: From Richardson to George Eliot* (Cambridge: Cambridge University Press, 2000), pp. 13–42.

14. See Rita Goldberg, *Sex and Enlightenment: Women in Richardson and Diderot* (Cambridge: Cambridge University Press, 1984), pp. 137–45.

15. This tension is analyzed in William Beatty Warner, *Reading Clarissa: The Struggles of Interpretation* (New Haven, Conn.: Yale University Press, 1979), pp. 221–32.

16. B. W. Ife, *Reading and Fiction in Golden-Age Spain: A Platonist Critique and Some Picaresque Replies* (Cambridge: Cambridge University Press, 1985), pp. 49–83.

17. Cf. Samuel Tissot, *De la santé des gens de lettres* (1768), Intro. François Azouvi (Geneva: Slatkine, 1981), and Roger Chartier, "L'homme de lettres," in *L'Homme des lumières*, ed. Michel Vovelle (Paris: Éditions du Seuil, 1996), pp. 159–209 (esp. pp. 196–99). English translation: "The Man of Letters," in *Enlightenment Portraits*, ed. Michel Vovelle, trans. Lydia Cochrane (Chicago: University of Chicago Press, 1997, pp. 142–89).

18. Thomas Laqueur, *Solitary Sex: A Cultural History of Masturbation* (New York: Zone Books, 2003).

19. Rolf Engelsing, "Die Perioden der Lesergeschichte in der Neuzeit. Das statistische Ausmass und die soziokulturelle Bedeutung der Lektüre," *Archiv für Geschichte des Buchwesens* 10 (1970): 944–1002.

20. Robert Darnton, *The Forbidden Best-Sellers of Pre-Revolutionary France* (New York: W.W. Norton, 1995), p. 219.

21. Hans Erich Bödeker, "D'une 'histoire littéraire' du lecteur à l'histoire du lecteur': Bilan et perspectives," in *Histoires de la lecture: Un bilan des recherches*, ed. Roger Chartier (Paris: IMEC/Editions de la Maison des Sciences de l'Homme, 1995), pp. 93–124 (quote p. 98).

22. Reinhart Wittmann, "Une révolution de la lecture à la fin du XVIIIe siècle?" in *Histoire de la lecture dans le monde occidental*, ed. Guglielmo Cavallo and Roger Chartier (Paris: Éditions du Seuil, 1997), pp. 331–64 (quote p. 364). English translation: "Was There a Reading Revolution at the End of the Eigteenth Century?" in *A History of Reading in the West*, ed. Guglielmo Cavallo and Roger Chartier (Amherst: University of Massachusetts Press, 1999), pp. 284–312 (quote p. 311).

23. These themes are developed in Roger Chartier, "Livres, lecteurs, lectures," in *Le Monde des Lumières*, ed. Vincenzo Ferrone and Daniel Roche (Paris: Fayard, 1999), pp. 285–93.

24. Pierre Bourdieu, "Lecture, lecteurs, lettrés, littérature," in *Choses dites* (Paris: Éditions de Minuit, 1987), pp. 132–43 (quote p. 133). English translation: *On Other Words: Essays Towards a Reflexive Sociology*, trans. Matthew Adamson (Cambridge: Polity Press, 1990). French text: "s'interroger sur les conditions de possibilité de la lecture, c'est s'interroger sur les conditions sociales de possibilité des situations dans lesquelles on lit . . . et aussi sur les conditions sociales de production des *lectores*. Une des illusions du *lector* est celle qui consiste à oublier ses propres conditions sociales de production, à universaliser inconsciemment les conditions de possibilité de sa lecture."

25. The formula is singled out by Herbert Josephs, "Diderot's *Eloge de Richardson*: A Paradox on Praising," in *Essays on the Age of Enlightenment in Honor of Ora O. Wade*, ed. Jean Macary (Geneva: Droz, 1977), pp. 169–82 (esp p. 174).

26. Michael Fried, *Absorption and Theatricality: Painting and Beholder in the Age of Diderot* (Berkeley: University of California Press, 1980), p. 104.

27. On reading Richardson in America, see Cathy N. Davidson, *Revolution and the Word: The Rise of the Novel in America* (New York: Oxford University Press, 1986), pp. 22, 114, and Elizabeth Carroll Reilly and David. D. Hall, "Customers and the Market for Book," in *A History of the Book in America*, vol. 1, *The Colonial Book in the Atlantic World*, ed. Hugh Amory and David D. Hall (Cambridge: Cambridge University Press, 2000), pp. 387–99. On Benjamin Franklin's edition of *Pamela*, see James N. Green, "English Books and Printing in the Age of Franklin," in *A History of the Book in America*, pp. 267–68.

28. Carlo Goldoni, *Pamela fanciulla, Pamela maritata*, ed. Ilaria Crotti, Le Opere, Edizione Nazionale (Venice: Marsilio, 1995).

29. On the wax theater, the Vauxhall paintings, and the fan, see Stephanie Fysh, *The Work(s) of Samuel Richardson* (Newark: University of Delaware Press, 1977), pp. 67–79. On the relation between the novel and its female readers, see the classic work by Ian Watt, *The Rise of the Novel. Studies in Defoe, Richardson, and Fielding* (1957; Berkeley: University of California Press, 1984), pp. 151–73.

30. Ibid., p. 78.

31. On the paintings by Highmore and Mercier, see James Grantham Turner,

"Novel Panic: Picture and Performance in the Reception of Richardson's *Pamela*," *Representations* 48 (Fall 1994): 70–96 (esp. pp. 83–90).

32. Ibid., p. 82.

33. Ronald C. Rosbottom, "A Matter of Competence: The Relationship Between Reading and Novel-Making in Eighteenth-Century France," *Studies in Eighteenth-Century Culture* 6 (1977): 245–63 (esp. pp. 254–55).

34. T. C. Duncan Eaves and Ben D. Kimpel, "Richardson's Revisions of Pamela," *Studies in Bibliography: Papers of the Bibliographical Society of the University of Virginia* 20 (1967): 61–88, and Philip Gaskell, "Richardson, Pamela, 1741," in *Philip Gaskell, From Writer to Reader: Studies in Editorial Method* (Winchester: St Paul's Bibliographies, 1984), pp. 63–79.

35. In the third edition of *Clarissa* (1751), Richardson, who was a printer, defied typographic conventions in order to give the reader the impression of holding a handwritten text. See Steven R. Price, "The Autograph Manuscript in Print: Samuel Richardson's Type Font Manipulation in *Clarissa*," in *Illuminating Letters: Typography and Literary Interpretation*, ed. Paul C. Gutjahr and Megan L. Benton (Amherst: University of Massachusetts Press, 2001), pp. 117–35.

36. On this tension, see the subtle analysis by Tom Keyner, *Richardson's Clarissa and the Eighteenth-Century Reader* (Cambridge: Cambridge University Press, 1992), esp. pp. 56–84, "Richardson's Reader," where he notes: "It is precisely by first absenting himself, thereby allowing the exercise of reading its fullest and freest rein, that Richardson most convincingly fulfils his claim to educate" (p. 82).

37. Louis Marin, *Le Portrait du roi* (Paris: Éditions de Minuit, 1981), p. 95. English translation: *Portrait of the King*, trans. Martha Houle (Minneapolis: University of Minnesota Press, 1988). French text: "Ce qui n'est pas représenté dans le récit et par le narrateur l'est à la lecture par le narrataire, à titre d'effets du récit."

38. Louis Marin, *Le récit est un piège* (Paris: Éditions de Minuit, 1978).

39. Concerning the identity of the two friends who quarrel over Richardson, see Siegel, "Diderot and Richardson," pp. 163–66, which concludes that "Sophie's mother, the dread Morphyse of the correspondence, is most likely the outrageous mère-qui-rit of the second paragraph," and that the original letter must be attributed to Madame d'Epinay, but that "onto the real letter (or a pastiche of several real letters), Diderot seems to have grafted his own passionate oratory," while Jean Sgard, in his edition of the *Éloge* (Diderot, *Arts et lettres (1739–1766)*, p. 204, note 16), indicates that the "quoted passages very likely echo a letter Diderot to Madame d'Epinay" but that "the identity of the other [friend], who must have been a female friend of Diderot's and a mother, is unknown." French text: "les passages cités reprendraient les termes d'une lettre de Diderot à Madame d'Épinay," but "l'autre [amie], qui doit être une amie de Diderot, mère de famille, nous est inconnue."

40. In the second half of the eighteenth century, a number of German novelists (Johann Karl August Musäus, the author of *Grandison der Zweite* and of *Der deutschen Grandison* in 1781; Johann Karl Wezel with *Lebensgeschite Tobias Knauts* in 1773–76; Friedrich Nicolai with *Das Leben und die Meinungen des Herrn Magisters Sebaldus Nothanker*, also in 1773–76) portrayed characters who were readers of Richardson, and their reactions ranged from the most profound boredom to the most extreme emotion; see Valérie Le Vot, *Des livres à la vie: Lecteurs et lectures dans*

le roman allemand des Lumières (Bern: Peter Lang, 1999), esp. pp. 233–37, 290, 318, 322–23. For a French example, see Nathalie Ferrand, *Livre et lecture dans les romans français du XVIIIe siècle* (Paris: Presses Universitaires de France, 2002), pp. 122–23 (on the reading of *Clarisse Harlove* in a novel by Sénac de Meilhan, *L'Émigré*, 1797).

41. Jean Sgard, Introduction to the *Éloge de Richardson*, in Diderot, *Arts et lettres (1739–1766)*, p. 187: "Let us not be in too much haste to regard Dierot as an ingenious theorist of the novel. What should astonish us instead about the *Eloge de Richardson*, is the outmoded nature of its arguments and the influence of contemporary prejudices." French text: "Ne nous hâtons pas de considérer Diderot comme un génial théoricien du roman. Ce qui étonnerait plutôt dans *l'Éloge de Richardson*, c'est l'archaïsme des arguments et l'emprise des préjugés."

42. Turner, "Novel Panic," esp. pp. 70–78.

43. Jean Starobinski, "'Se mettre à la place' (La mutation de la critique, de l'âge classique à Diderot)," *Cahiers Vilfredo Pareto* 38–39 (1976): 364–78. Another version of this essay can be found in Starobinski, *L'œil vivant: Corneille, Racine, La Bruyère, Rousseau, Stendhal* (Paris: Gallimard, 1961), pp. 93–128 (esp. pp. 117–28). English translation: *The Living Eye*, trans. Arthur Goldhammer (Cambridge, Mass.: Harvard University Press, 1989).

44. Ibid., p. 377. French text: "La preuve de la beauté, de la bonté, de la vérité du roman ne doit donc pas être donnée par une critique (fût-elle élogieuse) du roman lui-même, mais par l'affirmation que l'énergie dont il est la source peut être intégralement reversée sur la vie réelle."

45. Starobinski, ibid., p. 378, writes: "The identification is felt in the reader's relation to things by way of a gaze which, abandoning the book so often read and re-read, turns to the world to confirm the persistent presence of the book." French text: "L'identification retentit dans le rapport avec les choses, à travers le regard qui, abandonnant le livre lu et relu, se reporte sur le monde, pour y constater la présence persistante du livre."

46. On visiting writers, see Jean-Claude Bonnet, *Naissance du Panthéon: Essai sur le culte des grands hommes* (Paris: Fayard, 1998), pp. 209–15 (Rousseau), pp. 226–32 (Voltaire), pp. 246–48, and on its corollary, writing to writers, see Jean M. Goulemot and Didier Masseau, "Lettres au grand homme ou quand les lecteurs écrivent," in *La lettre à la croisée de l'individuel et du social*, ed. Mireille Bossis (Paris: Éditions Kimé, 1994), pp. 39–47.

47. Diderot's letter can be found in Diderot, *Œuvres complètes*, vol. 8, *Encyclopédie IV et Lettre sur le commerce de la librairie*, ed. John Lough and Jacques Proust (Paris: Hermann, 1976), pp. 465–567. See here the epilogue, "Diderot and His Pirates."

48. Price, *The Anthology and the Rise of the Novel*, p. 36.

49. Quoted in Mark Rose, "The Author as Proprietor: *Donaldson v. Becket* and the Genealogy of Modern Authorship," *Representations* 23 (1988): 51–85 (quote p. 62). See also Mark Rose, *Authors and Owners: The Invention of Copyright* (Cambridge, Mass.: Harvard University Press, 1993), pp. 117–21.

50. Paul Bénichou, *Le sacre de l'écrivain, 1750–1830: Essai sur l'avènement d'un pouvoir spirituel laïque dans la France moderne* (1973; Paris: Gallimard, 1986), pp. 23–77. English translation: *The Consecration of the Writer*, trans. Mark K. Jensen (Lincoln: University of Nebraska Press, 1999).

Epilogue

1. On Sartine, see Daniel Roche, "La police du livre," in *Histoire de l'Édition française*, vol. 2, *Le livre triomphant: 1660–1830*, ed. Roger Chartier and Henri-Jean Martin (Paris: Fayard/Cercle de la Librairie, 1990), pp. 99–109.

2. Diderot's brief was partially reprinted in Diderot, *Sur la liberté de la presse*, ed. Jacques Proust (Paris: Éditions Sociales, 1964), and fully reprinted in Diderot, *Œuvres complètes*, vol. 8, *Encyclopédie IV (Lettres M–Z): Lettre sur le commerce de la librairie*, ed. John Lough and Jacques Proust (Paris: Hermann, 1976), pp. 465–67. I quote here from this edition. On the history of the text, see Jacques Proust, "Pour servir à une édition de la *Lettre sur le commerce de la librairie*," *Diderot Studies* 3 (1961): 321–45. The letter to Madame de Meaux is quoted from *Sur la liberté de la presse*, p. 7.

3. On the underground book trade, see Robert Darnton, *The Forbidden Best-Sellers of Pre-Revolutionary France* (New York: W.W. Norton, 1995).

4. On tacit permissions, see Malesherbes, *Mémoires sur la librairie: Mémoires sur la liberté de la presse*, intro. Roger Chartier (Paris: Imprimerie Nationale, 1994), pp. 203–9, and Robert Estivals, *La Statistique bibliographique de la France sous la monarchie au XVIIIe siècle* (Paris: Mouton, 1965), pp. 107–20, 275–91.

5. For a similar tension in England in the late seventeenth century, see Peter Lindenbaum, "Authors and Publishers in the Late Seventeenth Century: New Evidence on their Relation," *The Library* 6th ser. 3 (September 1995): 250–69.

6. Jacques Proust, *Diderot et l'Encyclopédie* (Paris: Armand Colin 1967), pp. 81–116.

7. On the history of *privilèges de librairie* between the sixteenth and eighteenth centuries, see Elizabeth Armstrong, *Before Copyright: The French Book-Privilege System, 1498–1526* (Cambridge: Cambridge University Press, 1990); Henri-Jean Martin, *Livre, pouvoirs et société à Paris au XVIIe siècle (1598–1701)* (Geneva: Droz, 1969), vol. 1, pp. 440–60, vol. 2, pp. 690–95. English translation: *Print, Power, and People in 17th Century France*, trans. David Gerard (Metuchen, N.J.: Scarecrow Press, 1993); Raymond Birn, "Profit on Ideas: *Privilèges en librairie* in Eighteenth-Century France," *Eighteenth-Century Studies* 4, 2 (Winter 1970–1971): pp. 131–68, and Laurent Pfister, "L'auteur, propriétaire de son oeuvre? La formation du droit d'auteur du XVIe siècle à la loi de 1957", thesis, Université Robert Schumann (Strasbourg III), 1999, vol. 1, pp. 22–205.

8. Cf. Daniel Roche, *Les Républicains des lettres: Gens de culture et Lumières au XVIIIe siècle* (Paris: Fayard, 1988); Eric Walter, "Les auteurs et le champ littéraire," in *Histoire de l'Édition française*, vol. 2, pp. 499–518; and Roger Chartier, "L'homme de lettres," in *L'Homme des Lumières*, ed. Michel Vovelle (Paris: Éditions du Seuil, 1996), pp. 159–209. English translation: "The Man of Letters," in *Enlightenment Portraits*, ed. Michel Vovelle, trans. Lydia Cochrane (Chicago: University of Chicago Press, 1997), pp. 142–89.

9. This brief was published in Edouard Laboulaye and Georges Guiffrey, *La Propriété littéraire au XVIIIe siècle: Recueil de documents* (Paris: Hachette, 1859), pp. 55–120.

10. Denis Diderot, *La Proprété littéraire au XVIIIe siècle: Lettre sur le commerce de la librairie par Diderot*, ed. M. G. Guiffrey (Paris: L. Hachette, 1861).

11. On this abolition, see Steven L. Kaplan, *La Fin des corporations* (Paris: Fayard, 2001).

12. The complete text of *Fragments sur la liberté de la presse* can be found in Marie-Jean-Antoine Caritat, marquis de Condorcet, *Œuvres complètes* (Paris, 1847), vol. 11, pp. 257–314. On these "Fragments," see Carla Hesse, "Enlightenment Epistemology and the Laws of Authorship in Revolutionary France, 1777–1793," *Representations* 30 (1990): 109–38.

13. On the subscription system in eighteenth-century Europe, see Wallace Kirsop, "Les mécanismes éditoriaux," in *Histoire de l'Édition française*, vol. 2, pp. 15–34 (esp. pp. 30–31).

14. Cf. Hesse, "Enlightenment Epistemology and the Laws of Authorship"; and Bernard Edelman, *Le Sacre de l'auteur* (Paris: Éditions du Seuil, 2004), pp. 356–78.

15. On the key transition from ownership of the manuscript to ownership of the text, Diderot had predecessors, such as Louis d'Héricourt in 1725, as well as successors, such as Linguet and abbé Pluquet, see Pfister, *L'auteur, propriétaire de son oeuvre?* vol. 1, pp. 212–24.

16. Concerning the law of "rights in copy" and "patents" in England before 1710, see Adrian Johns, *The Nature of the Book: Print and Knowledge in the Making* (Chicago: University of Chicago Press, 1998), pp. 213–62 and Joseph Loewenstein, *The Author's Due: Printing and the Prehistory of Copyright* (Chicago: University of Chicago Press, 2002).

17. William Enfield, *Observations on Literary Property* (London, 1774), quoted in Edelman, *Le Sacre de l'auteur*, p. 221.

18. William Blackstone, *Commentaries on the Laws of England* (Oxford, 1765–1769), quoted in Mark Rose, *Authors and Owners: The Invention of Copyright* (Cambridge, Mass.: Harvard University Press, 1993), pp. 89–90.

19. Johann Gottlieb Fichte, *Beweis der Unrechtmässigkeit der Büchernadrucks. Ein Räsonnement und eine Parabel*, 1791. This text is quoted and commented on by Martha Woodmansee, *The Author, Art, and the Market: Rereading the History of Aesthetics* (New York: Columbia University Press, 1994), pp. 51–53 (quote p, 52).

20. Jorge Luis Borges, "Nota sobre (hacia) Bernard Shaw," in *Otras inquisiciones* (1952 Madrid: Alianza Editorial, 1997), pp. 237–42. Spanish text, p. 238: "Un libro es más que una estructura verbal, o que una serie de estructuras verbales; es el diálogo que entabla con su lector y la entonación que impone a su voz y las cambiantes y durables imágenes que dejan en su memoria. Ese diálogo es infinito; las palabras *amica silentia lunae* significan ahora la luna íntima, silenciosa y luciente, y en la *Eneida* significaron el interlunio, la oscuridad que permitió a los griegos entrar en la ciudadela de Troya . . . La literatura no es agotable, por la suficiente y simple razón de que un solo libro no lo es. El libro no es un ente incomunicado: es una relación, es un eje de innumerables relaciones." English translation: "For Bernard Shaw," in *Other Inquisitions, 1937–1952*, trans. Ruth L. C. Simms (Austin: University of Texas Press, 1964], pp. 163–64; translation modified.

Index